IDEOLOGIES AND MENTALITIES

IDEOLOGIES AND MENTALITIES

Michel Vovelle

translated by Eamon O'Flaherty

Polity Press

This translation first published 1990 by Polity Press in association with Basil Blackwell.

Published with the assistance of the French Ministry of Culture and Communication.

Editorial office: Polity Press, 65 Bridge Street, Cambridge CB2 1UR, UK

Marketing and production: Basil Blackwell Ltd, 108 Cowley Road, Oxford OX4 1JF, UK

British Library Cataloguing in Publication Data

A CIP catalogue record of this book is available from the British Library.

ISBN 0 7456 0344 0

Typeset in 10½ on 12 pt Sabon by
Wearside Tradespools, Fulwell, Sunderland
Printed in Great Britain by
Billings & Sons, Worcester

Contents

Acknowledgements

The author and publishers wish to thank the following for permission to use copyright material:

Armand Colin for maps on pages 158 and 160 from J. Dupleix, *Atlas de la France Rurale*, 1968;

The Past and Present Society for graph on page 182 from Lawrence Stone, 'Literacy and Education in England, 1640–1900', *Past and Present: A Journal of Historical Studies*, No. 42 (February 1969). Copyright © The Past and Present Society;

Plon, Paris, for graphs on pages 190 and 197 from M. Vovelle, *Piété baroque et déchristianisation, les attitudes devant le mort en Provence au XVIII siècle*, 1973;

Every effort has been made to trace all the copyright holders but if any have been inadvertently overlooked the publishers will be pleased to make the necessary arrangement at the first opportunity.

Introduction

Ideologies and Mentalities – a Necessary Clarification

This is a discussion which might seem naive and which, in fact, assumes such a naivety without any shame or false modesty. As a historian trained in Marxist methods, which I do not reject (far from it), I find myself classed among the ranks of the historians of mentalities. This is no doubt correct, if one thinks of the books by which I have become known, whether studies on collective attitudes to death, on the festival or on events in religious history, such as the dechristianization of the Year II, which was treated in terms of rapid change at the climax of the revolutionary process.

This being so, I do not believe that I have been unfaithful – if I may be allowed the term – to my earlier beliefs, even if my development has seemed paradoxical to many. Among these are historians who do not, or no longer, see themselves as Marxists, like Emmanuel Le Roy Ladurie, who expressed surprise, in his review of my book *Baroque Piety and Dechristianization: attitudes to death in eighteenth-century Provence*, at finding a Marxist historian capable of describing the 'how' and refusing to supply the 'why'. This observation may be as naive as my own, since it seems to invest the Marxist historian with the formidable responsibility of supplying the 'why' – itself a considerable tribute.

Conversely, I have sometimes surprised more than one Marxist historian by an apparent tendency to indulge in incongruous themes. I cherish the memory of Pierre Vilar's amicable question as to why, instead of being drawn to themes such as the history of death or of the festival, I did not find it preferable to study the processes of the awakening of consciousness among the mass of the people, which is certainly a less ambiguous calling for a Marxist historian. In their different ways, both these anecdotes reflect at least one, and possibly more than one, misunderstanding. Quite apart from my personal development I see here a deeper and wider-ranging question: that Marxist historians, when confronted with the refinements of their own problematic and with promptings from outside, need to clarify their concepts. It also involves the need for a new generation of historians of mentalities quite simply and yet quite strictly to define the very notion of mentality which has become widely used, while still retaining a vagueness which is, to say the least, artistic.

In order to do this, we need to be aware of the coexistence in the same field of two rival concepts which, in addition, are the legacies of two different traditions. As such, they are hard to reconcile, even though they undeniably show a real area of overlap. Yet, clearly, ideology and mentality are not one and the same thing.

Ideology

I will not fall into the trap of starting with a new definition of the Marxist concept of ideology. Others have done this, from the founding fathers to recent writers like Louis Althusser, who in his 'Ideology and ideological state apparatuses'[1] defined ideology as 'the imaginary relationship of individuals to their real conditions of existence'. It is thus a collection of representations, but also a collection of practices and forms of behaviour, whether conscious or unconscious. The very general character of this definition seems to be of a kind which can group Marxists and even non-Marxists around a common working hypothesis. If objections are raised to its undeniably vague character, it can be replied that ideology was deliberately vaguely defined by Marx himself, concerned in the 1857 *Introduction to a Critique of Political Economy*, to respond to the accusations of reductionist economism to which *The German Ideology* had lent itself. There he defined the mode of production in terms which are perhaps too frequently quoted, but which are nevertheless essential: 'There is in every social formation a particular branch of production which determines the position and importance of all the others, and the relations obtaining in this branch accordingly determine the relations of all other branches as well. It is as though light of a particular hue were cast upon everything, tingeing all other colours and modifying their specific features; or as if a special ether determined the specific gravity of everything found in it.'[2]

A particular hue, a special ether – we don't have to be particularly iconoclastic to agree with Pierre Vilar that, stylistically, it is 'not the best Marx'. Yet this matters little if the intention can be clearly discerned, as it was by Engels in his subsequent commentary on the passage in a letter to Ernst Bloch: 'In the materialist conception of history, the determining factor is, in the final instance, the production and reproduction of real life. Neither Marx nor I have ever asserted anything more. If anyone subsequently tortures the proposition to make it mean that the economic factor is the sole determinant, then he transforms it into an empty, abstract, absurd phrase . . .'

Engels, following Marx, thus replied in advance to an entire critique which is both opinionated and so elementary that we should not delay too long over it. This is the critique of 'vulgar Marxism' as a mechanical, economistic explanation, in a world where ideological superstructures respond automatically to the promptings of the infrastructure. This is surely an academic debate, which we can leave to the vulgar critics of 'vulgar' Marxism. Yet we should realize that such stereotypes have an enduring life and a real effectiveness. I do not know whether this criticism has led, in French historiography, to the kind of caution, even embarrassment felt by Marxist historians in approaching subjects which might expose them to such a reproach. Up until recently, one had the impression of an implicit division of labour to which a number of Marxist historians seemed to subscribe, if only by their silence; one which confined them to the domain of the economy and social structures (but within closely supervised limits) reserving the more complex fields of religious history and the history of mentalities and sensibilities to others who were better qualified. Thus Goldmann, in *The Hidden God*, long remained the exception who proved the rule of nonintervention by Marxist scholars in areas which were regarded as beyond their competence.

Confined to the basement and leaving the nobler storeys to others, Marxist historians were not even rewarded for their caution, having to face objections that, in the new fields which were being opened up, research invariably led to a supposedly Marxist interpretation.

Such objections were strong – a fortiori when they were not made by opponents of Marxism. This can be seen, to stay in my own field of eighteenth-century studies, in the major reappraisal constituted recently by the study of the discrepancy between the 'bourgeois' ideology of the Enlightenment and the sociology of its spokesmen in the provincial academies, the world of learning and the masonic lodges. In the irrefutable statistics provided by Daniel Roche, the bourgeoisie is hidden, leaving the centre of the stage to aristocrats or to representatives of an 'elite' of talents. What kind of ideology is it, we ask, that is not promoted by its rightful possessors, and that is even found being promoted by a group the seed of whose destruction it contains? Hence the success, formerly, of the French version of the theory of elites, which tried to break the 'mechanical' linkage of affiliations and beliefs, or of the awakening of consciousness.

As one proceeds to more complex levels of representation, the difficulty of correctly explaining, or even taking account of, a certain number of given elements increases. A very recent social history thesis, based on a Marxist approach, came up against this difficulty in trying to reconstitute the parliamentary aristocracy of eighteenth-century Aix, in all its opacity. Even though it brilliantly assembled all parts of the file, it came up against obstacles which it could neither eliminate nor whittle away, as with the case of the persistence of Jansenist beliefs among eighteenth-century judges. Are we, then, left only with a memory, an empty form?

These are the 'noble' forms of ideological expression. Yet a history which is constantly widening its scope is dealing with forms of behaviour by which all of humanity is defined – the family, morality and customs, dreams, language, fashion. In these areas it comes up against the apparently gratuitous, which is nevertheless not at all meaningless.

But what meaning can be assigned to it? Furthermore, is there an element in human behaviour which eludes ideology, which is beneath it or tangential to it? This proposition would seem absurd, given our original definition. The common usage of the term in everyday speech might be misleading in this area. 'That's ideology!' is a common accusation arising out of a common-sense image of ideology (based on a certain social practice and discourse) as an organized and polarized formulation, in contrast to a certain good sense which reflects the mood of the time – its mentality, perhaps?

Mentality

The notion of mentality, as it is used today, derives from a very different and much more recent tradition – twenty or thirty years old, we could say, if referring to its widespread use. We must also recognize that the concept is far from being universally accepted. We have only to look at the difficulty with which historians outside France have adapted to the notion, and even translated the word. German historians have tried to find an equivalent, while English historians, following the example of the Italians, have, for practical purposes, resigned themselves to using the French word.

Conversely, I am well aware that a whole prehistory in the historiography of mentalities can be described. It is clear that, just as M. Jourdin wrote prose without realizing it, the history of mentalities was also written before the concept was formally defined. What is George Lefebvre's *Great Fear* if not a study of one of the great old-style panics of French society, written with a modernity which is still surprising? Then we can point to some of the great classics. Huizinga's *Waning of the Middle Ages* is indisputably one of the founding works of this new approach to history. But, although we can begin to speak of a history of mentalities *stricto sensu* with Lucien Febvre and the *Annales* school – as in his *Problem of Unbelief in the Sixteenth Century: the religion of Rabelais*[3] – it was not really until the work of Robert Mandrou and Georges Duby in the 1960s that we began to see the official recognition of a new historical field, though not without some notable resistance. One might say that it compensated for the initial difficulties it encountered with a dominant aggressiveness. In the hit parade of publishing successes at present, the history of mentalities seems to be a repeat of or an alternative, in current French historiography, to the former successes of serial history. The curiosity and the sense of attraction felt in other schools of history shows that here, undoubtedly, is something more than a temporary fashion.

Yet here we come up against the first paradox – a prevailing idea which at the same time preserves, at the very least, an extremely vague character. Attempts have, of course, been made, over the past twenty years, to provide a definition for the notion of 'mentality'. Yet I know of no better definition than the one offered by Robert Mandrou when he was asked about this very point, defining it as a history of 'visions of the world'. This definition is attractive and satisfies my own tastes, and yet it is undeniably vague.

Will we upset Robert Mandrou by stressing the way in which even the contents of this kind of history have changed over the past twenty years? Given that such a summary will have much that is impoverished, and even caricatural, it seems to me to be very much the case that we have progressed from a history of mentalities which, in its beginnings, essentially stuck to the level of culture, or of clear thought (as in Febvre's *Rabelais*, but also in Mandrou's *Popular Culture in the Seventeenth and Eighteenth Centuries*), to a history of attitudes, forms of behaviour and unconscious collective representations. This is precisely what is registered in the trends of new research – childhood, the mother, the family, love, sexuality and death.

To grasp this development, we only need to follow one or two themes among the rest, which can illustrate the constants in the writing of the history of mentalities. Thus, in the area of witchcraft, between Robert Mandrou's *Judges and Witches in Seventeenth-century France*, whose merit can never be overstated, and the recent work of Carlo Ginzburg and Robert Muchembled, the historian's outlook has changed. Mandrou described a historical change in the attitude of the elites and those in power when the members of the *parlements*, sometime around 1660, decided to put an end to the burning of witches. Nowadays, we are trying to cross to the other side of the barrier in an attempt to analyse the internal mental universe of marginal and deviant people. Similarly, it would be very easy to show the change which took place between the appearance of Febvre's *Rabelais*, now historically dated, reflecting a history which was still concerned with the elite, located halfway between the history of ideas and the history of mentalities, and Mikhail Bakhtine's *Rabelais*, which was the expression and reflection of an appropriation of popular culture. The history of mentalities has changed in a very short period of time. One nowadays has the feeling of dealing with a voracious discipline, which is ready to annex entire swathes of history without hesitation, including religious and literary history, the history of ideas, but also folklore and a whole dimension of ethnography. Is this voracity dangerous? Who will eat whom?

It is time to pause and focus on the problem in hand: mentality and ideology. It is not easy to reach an adjustment between these two concepts. The concept of ideology has been elaborated and matured over a long period, even if the last word has not been said (far from it), whereas the notion of mentality is a conceptualized reflection of a progressive practice, or process of discovery, which is of recent origin and is still undeniably vague and charged with successive meanings. The two concepts come from two different traditions and two different modes of thought – one more systematic, the other deliberately empirical, with all the risks which this entails.

Nevertheless, there is unquestionably a large area of overlap between the two. If we look at the current state of both terms, it might appear to some people – in what risks becoming a dialogue of the deaf – that mentalities are naturally registered in the field of ideology and to others, that ideology, in the restrictive sense of the term, can only be one aspect or one level of the field of mentalities: that which involves the awakening of consciousness, and formulated or clear thought. This double assessment still harbours a great many fundamental misunderstandings. Those who want to rid the notion of ideology of the stain of being a Marxist concept, which is often too heavy a burden to carry, speak of a 'third level', without always referring explicitly to hierarchical organization, economic infrastructures and ideological superstructures. This may be a bourgeois compromise, but it at least has the merit of drawing our attention, as was done in Pierre Chaunu's work, to the important place occupied in recent years by history 'at the third level' in the collective concerns of researchers.

In Western liberal countries, and especially in France, the notion of mentality, defined more indulgently and freed from all 'ideological' connotations, seems to emerge as the winner in terms of collective historiographical interest, more adaptable and capable by its very vagueness of responding to the needs of a research undertaken without presuppositions.

Mentality versus ideology

Is the history of mentalities anti-Marxist? To be clearly appreciated, this problem can only be approached from a historical perspective. It is undeniable that Marxist historians have long felt a real anxiety about a development which has been suspected, consciously or not, of being mystifying. Was such an attitude justified? Certainly not as regards a whole section of the founders of the French school, like Mandrou or Duby, who were particularly alive to the need to hold onto both ends of the chain – the social and the mental – and who were therefore open to all confrontations. One cannot, perhaps, say the same for the previous generation, including Lucien Febvre and a section of the first *Annales* school. Although the founding fathers of the journal were careful to maintain the emphasis on the trilogy of economy, society, civilization (the last term recalling an older terminology which was to open the way to the study of the superstructure), and although Fernand Braudel maintained the emphasis on the importance of social mediation ('Material life *and* capitalism'), we can nevertheless see in the spirit of the *Annales* founders a concern to distance themselves from what was seen as a dated Marxist historiography which was locked into the dogmatic schemes of socioeconomic reductionism. Conversely, Braudel's emphasis on the mental universe and on the specific character of this 'prison of the *longue durée*' showed his concern to affirm, if not the autonomy of the mental universe, at least the originality of the rhythms which it obeys.

In this historical perspective, although it is true, as we have seen, that a good many contemporary French historians of mentalities came to it via social history, which they have not, naturally, repudiated, one can also see the gradual emergence, on both sides of the Atlantic, of a new generation of specialists who have not approached the subject via the traditionally prescribed paths, and who have preferred to take the 'short cut to prayer'. These new historians of mentalities, open to all the temptations of psychohistory, will, no doubt, unhappily adopt one of its major characteristics, and insist on the autonomy of the mental universe.

At a first level, the concept of mentality, as we have seen, is wider in scope than the notion of ideology. It includes those mental realities which are unformulated, those which are apparently 'meaningless' and those which lead an underground existence at the level of unconscious motivation. Hence, possibly, the advantage of such a resource in the quest for a total history.

In continuity with this first distinction, mentalities differ from other registers of history by virtue of what Robert Mandrou has called 'the longer time-frame', alluding to Braudel's *longue durée* and his 'prisons of the *longue durée*'. Mentalities thus lead back in a vital way to memory and to forms of resistance – in a word, to what has become commonly defined as 'the force of inertia of mental structures', even if this only constitutes a verbal explanation. Moreover, in the perspective which interests us here, this assessment of the inertia of mentalities, which is at first sight irrefutable, leads to many kinds of interpretations and working hypotheses.

The first – which may be a means of reconciling ideology and mentality – sees in one whole group of the characteristics of mentality the translation of an inferior level of ideology, the traces, if you like, of ideologies 'in fragments'. This is what survives of ideologies which were once firmly rooted in a precise historical context when they have become discordant and have ceased to be based in reality, having become formal, displaced, even derisory structures. This first explanatory mode, which I do not find entirely satisfactory, at least has the merit of trying to integrate the factors encountered in the study of mentalities into a coherent vision. Yet this might also be a source of criticism.

There is another way of taking stock of the specific relationship between the time-frame of mentalities and that of history, and the 'inertial force of mental structures'. Whereas the preceding hypothesis makes mentality a vehicle for the ashes of dead ideologies, more than one contemporary scholar is, on the other hand, disposed to see in these resistant memories the repository of a preserved identity, of intangible and deeply rooted structures, the most authentic expression of collective temperaments – in all, of everything which is most valuable. In a recent debate entitled History of Mentalities, History of Resistances, or the Prisons of the *Longue Durée*, held at Aix in 1980, this theme emerged unexpectedly from the discussion. This is a sign of the times, in a society in search of its 'roots'. In opening grandmother's wardrobe, we found just what we were looking for. This is one of the paths most likely to lead us to the area where the apparent incompatibility of the concepts of ideology and mentality is most clearly visible. By this I mean the affirmation of the autonomy of the mental universe and its irreducibility to economic and social factors. This is an old idea, and I am not claiming that it was invented yesterday. But it also contains new ideas, which are nowadays expressed in concepts such as the 'collective unconscious' or the 'collective imagination'.

To explain the last of these, we can refer to Philippe Ariès's contribution to *The New History*, dealing with the history of mentalities. The collective unconscious, as he defines the term, is not based on psychoanalysis – Jung, perhaps, in this case – nor on the criteria of Claude Lévi-Strauss's anthropology. It is an idea which is deliberately and openly more empirical, referring back to the autonomy of a collective mental experience which obeys its own rhythms and causalities. In his own favourite field of collective attitudes towards death, Ariès deciphers the elements of an experience which is apparently independent of any socioeconomic determinism, even via the medium of demography. But the intermediary strata of gestures, attitudes and collective representations on which he focuses are also defined without reference to constituted ideologies – neither religious discourse, whether Protestant or Catholic, nor philosophical discourse is considered important, nor even really taken into account. Both are seen as superfluous hypotheses in a history whose lines of force are woven through the collective unconscious.

I have said many times elsewhere why this kind of history, moving, as it were, 'on a cushion of air', and refusing to risk making patient correlations for fear, perhaps, of falling into reductionist mechanisms, leaves me perplexed and dissatisfied. In the current state of the problem, I have less hesitation in using the term 'collective imagination' as others, notably Georges Duby in his recent work, have done. This term seems more manageable to my way of thinking and is always susceptible to producing hazardous ventures into the field of psychoanalysis.

Where the Marxist historian becomes a historian of mentalities

In dealing with the current questions which are woven around the history of mentalities – and we have yet to take account of the field of psychohistory, lest we be criticized! – we have the impression that here is an area of study which directly concerns Marxist historians. They, moreover, are quite aware of this, and have not been idle. For my part, I gave one of my recent books the title *From the Cellar to the Loft*, echoing a discussion held some time ago with Emmanuel Le Roy Ladurie, the future author of *Montaillou, an Occitan Village, 1294–1324*, who was surprised by the route which took me from the 'cellar' – meaning social structures – to the 'loft' – meaning my work on dechristianization and on attitudes to death. Le Roy Ladurie, on his side, affirmed his determination to remain in the cellar, and we know with what brilliance he has gone back on this resolution.

But Le Roy Ladurie and I are not the only examples of such an itinerary. Other historians, both Marxists and non-Marxists, moved from social history to the new fields of mentalities between 1960 and 1980, including Georges Duby, Maurice Agulhon and Pierre Chaunu in his own way. Each one had particular reasons for doing so and each followed a specific route. For some, it was a permanent split with former concerns; for others, however, there was a consciousness of continuity which was expressed in a firm resolution to remain in control of both ends of the chain – from the history of structures to that of the most highly elaborated attitudes.

We can ask why such a collective movement took place, the importance of which proves that it was significant and not contingent in character and which, we note, involved historians of widely different orientation (if not of different training). There is no shortage of answers, of which the most elaborate was Pierre Chaunu's analysis, in his essay 'The quantitative at the third level', of the great waves of change which have affected historiography in recent decades. We can acknowledge, with Chaunu, that each phase of historiography dealt with the problems which were most in need of attention. And this explanation, to which everybody involved will add their own piece of hindsight, might just possibly suffice.

I will add a personal recollection based on my own starting point, at the beginning of the 1960s. A whole generation of historians was then formed in the discipline of social history as taught by Ernest Labrousse – quantitive social history which 'counts, measures and weighs'. Then came the time of debates; the 'society of orders' urged by Roland Mousnier and his school against the concept of class-based society. This quarrel might have been sterile, and to some extent it was, freezing the initiative and forcing part of my generation to become inventive in order to move forward.

Seen in hindsight, this was a beneficial digression. Without rejecting their existing methods or their working hypotheses, historians went beyond the analysis of social structures to attempt to explain collective choices, attitudes and forms of behaviour. Having done so, they found themselves confronted with a much heavier workload, but this, of course, was what they were looking for.

Moving from social structures to collective attitudes and representations involves the whole problem of the complex mediators between real human life and the images, or even the fantastic representations, which people construct and which are a basic part of the approach to the history of mentalities. This approach rejects any mechanical reductionism and deals with the interlacing of historical time, to use Althusser's expression, meaning both inertia in the diffusion of key ideas and the coexistence, at various stratified levels, of models of behaviour inherited from different traditions.

Having signposted some of the problems, historians ran into new ones along the way. It was because I wanted to explain the Counter-Revolution in the South of France that I decided to study two aspects of the process of dechristianization: the violent and explosive aspect of the Year II and the spontaneous and gradual change which took place in the century of the Enlightenment. Yet in trying to study this latter phenomenon in the flesh, through the analysis of eighteenth-century Provençal wills, I found something else, which ran deeper and was perhaps more essential. This was a change in the sensibility of death, and by the same token, of the vision of the world which Robert Mandrou spoke.

Having come to the end of the road, to the point at which the history of mentalities meets historical ethnography, without merging into it, the historian must pause and reflect. In moving from mediations to mediations, have we lost the thread of the over-clear over-linear history with which we started?

In fact we only left ideology behind in order to rediscover it, in a more refined and precise interpretation based on more information. Of course we need to avoid making too much of the commodities of Marx's formula, the 'particular hue' or 'special ether' of a period. Such reference points allow a far too lax interpretation, even if a recourse to the means of production as the all-embracing overdeterminant leads us back to a certain unity in the historical field.

The history of mentalities can be defined as the study of the mediations and of the dialectical relationship between the objective conditions of human life and the ways in which people narrate it, and even live it. At this level, the contradictions between the two notional systems which we have contrasted here – ideology and mentality – fade away. The exploration of mentalities, far from being a mystifying process, can ultimately lead to an essential widening of the field of research, not as a venture into foreign, exotic territory, but as the natural extension and the cutting edge of all social history.

Some debates are very serviceable. The great debate about the elite and the old-style bourgeoisie made possible a considerable advance in the process of conceptualization. The flourishing of the history of mentalities in the last twenty or thirty years, even if it is only just such a salutary digression – which I do not believe – will, at the very least, have had the immense merit of teaching us to come to terms more directly with the real, in all its complexity and in its totality.

Notes

This paper was originally presented at a conference on mentalities in the revolutionary period held at the University of Dijon in December 1980.

1 In Louis Althusser, *Lenin and Philosophy, and Other Essays* (London, 1971).
2 Karl Marx, 'Introduction to a critique of political economy', in C. J. Arthur (ed.), *The German Ideology, part I* (London, 1977), p. 146.
3 Hereafter referred to as *Rabelais*.

1

Hearts and Minds: Can We Write Religious History from the Traces?

It is in the field of religious history, which in many places merges into the history of mentalities – to the great horror of some people – that one question is most insistently asked. What do the 'traces' and 'indicators' of collective behaviour reveal, beyond the weight of social pressure and the conventions of the hour? Perhaps they provide an indiscreet confession whose significance needs to be assessed. Yet we should not be surprised if the question arises in this particular field, even if the problem is a general one.

The debate which I wanted to open here is, despite appearances, not at all academic. It should lead to a reflection on or, even better, to a view of the current state of a question which is now particularly fluid – the question of the methodology suitable for an approach to religious attitudes and practices.

This is a field which has been completely transformed in recent decades. Obviously, religious history is no longer written as it formerly was. But if areas of research are multiplying, new methods are being tested and change is apparent all round, we are still a long way from a methodological consensus, which is nevertheless indispensable. Yet even given this proliferation of openings in all directions, we are justified in asking, as Jean Delumeau did about Christianity, if religious history is dying out. By this we mean, is it going to merge into the history of mentalities, or even into historical ethnography, whose annexationism is obvious?

Such a question is unavoidable, as the basis of an inquiry which will more cautiously be restricted to methods and techniques. Yet everything is connected here.

The discovery of the quantitive in religious history

Without going back to the Flood, it is clear that when the Abbé
Brémond, now more than half a century ago, worked as an intrepid
explorer on the literary history of religious feeling, the question was
posed in quite different terms. He analysed elaborate and formal
varieties of evidence rather than frequently infinitesimal traces, even if
he showed great methodological originality in working on the
anonymous host of little known or badly known texts of everyday
religious literature. A potentially vast corpus, we would now say, was
outlined in broad terms, even if the mode of treatment, eschewing
systematization, remained impressionistic.

Brémond blazed a trail which is not wholly outmoded, leading to
the most recent products of the history of spirituality, which concentrated on the individual experiences of the small minority of the
'elect'.

In introducing our theme, however, it is necessary to begin with
another methodological revolution which itself needs to be appreciated historically. This is the field of religious sociology, where Le Bras
and Boulard paved the way and developed the techniques. In 1980,
François Isambart, helped by Jean-Paul Terrenoire, published the
Atlas of Catholic Religious Practice in France, based on the papers
and documents of Canon Boulard. This was certainly a monumental
piece of scholarship which is still being used and is still raising
questions, based on its series of maps showing participation in the
Easter ceremonies, attendance at Mass and communicants, analysed
according to gender, distribution between town and country and
position in the social hierarchy. We are still astonished by the wealth
of this scientific harvest, which is narrowly linked to one phase of
pastoral activity – between 1955 and 1970 at its widest – offering a
flash photograph of French religious practice at an essential point in
its history. Yet we cannot help remarking that this is a kind of history
which will never be repeated. This is true if only, we can add
somewhat wickedly, because such head counts are no longer conducted at the end of Mass when the congregation is leaving the
church, and the pastoral activism of the 1950s, which was keen to
compile an inventory of the domestic missionary field, no longer
exists in the same form today. But if the monument constructed by
Isambart, and by the publication, currently taking place, of Boulard's
papers, seems to be more commemorative than forward-looking in
scope and if, dare we say it, we are currently in the process of singeing

Gabriel Le Bras's beard, we can still rely on the revolutionary support of a religious sociology which had such difficulties in establishing its right to exist thirty or forty years ago.

In the first place we have a working hypothesis – or fertile lack of methodological caution – which asserts that there is a crude, but positive and indisputable correlation between the gestures of religious practice and religious belief. This is the first, at least implicit, answer to the central problem of this inquiry. On this basis, it becomes legitimate to count Mass attendance, Easter practitioners, communicants, delayed baptisms, marriages and religious obsequies, ordination rates and monastic vocations. These are so many 'traces' which are similar to others with which we shall be dealing in due course in that they are a massive, impoverished, but also direct and undistorted measure of religious affiliation.

I believe that a certain turning point occurred during the 1960s – at least in France – at the very time when the survey methods of religious sociology reached a sort of apogee in the context of a pastoral system which had begun to question them. This turning point was first marked by a wider historical perspective on what had hitherto been an investigative technique applied to a contemporary context. Gabriel Le Bras, indeed, was the first to have encouraged historians to undertake regressive studies in the modern, and even medieval period, by his insistence on the potential riches contained in the pastoral visitations of the *ancien régime*.

But this discovery took place in stages. For more than one French scholar, the French Revolution represented a kind of starting point, prior to which existed a state of Christianity characterized by a unanimity, or near-unanimity, of significant gestures, as in the great 'seasonal' sacraments such as Easter communion. The first scholars to have ventured into this type of research, like L. Perouas in his thesis on the diocese of La Rochelle in the seventeenth and eighteenth centuries, ran up against the enormity of statistics of the order of 97 or 98 per cent for attendance at Easter communion, or for seasonal practice, which seemed to deprive them of any meaning.

Regressive extension over a long historical period thus confronted the historian with the need to reassess the value of the battery of indicators available for the contemporary period and to discover other, more appropriate indices. This was the stimulating obstacle which, by making the relative character of the available 'traces' apparent, led to the search for others.

The two other elements which, in my view, characterized the turning point of the 1960s are fairly directly associated with the first.

First of all, there was the widespread acceptance of techniques of enumeration and measurement, which had ceased to appear shocking or incongruous. Religious history thus became reconciled to historical sociology and began to emerge from the deliberate framework of elites and spirituality, to focus on mass attitudes and behaviour. This was not without surprises in some cases, as with Toussaert's discovery of an unexpected resistance to Christianity by the peasantry of French-speaking Flanders in the fifteenth century. At this stage, moreover, there was as yet none of the later reticence with regard to the quantification of gestures, and the practice was taken up with confidence. The widespread acceptance of these methods was also accompanied by a change in the spirit of research which involved, if I may use the expression in its most neutral sense, its 'declericalization'. The underlying pastoral concern, whether conscious or not, of the majority of studies of the present or the recent past, which produced an anxious meditation on the problem of dechristianization and its origins, became more blurred as the study went further back in time. In parallel, these years also saw the history of mentalities, more aggressive and with wider appetites, encroach more and more on the field of traditional religious history in the domain of collective attitudes to life, the family, love or death, all of which were so many invitations to further research.

The time of series and 'indicators'

The history of religious attitudes and practices became qualitative, or more precisely, serial, as it organized the 'indicators' which it selected or were available to it, in the *longue durée*. We do not claim to be exhaustive – a vain ambition – in describing some of the new fields which have been opened up in the past twenty years. The legacy of Le Bras's school of religious sociology has not been rejected. The methods for measuring the gestures of religious practice have simply been refined and made more sophisticated, if only to go beyond the monolithic impression which can be derived from the parish registers before the laicizing division produced by the Revolution. There has therefore been a tendency to use more indirect tests: the zeal for immediate baptism, the respect for the ban on marriage at certain times of the year (in Lent and Advent) and, as a consequence, requests for dispensation from marriage banns. In addition, there are the ebb and flow of religious and clerical vocations which, even if significant questions were asked about their relevance as an indicator of religious fervour or zeal (by Perouas), seem to have passed the test and we now possess a wide range of graphs of clerical ordinations and promotions for more than half the dioceses of France. The events experienced by the clergy during the Revolution – schism, the constitutional oath, the dechristianization and resignations from the priesthood – also give us mappable indices which often anticipate by nearly two centuries the maps based on Canon Boulard's findings on religious practice in the 1960s.

This might still constitute no more than a regressive extrapolation from the methods and problems of the sociology of religious practice. Yet it is important to note the increasing diversity of the new factors which were taken into account, both in the area of written sources and in those of archaeology and iconography.

As to written sources, ten years ago I provided the bad example in this regard by proposing an approach focusing on the system of 'baroque' devotionalism in Provence and its destructuring in the course of the eighteenth century, basing my research on many tens of thousands of wills. This was a clear and deliberate invasion of the analytical methods of religious history by the quantitative methods of social history which, as Simiand said, 'counts, measures and weighs'. This weighing has not been accepted without some hesitations. I was asked about the meaning of the range of indices which the wills allowed me to quantify, ranging from the erection of funeral monuments to funerary rituals, Masses for the dead, pious and charitable benefactions and membership of confraternities. One English historian was far from amused by the graph of the average weight of funeral candles in Provence which I could not resist provocatively slipping into my book.

Here we have reached the heart of this new kind of research, which develops a particular relevant 'indicator' so as to analyse a particular change in religious sensibility or feeling in the pluri-secular framework of the *longue durée*. In this kind of research the possibilities are manifold. I have personally gone back into one area of my own research to work on a collection of about 1000 American wills written between 1660 and 1813 which was compiled in the nineteenth century by Thomas Alden, a learned clergyman. Elsewhere, I have dealt with a collection of some hundreds of death notices of French aristocrats between the beginning of the nineteenth century and the twentieth century.

These are just so many examples to provide a specific illustration of the procedure which is now widely used. Where the use of wills allowed me to study the collective discourse of death, the serial study of requests for dispensations from marriage banns in cases of consanguinity or copaternity has led another scholar, J.-M. Gouesse, to reconstitute the discourse of the couple, marriage and the family. It is particularly significant to see how, and in what terms, the corpus of minor devotional literature used by the Abbé Brémond sixty years ago has been reused in our own day. Daniel Roche, in his remarkable article on the literature of death replaces the thematic, impressionistic analysis of the literary histories with an exhaustive and systematic inventory which is followed by an analysis of a certain number of the relevant characteristics of the corpus of Christian literature about death in the classical period.

In this process of exploration, the importance of written sources is relativized by the other 'traces' which are suggested by archaeology or iconography, for example. We cannot claim to have discovered America in this field. Studies of the evidence for religious sensibility did not begin in the last twenty years. Yet the nature of the approach has changed. One scholar, Bernard Cousin, has assembled an impressive collection of 5000 painted ex votos in Provence dating from the sixteenth to the nineteenth centuries and shows very clearly, in a serial study based on very elaborate criteria of treatment, the moments and stages of a relationship with the sacred expressed through the request and receipt of miracles.

On the basis of a comparable, if much more restricted series, Gaby Vovelle and I ventured to analyse representations of death and the hereafter in the altars and reredos to the souls in Purgatory, studied in their continuity in the South of France from the fifteenth to the twentieth centuries.

Very recently, to take a neighbouring yet different example, I myself directed a study of urban cemeteries from the nineteenth century to the present in the same region, in order to analyse what has sometimes been perhaps mistakenly but significantly defined as the 'new cult of the dead' centred on the cemetery. The synthesis which I constructed, entitled *The City of the Dead*, tried to understand the cult through the forest of signs and symbols deposited in the great necropolises of the Mediterranean region.

We have perhaps enough examples here, however partial this avowedly subjective inventory may be, to allow us to analyse the original characteristics shared by these new procedures, in which qualitative analysis is only one element.

More profoundly, I feel that what is essential in the bias of these new studies is their attempt to try to arrive at an understanding of the anonymous masses, beyond the discourse and religiosity of the elites.

The masses were unable to afford the luxury of an individual and literary expression, however basic. Our inquiry is located at this stratum of common religion, both in terms of its practices and of the collective representations which underlie it.

At this level, the study of popular religion doubtless reflects a factor illustrated in the work of Philippe Ariès, vital to which is what Ariès called 'the collective unconscious' operating at the level of the history of mentalities rather than the domain of clear thought or clearly formulated expressions. It is in this field that the indirect questioning or extracted confessions offered by our sources can be most profitable.

A list of tasks: the quantitive in question

We need to be well aware of the limits and the schedule of conditions involved in this kind of research. The first limitation is, of course, the poverty of these massive sources. Let me illustrate this with an example. The painted ex voto can be discouraging at first sight by its apparent repetitiveness; the stereotyped attitudes of the figures and the ultimately limited number of scenarios, such as interiors showing people 'prostrate on the sick-bed' and exterior scenes of aggression and violent death, which it illustrates and comments on. The same can be said about the iconography of cemeteries and a fortiori of death notices. We need a whole system of decoding to deal with the fragile indices provided by these repetitive sources, which were not created for the purposes which they are being made to serve. In scrutinizing ex votos, scholars patiently measure the respective surface areas of the celestial space occupied by the apparition and the terrestrial scene in the image, as they analyse the system of gestures and the exchange of looks which establish the links between the two worlds. Analysing the images of Purgatory can reveal characteristic changes in a pantheon of intercessors which was gradually being depopulated in the seventeenth and eighteenth centuries.

This list of tasks also demands a real ingenuity on the part of scholars, and a flawless knack in both the choice and interpretation of the legacy which history has placed at their disposal. Sources like wills, which have a growing importance and meaning in the sixteenth century and the classical period, during which the practice of making wills spread, abruptly lose their statistical basis and their intrinsic interest in post-revolutionary France (indeed in one whole part of Europe) with the sanctioning of the civil division of property by the

Napoleonic code, which was accompanied by an irreversible decline
in the traditional ways of bequeathing property.

We need to move from one source to another, following individual
expressions about the hereafter in funerary art from the churches to
the cemeteries, and even to the town squares, when the dead left the
holy places, between 1770 and 1850, to gather in other sites.

These difficulties and constraints, which tolerate neither error nor
impoverished or reductionist explanations, partly explain the reticence, even the radical objections, which this kind of research into the
traces has sometimes encountered as the areas of study increase in
number. Such criticisms can be very powerful and should not be
treated dismissively. The traces which we are recovering and attempting to organize into series are, by definition, reflections of social
practices. They pass through filters and mediations which are capable
of changing their meaning. Who writes the will – the testator or the
notary? Painted ex votos were often more than half prepared in
advance, and the journeyman painter only had to add the details on
demand. With so many possible mediations, distortions and constraints, can these massive and poor documents be anything more,
finally, than the reflection of the social pressure or conventions of the
moment? By the same token, will the very weakness of these serial
studies of the traces not be such as to leave us on the surface of things,
confined to a superficial and generalized understanding which is
limited to appearances? And can we really hope, on such a basis, to
approach a phenomenon as secret as faith?

The amicable debate between Philippe Ariès and myself on the
interpretation of the spectacular turning point in collective sensibility
which took place at some point in the eighteenth century, between
1730 and 1770, when devotional and religious clauses disappeared
from French wills, is very indicative of the state of the debate. My
hypothesis on this process was, and still is, to see it as the beginnings
of dechristianization. A change of convention, the reflection of a
modified sensibility, Ariès replied. In his view, in the Rousseau-esque
age of triumphant sensibility, the father of the family no longer
needed to stipulate egotistically what precautions were to be taken
with respect to his mortal remains and his soul, being certain that his
heirs would look after everything. Thus we have a process of
interiorization, rather than of real change. There is always an interior
reality, and who can boast of having unlocked its secrets? I have to
admit that, in over 20,000 wills, I never met one which opened with
'Joy, joy, tears of joy . . .'.

In all these studies, one of the major difficulties remains the interpretation of silences, which are so often charged with meaning. When the source becomes mute, what should we conclude? In my eighteenth-century Provençal wills there is a Jansenist silence as well as a libertine silence, which widens out into the more generalized silence of indifference in the second half of the century.

Quantitive historians are not totally devoid of an answer to these criticisms. They are aware of the fragility of an indicator taken in isolation and of the overriding necessity to correlate findings. It is not hard to answer Ariès's arguments with the statement that the change which took place in familial affectivity does not explain why the confraternities lost their members; nor why the nebula of clerics and religious, relatives and friends, which were so important in the late seventeenth and early eighteenth centuries, should dwindle away towards the end of the century.

It would be just as easy to interpret the return to the qualitative approach which partly characterizes very recent work in the history of mentalities, and especially in religious history, in terms of a historical conjuncture. The quantifying trend in French and European Catholic historiography corresponded to a stage of voluntarist pastoral work which accepted, as a working hypothesis, an equation of the vitality of faith and the regularity of religious practice. Hence the contemporary importance of religious sociology as practised by Gabriel Le Bras and his successors. But nowadays François Isambart, while presenting his *Atlas of Catholic Religious Practice in France* as the final stage in this field, has announced the launching of a new research group which will, significantly, be concerned with the theme of 'symbolic ethics and practices'.

There has clearly been a complete change of direction, and not just because the collapse of the formal gestures of religious practice in post-conciliar Christianity made such a fundamental revision necessary.

Arguing the case

As researchers of indices and quantifiers of anonymous traces, are we the survivors of another war, of a bygone era? I do not think so, and I believe that there is a possibility that these researches into anonymous traces conducted according to the methods of serial history can be very fruitfully used in the directions being taken by the new religious history.

This is partly because such sources, when suitably decoded, yield

elements which are not at all impoverished, and which go well beyond
the initial questions formulated at the beginning of the process.

I hope I will be forgiven for going back one last time to the wills,
which were my first research field. Starting from an initial problematic which can retrospectively be seen to have been rather narrow – an
inquiry into the origins of dechristianization in the age of Enlightenment – I found much more than I had expected in the sources. I found
the characteristics of a sensibility of death; the system of gestures
which surrounded it and the symbolic forms which accompanied it.

Might we not say the same for other sources, which are very
diverse, ranging from dispensations from marriage banns to illegitimacy statistics, or from death notices to funerary art in cemeteries,
and which nevertheless converge around the pole of the family and of
attitudes to life?

It might be retorted that this is an ambiguous and questionable way
of approaching religious history, which would seem to be thus
absorbed, amoeba-like, by the history of mentalities. I agree, but, at
the level of attitudes which are properly and deeply religious, if these
can be dissociated from the attitudes mentioned above, I believe that
there is a whole series of results which can only be arrived at by using
this methodological ruse or detour.

Firstly, this is the case from the perspective of the history of mass
behaviour, attitudes and collective representations – what I prefer to
call the diffusion of key ideas. The dialectic which links the emergence
of new themes and ideas among the spiritual elites and their diffusion
among the Christian people is a complex relationship, whose developments and inertias alike can only be perceived by recourse to tests
based on religious practice. Brémond located the great period of what
he called 'the mystical invasion' between 1620 and 1640. I found the
small change of this process occurring between 1660 and 1680 in the
devotional clauses of Provençal wills. Such intervals, or periods of
inertia, can be studied with precision in the convergent sources which
we have at our disposal. If the upward trend in the production of the
literature of the Last Things, which was such an important part of the
post-Tridentine pastoral system, was 'broken' from the beginning of
the eighteenth century in the statistics of book production established
by Daniel Roche, who showed that the eighteenth century was a
period of reprints, rather than original production, this change is not
registered in graphs of testimentary devotionalism before 1750, or
1730 at the earliest.

A comparable exercise to the one we have all too briefly summarized was carried out in the *longue durée* dealing with the dogma and

devotions of Purgatory. This devotional system was traditionally rooted in the clergy, and especially in the religious orders, during the Middle Ages, and only began to be diffused among the mass of the people from the fourteenth or, more notably, the fifteenth century, reaching its culmination in the period of the post-Tridentine reconquest. A recourse to written or iconographic sources of the kind just mentioned seems indispensable in order to grasp the realities of this process of diffusion, distortion and adaptation. This is what tempted Gaby Vovelle and myself to work on the altars of the souls in Purgatory.

I will go even further. I believe that there is a whole series of characteristics of collective representations whose structures and unconscious evolution can only be grasped with the help of this type of source material. The psychology of the miraculous, as it can be followed through the play of glances in the painted ex votos; the changes registered in the series of paintings depicting the souls in Purgatory and the unexpected confidence shown in the representations of the 'third place', represent so many discoveries which no text would have made possible. Nor is it paradoxical, having just spoken of inertias in the spread of innovations, to contrast the stability of a religious discourse which was put in place during the Counter-Reformation with the patient work of adaptation, distortion and even creativity which took place on the mass level. In order to grasp these obscure processes of change, which were, for the most part, unknown to contemporaries because they took place far beyond the level of formal awareness, the new methods of research which we have just described are more necessary than ever. Doubtless others will also be found.

I will not, I hope, be pushed into saying that the global and approximate truths to which this kind of research leads will deliver up the ultimate secret and allow us, as if by stealth, to look into hearts and minds. That is another affair.

Note

Paper read to the International Congress of Religious History, Winnipeg, August 1980.

2

The Relevance and Ambiguity of Literary Evidence

More than a variation on the theme of the difficulty of interdisciplinary dialogue, we have here an investigation of the problems raised by a kind of evidence whose uniqueness makes it both irreplaceable and impossible to classify – and therefore suspect. What can literature, at the opposite extreme from the quantitive history of collective attitudes, teach us? A whole series of questions arises from this investigation, which is not at all academic. These include the relationship between the history of ideas and the history of mentalities but also, more profoundly, the ultimate significance of the evidence contained in art and literature. In this ambiguous dialogue between the collective and the unique, the history of mentalities betrays both its annexationism . . . and its scruples.

Literary history, as it opens up new pathways for itself – much like the history of mentalities as I, among others, practise it – currently retains a secret or overt complicity with too many legacies of mutual misunderstanding inherited from different traditions. I believe that the study of death, in literary history and in the history of mentalities, offers us a valuable opportunity, not to carry on an academic quarrel in a closed arena, but to find an area of confrontation between various methods – all the more valuable as it extends well beyond the theme itself.

Both literary history and the history of mentalities bear witness to the rediscovery of death which has taken place in France over the past fifteen years, even though we have hardly begun to detach ourselves from the taboo which surrounds death in contemporary liberal societies. Whereas the English-speaking world, in particular, has seen a proliferation of studies by doctors, sociologists, psychologists and essayists which has reached considerable proportions, the exceptional role of the literary and historical disciplines seems to me to be one of the most original features of the French (and Italian) approach to the rediscovery of death. There is no need to recite the roll of honour of French historians in this respect, which includes F. Lebrun, Pierre Ariès, P. Chaunu, D. Roche and R. Chartier, to name but a few.

In the literary field, the impression of a breakthrough or turning point is less clear cut, possibly because the theme was never really ignored. Lucien Febvre might once have seemed to be trying to be deliberately provocative when he asked historians who was going to give us a history of wickedness, of death, of love . . . , but, whether in classical or current terms, the funerary or macabre motif has always had its place in literary studies. Even more so since, following the work of Mauzi, Ehrard or Duprun, thematic studies, on themes such as the idea of happiness, nature or anxiety, have opened up new fields in literary history. Robert Favre's brilliant synthesis, *Death in the Age of Enlightenment*, shows a direct continuity with these other works while also, it seems to me, introducing a new dimension. But at this shifting frontier between literary history and the history of ideas, which tends to merge with the history of mentalities, Brémond showed the way very early on when he reserved a place in the ninth volume of his *Literary History of Religious Sentiment* for a chapter on the history of the Last Things. Similarly, Tenenti, in his pioneering work, *The Sense of Death and the Love of Life in the Renaissance* opened up a whole new field in the 1950s which was common to literary history, art history and the history of mentalities under the accommodating label of the history of ideas.

There is therefore a long history of comradeship, even if we have only become fully conscious of it in the light of our current pre-occupations. Yet, at the same time, I feel that the recent growth of the history of mentalities, in its methods and perspectives, leads us to raise in new terms the problem of the use of literary sources and evidence.

It may be restating the obvious to underline how the approach based on mentalities has developed over the last fifteen years from a kind of history which was still, in the work of Lucien Febvre and Robert Mandrou, close to that of culture or of clear thought, towards a study of behaviour, gestures and attitudes as the unconscious, collective expressions of humanity.

In dealing with collective attitudes to the family, life, love and death, contemporary historians tend to study characteristics which were formerly approached via literary sources by using a battery of new 'indicators' – massive anonymous written sources like wills or iconographic and archaeological material. Even when they do not completely adopt the logic of a quantitive or serial approach, contemporary scholars seem to eschew the support of literary evidence, which has come to appear too facile.

Literature: a suspect source?

I hope I may be allowed, without trying to be exhaustive, to illustrate this remark with some significant examples. In his rich synthesis *The Hour of our Death*, Philippe Ariès seems to me to demonstrate the equivocal links which connect the current history of mentalities and literary history. His many references to a multi-faceted culture allow him to draw on a whole range of information taken from all available sources – from archaeology and iconography to religious and secular writing, whether anonymous or well known. The 'achronic death' which Ariès places at the beginning of his survey, and again at the end – the ageless death encountered in traditional societies – is equally well illustrated by the death of the heroes in the *Song of Roland* as by that of Tolstoy's peasant in *Ivan Illich*, who turns his face to the wall to die when his time has come.

Yet even though he delves liberally into all kinds of sources, following the impressionistic technique which he favours, it could be said that Ariès rejects literature as such. The baroque or Romantic sense of death, for example, is not fully present in his work, and although he does not categorically exclude material found in 'great' literature, he uses memoirs, diaries and anonymous accounts much more frequently. This is because Ariès, as he himself explains, wants to reach the level of what he calls – with a certain amount of ambiguity – 'the collective unconscious', thereby cutting off the two extremities of the total history of death and humanity: the demographic, economic and social conditions on the one hand – an absence which does not greatly concern us here – but also, on the other hand, everything which reverts to ideology, be it religious, political or philosophical, up to the level of literary or aesthetic expression, so as to locate his study in the middle ground where attitudes reflect an unconscious system of collective representations.

I am well aware that the bias which I have described in Ariès's work can, for very different reasons, be attributed to my own. In choosing thousands of Provençal wills as the basis for the most detailed study I have undertaken on death: *Baroque Piety and Dechristianization:*

attitudes to death in eighteenth-century Provence, I deliberately focused on the text in its most neutral, massive and anonymous form, in short the least 'literary' form. Although it is formulated very differently from that of Ariès, my justification for this rests on the same concern, common to all historians of mentalities nowadays, to rehabilitate the collective attitudes of the mass of the people at the expense of the privileged expression of the few.

My final example to illustrate the different view taken nowadays of the literary approach to attitudes towards death is the most clear cut and involves the research carried out by Daniel Roche under the title *The Literature of Death* on the literature of the Last Things and the final journey in the seventeenth and eighteenth centuries. This involves compiling as exhaustive an inventory as possible of this (more or less) religious literature, seen in the context of changes in its rate of production in order to evaluate the 'global weighting', to use Pierre Chaunu's term, of collective investment in death. Such a detailed account also makes possible a thematic analysis of titles in the time scale of the *longue durée*, quite apart from a valuable sociology of the authors.

Such a procedure, conceived in an attitude of deliberate simplicity which should not pose any problems of disorientation to contemporary literary historians, nevertheless bears witness to a willingness to redeploy literary sources so as to construct a new kind of history – the history of mentalities and sensibilities. Taken as a whole, by a process of quantification which is unashamedly simple, the statistics of literary production on death reveal how, at some point between 1680 and 1720, the upward trend of treatises on the Last Things came to a standstill as a prelude to the stagnation of the eighteenth century, which saw mainly the republication of older texts.

We have here three examples which, despite their differences, all illustrate some new approaches towards death in the history of mentalities. In each of them we can see, in different ways, the rejection of a kind of history which, as Lucien Febvre said, 'is no longer ours', that is, a literary approach to death which can, with some unavoidable injustice, be summed up under the theme of 'Death in the work of . . .'. The list is certainly fascinating, and I recall the interest with which I read the proliferation of essays and theses on death in the work of Martin du Gard, on death in Simone de Beauvoir, on the Angel of Death from Winckelmann to Thomas Mann. . . . And yet we are constantly confronted by the historian's preliminary question, in all its inescapable naivety: just who is giving evidence about what?

Even when the literary approach goes beyond the framework of an individual study to open out onto a wider canvas of collective sensibility, as in Favre's work on the eighteenth century, or in a more uneven way, in Dubruck's work on French poetry of the fifteenth and sixteenth centuries, one may justifiably ask what real significance or importance this flowering of literary discourse has for an attempt to understand a wider collective sensibility. In one of the essays, which he has since republished, on Huizinga and the theme of the macabre in the later Middle Ages, Philippe Ariès tried to exorcise the overbearing presence of iconography and literature. Doubtless he did so because it has no place in his explanatory model, which is based on gradual changes rather than abrupt breakthroughs. Yet, in a wider sense, he did so because it is part of 'the encumbrance of the emotional' which Braudel wanted to expel from the history of the *longue durée*. Here the historian of mentalities is forced to face up to an essential problematic, and having yielded to the temptation to dismiss literary evidence, he might actually be led to rediscover its importance at the centre of the problems to be tackled.

This, at least, was the method I felt obliged to adopt in my work *Death in the West from 1300 to the Present*, taking up the challenge of a vertical total history which would comprehend the brute fact of mortality, in its demographic aspects, so as to try to analyse it in all its ramifications in time, including the most complex and sophisticated products of the imagination, ranging over religion, literature, art and, in short, ideology in its most elaborate forms.

Such imprudence, or vaulting ambition, on which I will be judged, was necessitated in the course of my research by the ubiquity of death, which was constantly present in all literary expression, and consequently by the ubiquity of a literary evidence which cannot be scorned.

An unavoidable kind of evidence

Doubtless a project of this kind entails a whole series of difficulties and preliminary problems, some obvious from the outset, others less so. If the recourse to literary evidence seems to emerge naturally for earlier periods where sources are scarce and all material is grist to the mill, the proliferation, in modern times, of a literature which has freed itself from any religious framework has led to a multiplicity of forms of expression and of the discourses which they contain. From the nineteenth century to the present this has led to an inextricably entangled web of fragmentary messages conveyed by films, comic strips, songs, television and other media, all of which provide evidence which must be taken into account in their various ways. Nobody will be surprised if I admit, as a modernist fully aware of his own imprudence, that I have encountered fewer difficulties in improvising as a medievalist (whatever well-earned reproaches I might have to face) than in attempting to organize a coherent synthesis for the contemporary period where the history of mentalities must, significantly, make its way with far more difficulty amid a profusion of evidence which has yet to be organized.

I want to move away from these problems to some extent in order to try to show very simply how, and in what terms, I envisage the use of literary evidence in the approach to collective attitudes towards death. Can literature be suitably used in this way? Clearly, and without claiming to reveal novelties, I should say that I see two 'easy methods of prayer' – two ways of developing the use of texts. The first way, very simply, is to take them as elementary evidence, reflections of a lived social reality, of a kind of practice about which, whether innocently or not, they can provide us with information which we would be hard put to find elsewhere. This could be said to be obvious. Yet this method of interrogating texts, in which history and literary history cooperate at the primary level, is not so obvious that it is superfluous to mention it. When I read the account of Goutil's funeral procession in the *Roman de Renart* the corpse, 'whose head uncovered was', evokes a princely or knightly funerary style where the displaying of the corpse with the face exposed was the rule. Here is a specific, apparently pointless piece of information which, in its historical context, integrates, in my view, a whole system of written, archaeological and iconographical sources and throws an interesting light on the delicate problem of the relationship between human beings and the dead body, the cadaver which some people lock away all too quickly (in my opinion) under the hermetic lid of the coffin, whereas the illuminations of French and Flemish books of hours, like the *predelle* of Italian altars, are evidence of the long persistence of a tradition of displaying the corpse in the Mediterranean world and beyond.

Such erudite decoding is not always obvious: it demands a real caution in the handling of the concrete signs which it produces. I do not want to give the impression of multiplying small quarrels over points of detail in Ariès's imposing and stimulating work in borrowing another example illustrating the gestural system of death which is so pregnant with meaning. When dealing with achronic death, the tamed death of the early Middle Ages, Ariès borrows from the *chansons de geste* the image of the position which the heroes, such as Roland, adopt at the moment of death – the *commendatio animae* – which can be seen in the recumbent statues of the thirteenth century in the Latin West. As we have seen, he treats the death of Tolstoy's peasant Ivan Illich under the same heading, as he turns to the wall when the time comes to submit to death. But at this point we can ask a question. The gesture of turning to the wall to die is also found in many places in medieval literature. To mention only two examples, it is the image of Marsile's death in the *Song of Roland* and it is the same in the death of Tristan. But we can see one common factor in both of these – the image of a bad death, of salvation refused. So what can appear, in the peasant world of the nineteenth century to be an image of 'natural' death, exists for us, historically, in already precise and very complex forms with quite a different meaning.

One can find other examples without too much difficulty from a variety of times and places, though the reader may rest assured that I will do so with discretion! If such information is particularly valuable for periods where sources are scarce, it is equally rich, and occasionally indispensable, in much more recent texts. Thus, the last page of Voltaire's *Ingénu* describing the death of the beautiful Saint-Yves can, in this perspective, be usefully read as a source for the history of death in Paris in the first third of the eighteenth century which shows a relatively greater intimacy surrounding the last moments, but also the survival of the practice of exposing the corpse, with the face still uncovered, at the door of the house.

Certainly, the more we proceed in time, the more difficult it becomes to isolate this primary reading, which sees the literary text as a simple reflection of contemporary social practice, and here our task is to decode the latent meanings, from a much more complex discourse which is charged with ulterior motives.

Thus it is possible to analyse the ceremonial of bourgeois death in its development and construction by using the nineteenth- and twentieth-century European novel, culminating in the enormous *fin-de-siècle* sagas of Thomas Mann or Roger Martin du Gard. Such serial study can also benefit from a comparison with the parallel (or significantly discordant) discourses of death notices, obituaries, epitaphs and funerary monuments, as they proliferated between 1860 and 1920 in Genoa, Milan and elsewhere. Yet one feels that the novel, even in the age of realism and naturalism, offers us far more than just a simple reflection or inert evidence of common social practices and that it demands a far more elaborate reading.

I promised to discuss two levels of the direct reading of literary sources. Now it is time to move on to the second, which does not claim to be any more original than the first. This is the deliberate discourse of death, a stylistic exercise which was, for a long time, almost the exclusive domain of religious literature.

One might think that in this field the process of decoding, although not without its difficulties, is nevertheless direct. We possess a vast corpus of material, one of the great advantages of which is doubtless its continuity in the *longue durée*. This literature, whether major or minor (but where is the frontier which separates what can be called literature from what cannot? We will not get involved in this debate which is at once both essential and futile) consists of collections of sermons, apologetic tracts, *artes moriendi*, funeral orations and even wills. The discourse of death is presented here without masks, if not without digressions. It is open to the historian, as to the literary historian, to treat this literature as a whole or in detail; to organize it into series as Daniel Roche has done for texts from the classical period, or as in Roger Chartier's work on the *artes moriendi* of the fifteenth and sixteenth centuries.

The difficulties begin when we actually have to open these books and analyse their contents. But we are not devoid of useful reference points in this field, and the traditional history of ideas has cleared the way for us here. The official discourse of the churches, the deviant discourse of heretics and freethinkers and the various discourses of humanism and philosophy lead us into the new vulgates of the eighteenth and nineteenth centuries. If the work of organizing these ideological expressions in the *longue durée* is enormous, the fact remains that they come to us as they are: meditations on death, the Last Things and the life to come.

Much more than a reflection

If we confine ourselves to the two levels of reality which have just been discussed – two ways, in all, of staring death in the face – we will doubtless still be restricted to a relatively impoverished use of literary sources. The history of death is in fact the history of a whole series of tricks, masks and evasions, but also of products of the collective imagination brought face to face with this compulsory passage in all human experience.

It is at this level that literature, because it is much more than a simple reflection of a lived social practice, offers an elaborate and complex type of evidence. It can produce vivid contrasts with the system of conventions of the age. In a century which has seen the emergence in the Anglo-Saxon world and diffusion throughout the West – even the Catholic West – of a taboo which has made death a new category of obscenity, by a seemingly inexorable process, we are, by contrast, also experiencing a proliferation of cultural expressions about death, however 'un-literary' they may seem. Through this cathartic compensation for the rule of silence, we have been able to analyse the ubiquity of a fantastic and productive creativity surrounding death in all media, as Potel has done in his essay 'Death on display; death for sale'. I have surprised, if not quite shocked, some people by discussing comic strips in one of my articles. Potel and others deal with popular songs, film and television, all of which are saturated by the universal presence of death, from the weekly massacre on the roads to the other death, so real and yet so far away, in Vietnam and elsewhere, and the kind of death imagined in the nuclear or ecological apocalypse.

A relative, if not total autonomy of literary expression emerges from these examples drawn from current events, and one can find equivalents in history. To this extent we can ask whether death, seen as a compulsory passage, constant in all literary expression, has ever really been the subject of a taboo in this area. Robert Favre's excellent synthesis has shown that even at the heart of the attempt to exorcise the unseemly spectre, during the Enlightenment, death was always present at the heart of literary expression.

Without seeking to be deliberately paradoxical, I would suggest that in this area silence itself possesses a significance which is open to close scrutiny. To take only a few examples: we can ask what the significance is, in the neighbouring sphere of aesthetic expression, of the absolute silence of Ingres on death in a very considerable body of work, when one thinks of the bloody orgy which unfolds in the work of Delacroix. Even more naively, what does the total refusal of Impressionist painting, with the exception of Manet, to represent death signify? Is it simply, as Odilon Redon wrote, that they were 'low-brow painters'?

Our history of death is also a history of silences, but to deal with this other point would take us much further, and we must content ourselves with investigating the presence of death in literary discourse.

The difficulty felt by historians in taking into account these discourses into account is obviously related to the degree to which they go beyond the limits of that normal reality which historians are constantly trying to recapture by using a battery of sources associated with normality. Does not all literary expression, however monitored, contain a certain dramatization which makes it part of the 'importunate pathos' which Braudel wanted to banish from history? Hence the difficulty, in a history of the *longue durée*, of taking account of the growth of the macabre in the fifteenth century, the fever of the baroque between 1580 and 1650, the return of darker ideas at the twilight of the Enlightenment or the pervasive morbidity of the period around 1900 which is antithetically called the *belle époque*.

There is a great temptation to relegate artists pervaded by the presence of death to the margins, or to see in their work only an individual pathology. Philippe Ariès observed that macabre sepulchral monuments never represented more than 5 per cent of all tombs in the fifteenth century, and went so far as to state that the sense of the macabre at the end of the nineteenth century was only cultivated by a few Germans and Belgians.

I am far from denying the role of the individual pathology of the artist in the personal synthesis which he presents. Sade or Delacroix (and Ingres, in his own way) all reacted as a function of a very personal experience which was uniquely theirs. We would be restricting ourselves to a very impoverished view of Thomas Mann and Roger Martin du Gard if we were to analyse their bravura strokes as a flat illustration of bourgeois death around 1900, without taking into account the personal dimension in these authors, whom we know to have been pervaded by the fear of death throughout their lives.

These individual adventures, within the Brownian movement of collective sensibility, appear as so many privileged testimonies within a much larger context. They acquire an exceptional value, in my opinion, when seen against the background of the crises of collective sensibility articulated by the history of mentalities. I know that the idea of crisis is disputed by many scholars in this area. Paul Hazard is still being criticized for this, just as there are those who are at pains to demonstrate that the French Revolution never happened.

Stretches of the *longue durée* and crises of collective sensibility

Yet such crises do exist, and literary evidence provides a vital indicator of the burgeoning sensibility of death. I have already summarily described them, ranging from the sense of the macabre at the end of the Middle Ages to the present day and including the baroque sensibility, European Romanticism and the Symbolists and

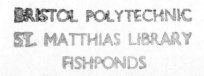

Decadents of the *fin de siècle*. These marginal figures testify, for many others besides themselves, to a malaise which was felt far beyond the narrow circles to which they belonged.

Does this mean that, as a historian, I should only take account of such expressions in times of abrupt change; times of tension and of sea changes in collective sensibilities?

Certainly not: between such sequences of redefinition and questioning, models or, if you prefer, stable structures develop and become prevalent which condition collective representations and attitudes – the rituals of an age – generally over long periods of time. It was in this way, based on a continuity between the end of the fourteenth and the middle of the seventeenth centuries, hardly troubled by the crisis of the Reformation, that what I call the 'baroque' model of death came into being, a model characterized by exteriorization, ostentation and by a wealth of multiple gestures. The baroque ceremonial of the seventeenth century diffused and gave currency to princely funerary practices of the fifteenth and sixteenth centuries. Likewise, Neoclassicism and Romanticism both reflected and contributed to the shaping of the new norms whereby bourgeois death was expressed in the nineteenth century. In this dialectic, it is clear that literature, like other expressions of ideology, both reflects, and at the same time helps to shape collective sensibility by providing it with a whole series of formal supports.

The result of such an investigation is that literary evidence is seen to be irreplaceable. Recapitulating the foregoing arguments, which have opened other doors along the way, I feel that its importance can already be seen on several levels.

First of all, it can be seen in the relative wealth of the information which it allows us to use. The serial sources which we have begun to exploit are poor, often univocal and demand a careful decoding. (I say all this as a convinced and long-standing practitioner of this method.) I am thinking here of tombs, wills and ex votos. Literary statements are still essential for understanding the hidden face of death. Thus, to take just one example, which is nowadays somewhat banal and hackneyed, the game of Eros and Thanatos existed long before Baldung Grien or Cranach, and would benefit by ceasing to be exclusively interpreted in terms of the Sadian revolution. Mario Praz's essay, *Death, the Flesh and the Devil*, so tardily translated into French, retains some of its provocative and suggestive power, but would certainly benefit from a new revision within a truly historical perspective. As a method of probing the inmost depths of the habitually not-said, the analysis of what has been hidden and obscured by the hegemony of a received model, literary evidence seems to provide excellent source material on at least two levels.

In the *longue durée*, which many see as the proper time scale for the history of mentalities, literature acts as a vehicle for images, clichés, memories and traditions – all the ceaselessly reworked and distorted products of the collective imagination. I have not discussed folklore or legends, but it is clear that all mythology is conveyed in a literary form. Under this heading one can underline the inertia or resistance of some persistent forms in the field of death, of which the religious discourse, as it became fixed sometime in the course of the seventeenth century by the struggles of post-Tridentine pastoral activity and transmitted *ne varietur* to the present day, is the supreme example.

Yet I prefer, in an apparent contradiction (which is really only apparent), primarily to emphasize another advantage of the literary source – its mobility. Literature, like a kind of electroscope, registers in its changes the equally rapid tremors of collective sensibility. The obsession with death, itself a metaphorical expression of an existential ill, is becoming one of the most vital indicators of the kind of history of sensibility which is currently coming into being. In discussing the innocent and yet crucial question as to how and why the image of death changes, Pierre Chaunu, who is very much aware of the great demographic cycles, once wrote that, in his opinion, collective investment in death was derived from life expectancy. I would not push this paradox so far as to convict Chaunu of flagrantly mechanistic reductionism! But I truly believe, without succumbing to lyricism, that this investment is really derived from the hope for happiness. All of which goes to explain why, in our ageing societies – where, in America, women have broken through the barrier of an eighty-year life expectancy – we now face death with anxiety.

On this level, the use of literature seems to offer the historian of mentalities a method which is not merely useful, but even indispensable for reintroducing the dimension of the short-term into a subject which is all too open to the attractions of an immobile history, losing itself in the realms of historical ethnography at the expense of a history which moves; one which registers those changes of sensibility which are much more than just 'the transient froth of days'.[1]

Notes

Paper delivered to the Conference on the History of Death in Literature, Nancy, October 1980.

1   The phrase is a reference to the title of Boris Vian's novel, *L'Écume des jours.* [translator]

3

Iconography and the History of Mentalities

Something more than an individual reflection, this paper offers a view of the state of the problem as it was collectively debated at a conference which brought together historians, art historians, ethnologists and semiologists. The problem discussed here arises out of the variety of sources used in the history of mentalities, where the privileged status of the written word is at least diminished, if not wholly called into question. Why the recourse to the image or, even more widely, to figurative expression, the importance of which is attested by a whole series of parallel studies? And how do we treat this material, given the specific questions which are being asked of it?

These reflections on the use of iconography in the history of mentalities reflect a process of collective research. The object was to present a synthesis, although this did not preclude the possibility of broadening the scope of the inquiry arising out of the discussions and conclusions of a conference held on 12 and 13 June 1976 under the aegis of the Centre Méridionale d'Histoire Sociale, des Mentalités et des Cultures. On this occasion, a group of scholars met to investigate how iconography has come to be seen as a vital source for the history of mentalities and why this use of iconography is particularly manifest among modern historians – although this proposition must be treated with caution, since it only has a provisional value. To what extent is this development linked to the trend towards the study of popular culture, providing a resource which can be used to obtain a knowledge of people who cannot be approached through the medium of written sources or discourses?

A 'flashback'

The first response to this preliminary question might be a kind of 'flashback' which briefly retraces the progress of this kind of research. The traditional bibliography is quite impressive. Briefly, it has two main directions. On the one hand, what I shall call traditional art history, without attaching any pejorative value to the label, has never been indifferent to the information about the sensibility of a period which is revealed in works of art. Yet this type of iconography, which focuses chiefly on the aesthetic qualities of a work of art (for which no one can criticize it), is nevertheless restricted to the qualitative iconography of elites and aesthetes. It is, to use a comparison which is commonplace but expressive, in the same position vis-à-vis history as traditional literary history, or, as the literary history of religious sensibility, as exemplified by Brémond, with its concentration on the commanding heights of spirituality, vis-à-vis the sociology of religion.

On the other hand, the erudite iconography of folklore, of the kind familiar to us from learned manuals on earthenware or popular printmakers, seems more appropriate to the interests of the collector than those of the historian. It is highly attentive to art forms which are often popular, but its perspectives are different. For different reasons, a certain kind of ethnographic iconography, which is in part the product of the researches of folklorists, has for long remained unassimilable by the historian, despite its merits.

Some stages are discernible on this canvas which can also be easily paralleled with equivalent developments in literary history. What Paul Hazard or Daniel Mornet were to the previous generation of historians, the elaborate monuments of Louis Réau's *Iconography of Christian Art* and, for modernists especially, Emile Mâle's *Religious Art after the Council of Trent*, are for art history. In the case of Emile Mâle, as his work unfolds, we can trace the influence of his work on earlier periods, from antiquity to the Middle Ages, where archaeology and iconography were essential tools, on his work on the post-Tridentine modern era where these techniques needed to establish their right to exist. The importance of these works should not be minimized. This derives not just from the irreplaceable wealth of their thematic repertoire, but also on the way in which iconography, at this level, truly comes to terms with history, especially the history of religious sensibility.

In the development from itemized iconography to iconology, a breakthrough was achieved which, for the French reading public, was symbolized by the publication in 1967 of the French translation of Erwin Panofsky's *Essays on Iconology* which had been first published in 1939. This important stage seems, appropriately, to have had many of the objectives of our own research. No longer is it a case of writing 'a history of cultural symptoms', or of 'symbols in general' such as 'time, love, death, or the creation of the world'. Yet, just as we feel we are coming close to touching the foundations of our own kind of research, this history, in the author's very words, seems to tail off in the face of an inquiry into the 'essential tendencies of the human spirit'. These adventures turn into 'little strange and learned odysseys' which stimulate us while still leaving us with the desire, stemming from the well-known annexationism of our discipline, to involve history in such projects. It will only be by getting away from the framework of the initiated and the complicitous that we can direct our attention to the problem of the diffusion of the key ideas and collective representations which are expressed by these systems of symbols.

It was at this level, or at this stage of the way, that the essential turning point, generally speaking located in the late 1960s, took place, after which iconography began to be used as one of the techniques of the history of mentalities. (Despite the important earlier work of Alberto Tenenti on *Life and Death in Fifteenth-century Art*, a swallow heralding the coming of spring.) The essential impetus came from a branch of history which was then at its formative stage and was working at the frontiers of discovery of popular culture. In the work of scholars like Robert Mandrou and Geneviève Bollème, the visual document took its place beside oral and written sources. In the light of this new problematic there was a reappraisal of the themes of art history, evident in Tenenti's work on life and death, Deyon on poverty (*The Representation of the Poor in Seventeenth-century French Painting*) and L. Marin on spirituality (*Philippe de Champaigne and Port Royal*).

Yet such a reworking could not have taken place without involving more or less drastic revisions. From art history to religious history or the history of mentalities, a totally modified reading was applied to the same objects. The works of art which were studied also changed as a pronounced migration took place from noble or great art to popular art, from the unique masterpiece to the anonymous series. That the methods used were also influenced by this reversal of perspective was inevitable. The quantification of material which was often profuse necessitated the development of a methodology of enumeration and the establishment of criteria of treatment.

From traditional methods of classification and description scholars have moved on into more sophisticated types of inquiry, sometimes in the most varied directions. The lure of structuralism proved particularly strong in the 1970s, as did that of historical psychoanalysis. These efforts, or experiments, by a discipline in search of techniques, have led increasingly in recent years to the search for a semiology which is appropriate to historical iconography. Some scholars have seen this kind of semiology as merely a technique for dealing with voluminous materials (notably the graphic semiology used by the cartographic laboratory of the École des Hautes Études) – a sort of short route to prayer, useful for the demands of computer programming. This was the case with the work of V.-L. Tapié's team investigating baroque reredoses in Brittany. The scale of their error was evident in the results of their work. This in itself led to a sense of the need to resolve a number of preliminary problems, such as the problem of knowing whether visual sources contain 'discourses' like other media.

By the same token, we are brought back to the tasks outlined at the beginning of this paper: the attempt to define our field, which was the purpose of our meeting in June 1976. We had a very real confidence which gave rise to a certain optimism – and also provoked a certain headiness. As far as the sources for the history of mentalities are concerned, iconography places a sizeable mass of documents at the disposal of scholars. It thereby permits us to look at very extensive social groupings and to recognize different attitudes. Without in the least devaluing the approach to the work of art as an object in the service of the elite (although it may need to be approached differently), popular iconography, dealing with pictures, sacred and secular furnishings and ex votos, provides the most abundant range of source material. When seen in this way, the very notion of iconography is expanded and the boundary demarcating it from everyday objects, or material culture, becomes ever more fluid.

These sources are not just abundant on the simple level of numbers; they also offer possibilities for new kinds of uses. At the risk of seeming to be deliberately paradoxical, I would say that they can seem to be more 'innocent' in some respects, and in all cases more revealing than written or oral sources, given the significance of what can be derived from them in the way of involuntary confessions. This, at least, is the feeling I was left with after studying Provençal altars and reredoses dedicated to the souls in Purgatory, which are a sort of whispered or exorted confession about collective representations for which we would be hard pressed to find a written equivalent.

These reasons for confidence have their counterpart in the sense of crisis felt by many scholars and the feeling that there is a further breakthrough which has yet to be made. Simple description or impressionistic, thematic analysis, although not obsolete within the limits of their usefulness, cannot provide an appropriate language for dealing with these newly discovered riches; all the more so because these new iconographic sources also have their own limitations. They can sometimes seem to be poor in terms of the content of what they can reveal. This is the case with ex votos, for example, at first sight, and it is necessary to manipulate the mute silence of these sources. More often, their hermeticism seems to demand a difficult process of decoding, and they are much less explicit than the written source. Finally, and here we are more concerned with their historical uses than their form, they follow a specific chronology as they change, which sometimes makes them quite mobile, singularly subject to changes in 'fashions' in elite forms of expression. At other times they are quite inert, as in the picture of religious attitudes which we get from popular imagery or even from reredoses. This may be partly because we find, in this domain, stratified expressions of sensibility which are superimposed on each other without being mutually exclusive.

The second order of problems, which concerns the current development of new techniques for treating the sheer volume of sources involved, is as much a technical as a methodological affair. The totally empirical character of the early procedures and methods of treatment convinced scholars that the use of massive sources might be unproductive if it only led to a sociography devoid of perspective. Deciphering, decoding, fashionable terms borrowed from neighbouring disciplines hide a real anxiety which is disguised as confidence. Is there a semiology adapted to the kind of sources which interest us? Or will we be forced to return, as we have been on occasion, to the method of intuitive analysis which we ought never to have abandoned?

It was to try to find answers to these questions that the Aix conference was divided up under several headings. The first session was deliberately devoted to listening to semiologists, theoreticians and practitioners of the use of the image. At this point practical exercises, so to speak, were used to illustrate the current state of research in certain areas of study, thus drawing general contributions from a number of participants on the complementarity of their source materials. In this way a number of themes were introduced and developed, including ex votos, sacred iconography in the spatial context of the parish, funerary monuments and, in a more abbreviated form, some specific illustrations such as the iconography of the shepherd or the representation of the stages of life.

Current fields of exploration in iconography and the history of mentalities

The meeting of scholars which took place at Aix was, like all conferences, dependent on too many contingencies to be truly representative of all directions of current research. Yet it was nevertheless suggestive of the various ways in which we nowadays have recourse to iconography. It would be too easy to juxtapose two different kinds of research: one in which a given theme, such as research into agricultural techniques and pastoral life, suggested which sources should be used – the image of the shepherd, for example, from Greek sculpture to Roman mosaics – and thence to the reformulation of a problematic – the paradoxical absence of the shepherd in Greek sculpture; and a second type based on a different approach which begins with a massive corpus of given material (reredoses, ex votos, funerary monuments, popular representations of the stages of life) in order to derive from them one or more series of facts: the representation of life after death in the reredoses dedicated to the souls in Purgatory; individual or collective heroic death in funerary monuments; sickness, accidents and miracles in the ex votos. Yet this is an artificial contrast of approaches, since all the authors involved started from an initial problematic in search of an appropriate source.

If we take research into collective religious representations among the common people in the classical period as an example, we can bring together complementary evidence from a whole range of iconographic sources. Ex votos and pious images each testify, in their own way, to individual piety: the first as an individual reaction, even if the object itself was displayed in public; the second as a stereotyped representation which therefore reflects a collective atmosphere but which is designed for domestic use. On a higher level we proceed from the sacred furnishings of devotional places (pictures, statues, reredoses) to the props of collective religiosity, but we can also begin to organize this collective sacred space more fully by investigating the hierarchical positioning of altars and images in the parish church, and the spatial organization of the devotional places of the countryside with its churches, chapels, crosses and oratories. A whole system takes shape, in which every iconographic source finds its appropriate place.

Under these circumstances, the studies which formed the basis for the discussions devoted to areas of research can still retain their specific character while at the same time being demonstrative and capable of giving rise to a collective reflection, even if they only deal with one part of this iconographic treasure. Adapted to research in the modern period, the wealth of this treasure has been pointed out to us by contemporary scholars on the one hand and classicists and ethnologists on the other.

Ex votos

In the present state of research, some areas are particularly valuable reference points, and the study of ex votos is one such area. At first glance this material may seem to be quite a poor resource, naive for the most part and generally stereotyped after a certain period as a response to a limited number of situations in traditional societies. Yet the ex voto compensates for these defects by some irreplaceable advantages. It is one of the rare means of investigating the silent world of those who had no recourse to the written word. It is also an individual confession, serving as an introduction, however small, to the secrets of conscience. Then again, it is a massive source. The 208 examples collected in the exhibition Maritime Ex Votos from the West of France, presented by Michel Mollat, are only a small sample of the thousands catalogued by his team of researchers from Dunkirk to Saint-Jean-de-Luz. In Provence, Bernard Cousin catalogued 5000 documents which form the basis of his work. In Nice, Mlle de Ville d'Avray counted more than 1000 at Notre-Dame-de-Laghet; at Oropa in Piedmont, Christine Loubet was able to select a sample of 600 ex votos from a total of 2500. These sources, still present in abundance, are also a resource which allow us to work in the *longue durée*. While not going as far back as antiquity, pilgrimage sites still preserve some which date from the sixteenth century. They are more numerous for the seventeenth and eighteenth centuries and are especially so for the nineteenth century. Although some pilgrimages went into decline in the second half of the last century, others showed a vitality which has persisted down to our own time. The majority of the examples from Oropa date from the period 1809–1975. This transalpine site is a happy exception to the general demise of the painted ex voto, which came about in France as a function of its replacement by engraved marble plaques, prior to its complete disappearance.

A massive source, ranging over a long time-frame, requires a good deal of preliminary work in cataloguing and, of course, conservation, before it can be exploited. In the various sites where ex votos are to be found, whose hierarchy ranges from important pilgrimage sites to small country shrines, the process of destruction or dispersal has gone so far that an inventory and a photographic record needs to be undertaken as a matter of urgency. This is what Michel Mollat and his team have undertaken, striving all the while to foster an awareness of and respect for these sources. The first task is the preparation of an inventory, but the work does not end there. The sheer size of the archive (which can, of course, be preserved archivally in slide form) necessitates the development of systematic treatment criteria, as a preliminary to the indispensable computerization of the material. This is the task which Bernard Cousin has taken on.

Cousin has stressed the need to define a truly historical method of analysis in order to go beyond the cataloguing systems which have been used up to now. This method, he argues, must be both broadly based and directional: directional in the sense that it is not primarily concerned with possible uses of the material from the perspective of a study of material culture, although it certainly contains potential for such a study; broadly based because it tries to collect all the material which can be of use in the history of mentalities in relation to the 'three spaces' of the image, namely the representation of the divine, the human scene and the text. The encoding of this information, tested in a large number of sample sites, has led to the development of a project which is already quite advanced and which offers many examples which show its potential uses, including the analysis of the gestures of prayer and of the divine, or of family behaviour. The application of statistical tests and indices (such as the classic chi-2 test) which, although common in the human sciences are less hackneyed in the historical disciplines, allows us to test the validity of connections made in the *longue durée*, as has been shown in the demonstration of the increased presence of the sick child as a theme in these sources.

In this area, where Bernard Cousin emphasizes the technical problems involved in a massive research project which is still in progress, Christine Loubet has brought us an armful of ideas suggested by her work on a rich but strictly defined site. The site is Oropa, near Biella in Piedmont. For the earlier periods, from the sixteenth to the eighteenth century, only a qualitative approach is possible, based on a narrow range of documents whose scarcity can be explained both by destruction and by the 'Jansenist reaction' between 1750 and 1850. By contrast, after 1868, one can see a 're-awakening of wonder' which marked the golden age of the ex voto in this area. The volume of examples allows a periodization to be established from this point onwards which highlights some significant developments. In terms of the specific objects of prayer, illness gave way to war between 1914 and 1945 and then, after 1945, to road accidents, which figure in 80 per cent of the current images. The sociology of the supplicants also changes. The disappearance of the rich and the very poor leads to the dominance, nowadays, of the lower middle class. Children, and especially women, command very little attention. Maybe this is because war – or the motor car – are still the preserve of men. And yet it is the women who pray – up to a point – because, as Christine Loubet argues, in the contemporary ex voto representing the motor car, the link with the divine has tended to disappear, as has prayer. The classic diagonal composition has given way to the practice of a religious 'magic' which is restricted to capturing the moment of the accident and the miracle. This marks the return of a panic sensibility in which gratuitous miracles compensate for a deeply felt sense of loss.

Seen in the light of these varied interpretations which operate on different levels of treatment, the reliability of the ex voto as a means of investigating an essentially popular sensibility is apparent. Its relative stability, and its 'poverty' as a resource make it a valuable means of approaching the problems of classification and serial treatment of iconographic sources.

Reredoses and the geography of the sacred

L. Chatellier (in 'Iconography and parish structure') and Marie-Hélène Froeschlé-Chopard in her work on pilgrim chapels, demonstrated the uses of another type of methodology. Both scholars refer to the work of Professor Dupront and, by the same token, more remotely to the research on altarpieces carried out by V.-L. Tapié.

It is important, in order fully to appreciate the significance of their work, to see it as part of a progressive discovery of the potential value of the study of sacred furnishings (the reredos in particular) and of the sacred space itself. When Gaby Vovelle and I combed the churches of Provence between 1966 and 1969 to catalogue and photograph the altars to the souls in Purgatory, we had to invent our methods. To some extent we followed a traditional path, since we took the easy route of following a single thematic series (even if our choice was more of a response to a specific problem than a desire for an easy method). Yet we also made the compiling of a catalogue designed to be as exhaustive as possible in the *longue durée* into the basis for a serial study. The thematic demarcation of the subject made possible an analysis of the object which was both simple and empirical and was, moreover, total, integrating the data of the reredos and of the pictures themselves, which could then be analysed according to their themes and internal structure.

The next stage was represented by the work of V.-L. Tapié, J.-P. Le Flem and A. Pardailhé-Galabrun on baroque reredoses from Brittany. The objective of that inquiry, carried out by means quite different from our own, was much more ambitious and, all in all, more reasonable. Rather than selecting a single thematic series, it involved the compilation of an exhaustive inventory of altars and reredoses (at least for parish churches), for a particularly representative province. The difficulties arose from the sheer volume of the corpus which was thus assembled, involving more than 1500 reredoses, and from the variety of questions which could be formulated about each one. These ranged from problems of external attribution (a catalogue card showing date, authorship and location) to architectural (plain, wreathed or fluted columns . . .) or thematic descriptions (the artistic subject, even if the authors decided not to undertake an internal analysis of artistic representations). The use of a pictorial card catalogue prepared by the cartographic laboratory of the École Pratique des Hautes Études seemed a most appropriate way of mastering this large corpus of material. I have said elsewhere why I thought this whole enterprise miscarried.[1] Without going into the whole argument again, the reason is clear: in the fifteen pages of iconographic commentary, the authors practically ignored the pictorial catalogue, which they were unable to program properly or to exploit adequately. This judgement, which may seem severe, is only recalled here because the failure of the project testifies to a collective difficulty in mastering the massive resources offered by serial iconography.

A considerable number of the obstacles on which the Breton reredos project foundered seem to have been overcome in the work currently being pursued by L. Chatellier and Marie-Hélène Froeschlé-Chopard. Not all, of course, as we have still not developed a method of reading which is suitable to images taken individually – which could be the equivalent of what has been attempted in the case of ex votos, for a kind of material which is much more rebellious by its very diversity. But these two authors do show us how, on the basis of the distribution of iconographic elements in the parochial space, a great deal of information can be gleaned about the forms of religious life itself. A new problematic has been developed by this spatial positioning of objects. We now need to find a technique for handling the material, whether by the use of computers or of a pictorial index, which would no longer run the risk of distortion.

Marie-Hélène Froeschlé-Chopard, in her previous articles, has already shown, in the case of the dioceses of Vence and Grasse, how the overall structure of the reredos was modified in the classical period and, in particular, how its place in the body of the parish church developed. A strict hierarchy of place, descending from the high altar, the two side altars flanking it, via the nave, right down to the 'saints at the church door', to use Alphonse Dupront's happy phrase, saw the revived themes of post-Tridentine pastoral religion such as the Blessed Sacrament, the Rosary and St Joseph, occupy the places of honour, while the traditional intercessors were driven back and marginalized. L. Chatellier also applies this principle and widens it to encompass the whole iconographic system of the parishes which he has studied in the Kochesberg area of Lower Alsace, based on pastoral visits conducted between 1760 and 1780 and his own investigations *in situ*. From the elements which he listed in the parish church, the cemetery, the Way of the Cross and the smaller chapels and wayside crosses of the countryside, he analysed their relative situation and importance, reflected in a system of interconnected images.

The catalogue presented by Chatellier, covering the period which saw the growth of parish churches in Alsace in the second half of the eighteenth century, stressed the rigidly controlled ('Sulpician' the author calls it) aspect of religious practice, striking in its Christocentrism and hardly going beyond the holy triad of Jesus, Mary and Joseph, and the depopulation of a pantheon from which the old agrarian saints had long been banished. Yet, if we look a little further, we rediscover the traditional patron saints on the side altars, and find that the local saints have migrated to the rural chapels or the cemeteries, then being established in large numbers. In this way, an important stage in the development of the modern parish has been visualized, making the parish church the unique centre of religious life although without depriving the peripheral establishments of all their vitality.

Marie-Hélène Froeschlé-Chopard describes such peripheral rural sites in her paper, 'Function and iconography of Provençal pilgrim chapels'. The *romerage*, in the sense in which the word was used in

Provence during the eighteenth century, no longer meant a pilgrimage
to Rome, but a collective pilgrimage in the form of a procession into
the countryside which took place once a year. It was a rite of
regeneration, combining official sacred ceremonies and elements
which were not at all without purpose, such as games, competitions
and cathartic brawls between youths from different villages.

Half of these chapels seem to have been linked to older cults,
sometimes simply because they perpetuated an older parish or the site
of an older cult. Of relatively recent origin are those dedicated to
healing saints, although this may mean that the new saint (usually St
Roch) supplanted an older one. But in all cases the chapels retain a
central function, which is to house 'the protector of the community,
the saint associated with the land for centuries past, or the saint
responsible for keeping contagious diseases at bay'. The geography of
these functions is specific; therapeutic saints are found on the roads
which are under their protection; the traditional intercessors are still
further away, at the limits of the district, at the heart of another
sacred world in which 'the community regenerated itself by contact
with trees, water and rocks – the sources of life; or by contact with
the old cemetery, the old village – places imbued with sacred power'.
But the very decoration of these sites reflects the poverty that is often
typical of these places, which are only visited once a year: old
reredoses showing, in rigid and immobile postures, the three saints in
a static display of the presence of the sacred, untouched, in most
cases, by the changes which can be noticed in the parish churches.
The presence of a reliquary, sometimes permanent, but generally
occasional, contributes to this impression. Yet, in some sites, the
growing importance of a pilgrimage drawing large crowds adds to the
richness of the decor, which begins to mimic that of the parish
church. The latter, although victorious, is nevertheless still involved in
a rivalry with these places of refuge of popular religion, where the
community enters into direct contact with the deity through the
mediation of a saint.

At the conclusion of these studies, we can see how the very idea of a
recourse to iconography is capable of being extended to open out into
a global view of the entire sacred space. In this way we can form a
better estimate of the necessary dialectic between the methods of
collection and inventory of material and the fruitful hypotheses which
can animate it. At this level there is no discrepancy, rather continuity,
between the analyses and interpretations which have been presented
on funerary monuments as evidence for collective mentality. Monuments to the dead certainly form part of an essentially laicized

sensibility in the nineteenth century, but do they not also occupy an essential place in any inventory of the 'sacral' monuments of village life?

Funerary art and monuments to the dead

These studies can also be seen as part of a process of discovery, some aspects of which should also be mentioned here, including the history of attitudes towards death, both individual and archaeological. We have seen with some surprise how, in Provençal churches in the twentieth century, plaques or bas-reliefs to the dead of the Great War often displaced the 'poor souls' from the Purgatory altars. More generally, there is still a great deal of work to be done on the history of cemeteries, even if some aspects have begun to be clarified, as in M. Foisil's work on Parisian cemeteries in the nineteenth century. M. Bée's article on cemeteries in Calvados, based on the reports of prefects under the Empire,[2] opens up several interesting pathways in this field of research, interpreting a specific document which was the ancestor of the monumental catalogue. But much more work still has to be done in the field, so to speak, by developing a stylistic and thematic interpretation of the various aspects of burial places from the fourteenth century to the present. This is a theme which art historians have generally neglected, and which historians of mentality have only just begun to discover.

From another perspective – which is very close, though quite different – research into monuments to the dead, chiefly for the period beginning in the nineteenth century, blends with recent work, particularly that of Maurice Agulhon, on the representation of symbolic figures in this period. The figure of the Republic, Marianne, has provided the theme of many of his publications and he has written more widely on the 'Origins and significance of the fashion for statues in modern France'. Such work shows the degree to which contemporary history, which has clung for a long time to traditional methods, is gradually beginning to discover the importance of everyday works of art, though these have been the normal fare of classicists and medievalists for quite a while.

R. Koselleck, of Bielefeld, invited us to join in quite a new kind of reflection as a prelude to a study carried out in a European framework (ranging over Germany, Italy and France) with the title *Monuments to the Dead; a study of a modern visual form*. In the temporary absence of a massive series of sources, Koselleck already disposes of an ample photographic repertoire of illustrations drawn from a wide geographical range – from Europe to America – and, historically, in the *longue durée* extending from the Thirty Years' War to the present. He introduces his work by stressing the particular value of the system of signs and landmarks provided by monuments to the dead for the study of 'political sensibility'. He invites us to think about the collective hecatomb rather than the individual monument as a means of directing our attention towards a given political project.

Although this work mainly concentrates on the nineteenth century, there is also a prehistory which is interesting and relevant. The traditional mercenary soldier did not even have the right to a tomb. The anonymous military hordes of the Thirty Years' War were at best commemorated by crosses built to expiate the crimes of humanity. At the same time, the princes or the victorious generals rewarded themselves with monuments designed to immortalize their triumphs. The tombs of Maurice of Saxony in Strasbourg and of Canova in Vienna are the culmination of a continuous series, and part of such series. Koselleck sees the development of the modern practice of erecting monuments to the dead as having been accompanied by two essential transformations. Firstly, there was a progressive equalization which blurred the outlines of a hitherto cruelly hierarchical practice and, in addition, there was an increasingly wide distribution of such monuments linked to the fact that the decreasing importance of the religious (or expiatory) nature of the collective monument made it a more fitting vehicle for a functional political message.

What the author calls 'the functionalization of the representation of death in the service of the survivors' is illustrated by reference to the unconsciously grating, but very British joke in William Wood's 1806 proposal for the erection of a giant pyramid to stimulate the ardour of British merchantmen during the Napoleonic wars. Wood stressed the profitability, in economic terms, of an investment equivalent to the cost of three days' warfare. Wood's project achieved a remarkable posthumous success in the form of the lion which dominated the plain of Waterloo with the inscription composed by Frederick William III of Prussia, and which survived until 1871: 'Den Gefallenen zur Erinnerung, den Lebenden zur Mahnung, Den Kommenden zur Nacheiferung'.[3] This exhortation to the coming generations, who inherit the duties of the dead, is the common denominator of all such monuments to the fallen, wherever they were built, right down to 1918. The position of victor or vanquished is only a secondary consideration in the face of a call to duty which was addressed to everyone. Hence we find a remarkable homogeneity in the symbolic accessories of this neoclassical lay piety in different countries – even if the author very properly notes the marked variations between nations, including the 'familial' tradition in French monuments, as compared to the moralizing triumphalism of the American monuments, representing the conflict of good and evil.

Parallel with this functionalization of the monuments to the dead was their democratization. Koselleck follows the stages of this process from the older, not quite defunct tradition of monuments to victorious generals (from Scharnhorst to Kellermann or Patton), through the intermediate stage which commemorates the officers, as, for example, the monument to the Hanovarian officers at Waterloo, and ignores the common soldiers. At a further stage, the names of officers and men were placed on the same plaques, but in order of rank. The American Civil War abolished rank *post mortem* and Europe followed the American way in 1918, at the very moment when technological progress, by swelling the ranks of the unknown dead, made individual identification impossible. Hence the practice, alongside the custom of burial in village cemeteries, of erecting simple, anonymous memorials on the battlefields of the two world wars. The last war made triumphalist memorials, stamped with the seal of good conscience, obsolete. Abstract memorials, hollow forms, like Zadkine's at Amsterdam, or the anti-monument, of which Keinholz's parody of the Arlington War Memorial is the classic example, show clearly that the life cycle of the commemorative monument, from birth to death, has been completed. It is now time to write its history.

Geneviève Richier and Bernard Cousin's paper on the attempt to compile a thematic inventory of the monuments to the dead of World War I in Bouches-du-Rhône suggests the various ways in which a systematic inventory based on a definite plan can be used to pursue the kind of research which Koselleck is calling for. Under the headings of place and conditions of construction; date; whether a single, double, or even triple monument – in the town square, the cemetery or the church – and thematic analysis, we already begin to see the outlines of a potential system of treating the material, material which is a practically universal testament of collective sensibility.

The other fields of research which emerged in this necessarily incomplete survey can be grouped together under the useful heading of 'Works and Days'. They are no less important as proofs of the ability of the iconographic approach to adapt to very different problematics, well beyond the relatively homogenous limits of the works already discussed, which focus on religious or civic iconography.

In discussing the iconography of the shepherd in Greek sources from the eighth to the third century BC, Marie-Claire Amouretti did not just offer the modernists at the conference a useful prompting from outside their own period. Her work was less distant than it might seem, since it was formulated in the context of a study of pastoral life in the *longue durée* being carried out by a group at the University of Provence which is working on material life in the Mediterranean world. She showed especially, how a study of the sources, beginning with Arcadian, Cretan and Boeotian sculpture and extending into ceramic art, yielded a realization of absence which, if not total, was certainly pronounced. The shepherd, as a human type, was not integrated into Greek iconography, which is especially intriguing if we think of the place of pastoral in Roman civilization. A whole series of questions springs from this. Why this silence, these tastes, fashions and developments? We need to formulate a whole series of questions about the socioeconomic context which should not be undertaken too mechanically, but we must also investigate a whole series of ideological mediations, based on collective representations, to understand why the Greeks, who made the Cyclops the antithesis of the civilized man, underrated the shepherd, and, conversely, the reasons for the importance of pastoral from the Middle Ages to *Astrée* or the Trianon. Iconography in this context is an invaluable method of following the dialectic between material realities and the attitudes adopted towards them.

Yvonne Knibiehler decided to confine her contribution to a short paper on a series of images of the stages of life ranging from the seventeenth to the end of the nineteenth centuries, which is part of her research on collective representations of women in images of the life cycle. This is a very appropriate subject, given the apparent inertia of the formal structures of figurative art: the ascending and descending staircases which couples tread between one age and the next; the underground arch between the cradle and the grave; the evocation of the Last Things in the imagery of the Final Judgement. This material has not been ignored in recent studies which have approached it from what I shall call, for the sake of simplicity, a structuralist perspective. Yvonne Knibiehler, by contrast, stresses the revealing changes which underlie the apparent continuity. This is true of the place of women, which has been seen so differently in various ages. The ladder of life is a good semiological theme, of course, because of the very rigidity of the formal categories in which figurative representation is enclosed, which permits the analysis of a finite number of significant elements.

This limited, but dense corpus of material brings us back to the image, and especially the popular image – although the notion is fluid, since we can detect a gradual process of popularization, from classical engravings to the Epinal prints. Other possible series of popular images which deserve to be studied were not discussed at this conference. There are many of them, ranging from the early woodcuts of the later Middle Ages down to lithographs, which spread the work of printmakers and card manufacturers in the nineteenth century. Some local studies, however, like the one carried out by M. Mus from Aix in the preparation of a catalogue of Avignon prints and images, indicate precisely what can be drawn from such a corpus of material by using a serial approach. The figures represented in the Avignon prints which Mus studied also feature in the pilgrim chapels dealt with by Marie-Hélène Froeschlé-Chopard. In these images, tradition is more important than innovation and in most cases they have no didactic function but are 'simple representations'. They represent hieratic saints whose presence alone is sufficient and whose role is to be put up on the wall as static intercessors, visual supports of prayer. It is therefore not surprising that compared with approximately 10 per cent of images of Christ, including the Crucifixion, but more frequently portraying the Infant Jesus, images of the Virgin account for nearly a third of examples, including Our Lady of Pilgrimage, but also Our Lady of Mercy, of the Seven Dolours and of the Scapular and Rosary. Images of the saints constitute nearly 55 per cent of all images and four-fifths of these are of traditional saints: the 'greats', including Sts Peter and Paul, St Joseph and St Anthony, but also many local intercessors, including Sts Gens, Benezet and Peter of Luxembourg, who are far more prominent than the saints and blesseds of the Counter-Reformation, sparingly represented here, even if some of the local figures (Fathers Bridaine, Yvan and Cayron) make a discreet appearance. This iconography is not immune to new languages. Although the figure of the martyr is absent, we can see the introduction of ecstatic and celestial visions, the figures of the guardian angel and the death of St Joseph. In spite of all this, we are staggered by the evidence of extraordinary stability. In an initial study covering the end of the seventeenth century, a second covering the eighteenth century and a third dealing with lithographs of the period 1820–80, the proportions were shown to be unchanged, or practically so. Some saints disappeared, like St Sebastian, St Barbara or St Anthony the Hermit but, all in all, the tradition shows signs of having gained strength rather than of having declined. Does this show a simple, often literal copying of the motifs of the early image-painters by the lithographers? Such an answer, which contains problems of its own, can only provide a partial explanation.

Along with this corpus of traditional images we need to juxtapose those which were the product of change and which were spread by the new vulgate of a more literate culture in the second half of the nineteenth century. Remi Maillet who works on the relations between learned and popular culture has introduced us to this material. He chose Henri Martin's *Popular History of France* published in 1875 as a subject, starting with an analysis of the two volumes relating to the Revolution and Empire. We immediately get a sense of change relative to the earlier series, in which images carried their own meanings. Here, on the other hand, we have illustrations linked to a text from which they cannot, apparently, be separated. Does this portend an ultimate redundance of the image? Apparently not, to judge by the author's argument, in which he presents a thematic analysis of 530 engravings which, although traditional, is very searching. He divides the engravings into two roughly equal groups comprising portraits and compositions. A deliberate, historicist didacticism is apparent in the importance attached to the portraits, views of villages and traditional historic scenes, and also in some documentary plates, such as those illustrating costume. But this was not just innocent pedagogy. Remi Maillet isolates several recurring themes which he analyses in detail, including that of violence, which might be said to be part and parcel of the period at which he is looking. Yet violence has two faces in this context. Violence is presented as a liberating and emancipating force as part of the epic of French conquest and, conversely, a different, fanatical violence is constantly linked to the image of the people: the cowardly and brutal violence of the Romans, Neapolitans and Spaniards; the dual fanaticism in France of the Vendée and the White Terror, on the one hand, and of the bloodbaths of the *journées populaires* on the other. The images juxtapose two different worlds much more clearly than the text. On the one side is France, representing liberty, justice and organization; on the other is the chaos of popular spontaneity and violence. The other major theme is hero worship, in the context of a history which is very much a history of battles, a history of events. The choices which are made, whether in the portrait gallery or in the development of themes like exemplary or heroic death, clearly betray Martin's bias as he glorifies the Girondins and Mirabeau, plays down Robespierre and Saint-Just, nails Marat to the pillory and leaves an ambiguous image of Bonaparte. The author's political philosophy, his religion of progress and of the omnipotence of the intellect and his confident belief in the role of France as the bearer of supreme values show themselves more discreetly. In this context, a history in which the people only figure as disturbing agents of the Counter-Revolution or the false Revolution enlists the visual image in the service of an ideological discourse conceived by the bourgeoisie for the use of the masses. It is perhaps in this sense that it is a popular history.

This initial approach highlights the need for a further stage of study in which images can be analysed in their internal structures. The idea springs to mind that a useful comparison might be made between the series just considered and engravings which were truly revolutionary, like the series created by Prieur, Duplessis-Berteaux and others. For the series studied by Maillet, there also arises the double problem of the relationship between text and image, as in the question of the extent to which the image is effective in visually fixing the themes and key ideas present at the level of oral transcription (or translation), as Philippe Joutard has recently shown in his work *The Legend of the Camisards, a study of the sense of the past.*

An abundance of problems, and some trails to follow

This general survey, at once both abundant and intermittent, has given us an insight into the dimensions of the field and its potential riches. Yet it is also necessary to define its frontiers. The dialectic between text and image to which we have just referred (and which can be found in other areas such as the ex voto where the text, at a certain point, kills the image) can be extended into the area of the relationship between the visual and the oral. This is the link which Philippe Joutard recognized in his work *Iconography and Oral Tradition.* Rejecting the obsolete belief of traditional folklorists in the autonomy of the oral, he underlined the intermediary role which the image plays between learned and popular culture, recalling the role played by the massive diffusion of images by pedlars in the nineteenth century. Now, as in the past, images have played an important role, not just in fixing, but even in adding to the oral tradition. We can point to examples like the legend that crosses were painted on the doors of Huguenot houses on the eve of the St Bartholomew's day massacre, which was inspired by visual imagery, and the figure of the Wandering Jew, which popular imagery endowed with giant, even Gargantuan, proportions. Fair-day parades and magic lantern shows were exceptional means of spreading and of fixing images in traditional societies, perhaps, as the author suggests, because the historical memory, by dividing reality into elemental sequences, finds quite a useful prop in popular iconography. This last point underlines the need for a study of the social diffusion of the image.

Whether we speak about sterilization by transmission or enrichment by contact, it is certain that the field opened up by the study of iconographic sources, with essential variations which reflect time, place and social environment, is at the heart of the concerns of the history of mentalities. We witnessed the beginning of a new awareness of the possibilities when Didier Lancien, in a provocative and fruitful detour from the normal paths of research, introduced the historians at the conference to the study of contemporary cinema in what might well be a historic contribution to this field of research. Everything, he argued before an audience accustomed to a more restricted kind of reading, is relevant, down to the most banal feature film or advertisement.

Our appetite is virtually limitless, but we must nevertheless reach agreement on the procedures to be adopted in this field, and confront a new teaching based on illustrative 'flashes' with a theoretical foundation which is in the process of being developed. A pathway is becoming apparent, though not always a direct one, both in the techniques for collecting documents and the use made of them.

What I call classical thematic analysis (without any pejorative connotation) is neither obsolete nor useless in the field of the history of mentalities. The studies which have been mentioned can be defined, for the most part, as searching thematic analyses. In fields ranging from studies of funerary monuments and visual images to specifically defined series – whether dealing with Purgatory, the shepherd or even the witch, as in some recent Italian work – the history of mentalities has everything to gain from the study of an iconology which has been defined in new ways.

Can we go further and make this 'reading' (a term I use with considerable caution, for reasons which will soon be apparent) more scientific, more searching and systematic? The question which was posed at the beginning of this paper echoes a growing concern: can we develop a real semiology of the image?

Some of the studies analysed above reflect both a real interest and a manifest unease. Bernard Cousin, in presenting his approach to ex votos, was not unaware of the fact that some semiological theorists (Roland Barthes, Umberto Eco and Louis Morin) have already proposed a system of concepts for the decoding of the image which the historians cannot ignore. Yet historians are nevertheless troubled by the current limits of the semiological approach – the preference for individual examples over a corpus of works and, linked to this attitude, a distrust of the historical approach revealed in Roland Barthes's statement: 'In principle, diachronic elements should be eliminated from the material to be used, which should coincide with a moment in time, a particular state of affairs.' Can history find any role here? Some recent approaches, which combine semiology and psychoanalysis, make one wonder (as, for example, B. Lamarche and G. Vadel's paper on ex votos)[4] and not just by their hermeticism.

A semiology of the image

The question has been posed, but the answers are far from uniform. The voice of prudence, in accents familiar to many historians, is that of Georges Mounin, in his essay 'Iconography and semiology'; this takes as its example Dr Bréhant's paper on 'Representations of the Crucifixion',[5] which is a particularly appropriate corpus of material to which to refer. Georges Mounin warns the reader against the literal transfer of linguistic concepts to semiology – the unreflecting use of terms like 'reading' or 'message', he argues, 'can be partially or totally misleading,' because there is not, by definition, a simple or unambiguous reading of a picture or an object, reflecting a code which can be deciphered. A painting of the Crucifixion is both a kind of *message* which conveys information and a *collection of stimuli* designed to provoke reactions. This makes it all the more difficult to select the relevant indicators. We can more usefully speak of interpretation than of decoding. This implies the selection of a certain number of characteristics as a function of a given criterion of use. The author, in fact, stresses the imperative, when dealing with complex cultural objects, to state what their significance might be, and for whom – for the producer, or for the onlooker, whether past or present, learned or uneducated.

Whether the contemporary viewer is a historian, art historian, doctor, anthropologist or psychoanalyst obviously determines the choice of what is relevant to a given object and this can be unthinkingly confused in the semiological approach. Is it reasonable, therefore, to speak of graphic semiology as 'a science capable of systematically extracting the meanings contained in images'? At the very least, this idea requires an initial agreement about terms. The links which bind the producer (the painter) and the viewers, both past and present, are the domain of the semiology of communication. The meanings which contemporary scholars, of whatever discipline, will draw from the indicators which they interpret is the domain of the semiology of meaning.

Given these precautions, Georges Mounin thinks it possible that we can proceed from this clarification 'to derive more rigorous methods of analysing and interpreting visual images'. He is interested in reformulating the much debated, but as yet imprecise question of the relationship between myth and history. Structuralist analysis has obstinately tried to remove the study of myth from the competence of history, 'asserting that myth is always composed of a closed system of non-variable elements, the underlying structures of which must be analysed'. If we apply this reading to a concrete myth, such as that of the Crucifixion, we are very quickly brought to affirm, if not the absence of structural constants, at least the extreme mobility which affects its essential determinants – the cross, the position of the body and its nakedness, the crown of thorns – and that this mobility is a function of determinants which are historical in the widest sense of the term, involving the history of religious thought, or of society. On the basis of this statement, we can share the optimism of the author's conclusion: 'Because iconography, by its very source material, gives more scope to historical research, scope which is often less haphazard than idiom and narrative, it offers a privileged field for demonstrating that changes in the structures of myths profoundly depend on history.'

It would doubtless be forcing the point to take Régine Robin's paper as a contrast to Georges Mounin's, but it would be also artificial to pretend that they were in complete agreement. Régine Robin approaches iconography both as a historian and as a semiologist, familiar with the study of discourses and discursive practices. Where Mounin dealt with a study of the Crucifixion, she uses a study of two libertine novels of the eighteenth century to illustrate her argument and to lead us into the strange world of the representation of women in the Enlightenment. We can summarize the major themes of this paper. Robin is certainly in agreement with Mounin in undertaking a project which can only be agreeable to historians: history must be applied to an area which has been hitherto consigned to a structuralist analysis which is not only incompatible with historical discourse, but which itself falls within a definite 'ideological, and ideological and theoretical conjuncture'. But Régine Robin does not believe that we can do without a fundamental theoretical debate, if not advocating a fully structuralist approach. She rejects the empiricism of current methods, while not criticizing the competence of historians who are trying to find a pathway in a new field without the help of landmarks. She is not unaware that a succession of short-lived 'fashions' and incompatible interpretations can have a discouraging effect. Yet she does not believe that there is a 'short cut to prayer' and she stresses the importance of Roland Barthes's work for those who wish to explore the connotative systems which relate to the corpus of visual images from the past. She gives one example from the history of eighteenth-century libertinism, based on two images on which she grounds an inquiry into the mobilization of the imaginary in the organization of social groupings. This may be part of the history of the imagination, with all the questions which it raises. What relationship can be established between fantasies and ideologies? Can we avoid resorting to psychoanalytic concepts, interpreted in a historical light, when dealing with a libertine eroticism which does not in the least resemble our own? Many scholars have shuddered at the idea of getting involved in an area where the landscape is still changing rapidly, with all the investment that this demands. Many, sometimes the same people, think that it might be limiting from the outset, and even an obstacle to further progress, to refuse to become involved in such an adventure.

Scholars are even more perplexed because the progress of current research is putting them in situations where there is a certain amount of ambiguity, and even some apparent contradictions. The semiology of the image, as we see it being practised, still refuses to emerge from the study of significant examples, or admits its inability to handle large bodies of material, which are indispensable for the adoption of any approach towards mass phenomena which characterize popular culture. Yet it is from such detailed studies that they derive a sense of the need for a less empirical and more sure approach. The examples dealt with over the past few days show that the essential stage of this kind of research lies in the establishment of criteria of treatment or, if you will, a pinpointing of relevant characteristics, of the kind described by Georges Mounin. This procedure is all the more necessary because scholars are increasingly using methods of analysis which do not involve a first-hand approach to the sources. Scholars are aware, and have said so, that a quantification without perspectives can only lead to derisory results, statements of the obvious or short-sighted descriptions. This can only lead to the transfer, to this field, of the kind of sterile sociology sometimes practised elsewhere.

In these conditions, the issue of quantification as a means of reaching an understanding of the behaviour of whole groups, is not at all called into question (except as La Palisse would say, by its opponents – but theirs is a lost cause). There is not even a real conflict about the techniques of treatment to be used. We are at a stage where, beyond the level of manual counting, which has been and continues to be the lot of many researchers, the first important step towards more sophisticated techniques was represented by the use of the pictorial card index and statistical matrix in the survey of baroque reredoses in Brittany, or the graphic semiology used by the École Pratique des Hautes Études (where we see semiological technology replacing the semiological reading!). The criticisms which have been aired about the results of this work do not apply at all to the techniques used; the fault lay at the programming level. These procedures, although giving working scholars the possibility of a more direct, almost manual contact with their sources – and therefore more satisfaction and, possibly, more independence – nevertheless still have technical limits of their own: a maximum of 100 items for a statistical matrix and less than 500 for a microfiche catalogue. This rules out a whole range of research referred to above, which requires computerized techniques. Between graphic semiology, the poor man's computer, and computerized treatment, the main difference is in the scale of the materials being studied.

Agendas and techniques

The real problem, which is not at all technical, is the establishment of an agenda and of modalities of treatment. Three complementary papers, presented by Christian Bromberger, Henri Hudrisier and Mario Borillo, gave the conference a lot to think about in this area.

Christian Bromberger, on the basis of a study of African, Oceanian and Amerindian anthropomorphic statues entitled 'A method for the ethnomorphological analysis of sculpture', brought the welcome contribution of the ethnologist to the debate. The historians present welcomed the suggestions which emerged from an encounter with a problematic similar to their own, but different, which already possesses a well-developed methodology provided by the work of Leroi-Gourhan and Perrois. The objectives of this method are to distinguish 'the formal and rhythmic canons defining a common ethnic style', and then to identify the sub-styles. It operates on the basis of an ordered questionnaire which examines modes of expression, the distinction of forms, movement and the framing and proportions of the objects. The paper, based on concrete examples, was able to suggest many ways of exploiting the material which went beyond the confines of a formal analysis, as in the study of the relation of the material to the symbolic vision of its users. In a prudent conclusion, the author stressed, however, that this useful method of classification, replacing traditional typologies, only represents a preparatory stage in every semantic inquiry.

Can one expect more from the treatment of a corpus of material, and if so by what means? Henri Hudrisier and Mario Borillo gave us two very different answers to the question. Henri Hudrisier is not a computer scientist, but as both a historian and an archivist he had to use computer techniques in dealing with a collection of 873 photographs taken in Algeria between 1954 and 1962. The results were delivered in his paper 'The application of multi-dimensional methods of analysis to the global study of an iconographic collection'. This method of analysis, relying on a factorial analysis of relationships, is intended to produce a means of presenting images which could be used for educational purposes – in a photographic or iconographic collection, or for research purposes – for setting up or refining working hypotheses. The author's approach is very attractive. Having analysed 'the semantic aspects of the objects in the collection according to analytic criteria which are as homogenous and non-hierarchical as possible, the total information is then subjected to a factorial analysis of relationships.'

The concretization of relationships in the synthetic universe of the factorial space allows visualization techniques to be developed whereby groups of relevant slides can be assembled and shown on a screen. This procedure is intended, according to the author, 'to escape ... from the cultural pressures which are inevitably introduced by the user in framing questions and which are also introduced by the documentary vocabulary, carrying with it hierarchical ideas which are aprioristically imposed by institutional pressures'. It is nonetheless important, in order to construct a preliminary system of analysis, to locate the relevant characteristics of the image – what the author calls the 'star features'. Furthermore, even if the criteria are left open, so as to be capable of enrichment, they nevertheless already constitute a preliminary selection, an inevitable infringement of the unbiased approach of the machine. As such, and reserving judgement on the results it may produce, the proposal is nevertheless representative of the current preoccupations of researchers confronted with problems associated with the use of massive iconographic sources.

Here, where Henri Hudrisier prides himself on setting off 'who knows where', to use the old libertine expression, Mario Borillo, in his essay 'Semiological analysis and the coherence of historical discourse', starts off from a very different working hypothesis. He begins by working on a well-known archaeological source: Richter's inventory of archaic Greek kouroi published in 1960. He is thus working on a completed study and on a working hypothesis which has already been formulated, by which Richter showed the continuous and irreversible development from a hieratic model to a much more elaborate and living plastic art form. What interests Borillo, starting with a reclassification of the material and proceeding by means of a method of treatment not far from factorial analysis, is to replace or reconstitute Richter's argument, to refute it if need be and sometimes to enrich it by new working hypotheses. Struck by the empirical nature of the research and by the implicit arguments which abound in archaeology, the computer expert offers two clear ideas which are very solidly founded. He defines the limitations of a method, the 'unthinking use' of which he indicts as being 'largely responsible for the calculatory obscurantism which is rampant in the human sciences', not in order to provide a sense of direction, but as a sort of simulation of the archaeologist's unconscious question.

We are left, after all these contributions and provocations, with more problems than solutions. Apart from some bridge-building, there was no coming together of historical iconographers and semiologists. But they did listen to each other with considerable interest. Some may regret the lack of homogeneity which resulted from this, as well as the intermittent character of the spotlights shone on work in progress.

All of this, in my view, reflects the reality of a continuing process of research on a theme which is clearly important in the context of the history of mentalities – a theme which has lately been undergoing an extraordinary renewal, where the scope of research has been widened and methods have been radically modified.

The term 'growing pains', which I thought an appropriate description of this stage of research, should not be misunderstood. The value of the research is not at all in doubt, but we have a greater awareness of the problems involved – not all of them of a technical kind. This awareness ought to lead to a real maturity. We have seen that it is not enough just to describe in order to understand, and that it is not enough just to count either.

Some historians are still perplexed by the contacts which have been suggested to them, including semiology (which semiology?) and, even more so, psychoanalysis. Yet they too are conscious of working in a field which is in full expansion and is experiencing a methodological renewal. (We need, for example, to extend the methods now being used in the field of popular iconography to the iconography of the elite.) To this extent, and without prejudice to what is yet to come, the questions posed today are an index of health rather than of sickness.

Notes

Introduction to the proceedings of the Conference on Iconography and the History of Mentalities, Aix-en-Provence, June 1976.

1   *Annales E.S.C.* (September-October 1973).
2   *Annales de Normandie* (1976).
3   A memorial to the fallen, a reminder to the living, a model for future generations.
4   'Does God signify?', *Communication*, no. 19.
5   *La Presse médicale* (1965).

4

On Death

Over the past ten years a whole series of different perspectives on death has been put forward: evidence of the new interest in collective attitudes and feelings. But each one sees death at his own door, as it were. The paper which is offered here is the thematic introduction to a longer work,[1] and may also serve as a statement of intent or a programme of research. Based on a theme which has long preoccupied me, and which I believe to be essential, it illustrates my approach to the history of mentalities, and its underlying rejection of the autonomy of a 'collective mentality'. In my view, without any reductionism, the history of mentalities, in all the complexity of the mechanisms which it enables us to analyse, remains the cutting edge of social history.

We have become suspicious of sensational effects, nowadays somewhat over-familiar and deprived of the terrorist impact they once had: in looking at themselves in a mirror, people discover death. The theme was illustrated by painters from the Renaissance to the Baroque, from Germany to Spain, and elsewhere. Painters knew how to achieve the effect of surprise: a young woman dressing, or the old Burgkmayr couple looking at themselves in a glass which reflects their image as a death's-head.

Perhaps this is what makes the history of death so fascinating. The historian's task is to reassess the given elements of the problem, to see this exchange of images in the looking-glass from the other side. Starting from death, and from the collective attitudes towards death, history wants to rediscover people and to catch them in their reactions to an event which allows no exceptions.

Thus defined, the history of death occupies a far from minor place in the new history of mentalities. It is situated in the direct line of evolution which has led researchers, interested in the first instance in the development of cultures, to become more and more involved, without leaving their first path, in an area where clear thought gives way to unconscious attitudes, where the characteristics of a mentality are registered in acts as much as and more than in statements. The study of collective attitudes is currently in full development. Its field of inquiry is in areas such as the history of attitudes to life, the history of family structure, the history of death and these are, to some extent, various aspects of the same inquiry. But the history of death retains a specific and exemplary value within this complex system: in the human adventure it stands as an ideal and essential constant. It is a constant which is quite relative, moreover, since people's relationships with death have changed, as have the ways in which it strikes them. Nevertheless, the conclusion is always the same ... death. This is why death, at the terminus of all human experience, is always a particularly sensitive indicator. Pierre Chaunu was right when he said that every society gauges and assesses itself in some way by its system of death.

The logical complement of such an evaluation is that this privileged moment of existence is surrounded, more than any other, by a whole system of masks, devices and taboos and, inversely, of fantastic creations and magical practices. The image of people which we see via the history of death is a peculiarly distorted one, the meaning of which needs to be deciphered. This is what makes the project so absorbing and which entails an approach at once prudent and ambitious. Prudent, because one must avoid coming up too quickly with a 'model', as Americans would call it, of the history of death, which would be too easy a way of escaping from the multi-faceted image which it reveals. Ambitious, because I believe that it is necessary to consider death in its entirety, going from biological or demographic death – the material, brute fact of death – to the most elaborate literary and aesthetic products of the sentiment of death. Thus it is a project which can only be carried on in the very long-term perspective, in the *longue durée*. These, then, are the two basic parts of my method, which I shall now proceed to explain in greater detail.

An approach on three levels

The first point on entering into a history of death is to see it as being vertical. By that I mean a history which will connect, without necessarily presupposing a link of mechanical causality, what I shall call physical death, the experience of death and the discourse of death; three essential units of explanation to which I have already had recourse and which I take up again now for the purpose of definition.

The first level, physical death, emerges as a matter of course, it is the brute fact of mortality. It is inscribed in demographic statistics from the point at which they become available. This brute fact registers the impact of classical mortality rates which lasted from the beginning of history until fairly recently. By that we mean an annual mortality rate of between 30 and 40 per cent on average, the result of a very short life expectancy of thirty to forty years in most cases. It was the product of a high levy on the younger age cohorts which allowed only half of any given generation, and sometimes fewer, to survive until the age of twenty. This was the old model, constantly maintained by convulsive and frequent eruptions of famine and disease.

In modern Western society where the mortality rate oscillates around 10 per cent where infant mortality has become very low and where life expectancy is higher then seventy years (and over eighty for women in the United States), these references to a past which is not so far away can seem horrifying. This is to avoid looking at the Third World, where these old-style realities are not so very far off and are often immediate.

To evaluate physical death at this first level is to study its parameters: the social composition of this human levy, beginning with differences based on sex and age; the death of a woman, of a man, of a child, were all very different and were very differently felt. It is also to appreciate the contrast between town and country. Should one speak of the privileged city or the deadly city? Such a contrast might help to explain how the countryside in the context of tradition-al societies was able to preserve ancient systems of folkloric or folklorized death. The major cleavage, of course, is that which divides the powerful from the powerless, rich from poor. Nevertheless the measuring of physical death is only the first stage of a process which leads to the measuring of death as experience.

The experience of death can be simply defined as the whole system of gestures and rites which accompany the passage from final illness to death, the grave and the next world. One can, of course, easily accommodate the reality of physical death within the roomy and reassuring framework of funerary, magical, religious and civic prac-tices which have always been used to domesticate death by giving to the rites of final passage, of funerals, burial and mourning, a structure which reveals a system, or more commonly, an entanglement of different systems. To reduce the experience of death to these elements is only to see its formal exterior. Behind this exterior we can discover expressions of sensitivity to death which are far from monolithic or constant. I do not believe that there has ever been a time when human death was 'natural', as has been claimed, that is accepted serenely, without fear or apprehension. Voltaire, it will be remembered, said that this serene death without fear or apprehension was only experienced by animals.

It is nevertheless the case that in the eyes of people who were spectators or actors, death has not always been of equal significance. This sensitivity to death marks advances or retreats. From what point did the death of a child come to be felt as a real loss, before becoming, in the course of the nineteenth century, an essential, particularly painful sorrow? From what moment did some equality manifest itself between men and women in the affective value of physical loss? These are naive questions to which there are no simple answers. Or perhaps there are. There are moments in history when the sentiment or simply the fear of death grows significantly. This is true of the panicky convulsions of periods of epidemic, but also, in a more diffuse way of periods when collective sensibility becomes obsessed with death. I believe that we are currently in one of those periods; just as we are in the process of admitting to our current taboo about death, the idea, nowadays all pervasive, that we have rejected or expelled death, shows paradoxically to what extent death has come to preoccupy us in a very real way.

The history of the experience of death is, for the most part, the history of these trends and it leads directly into the history of collective discourses on death.

One might say that the transition between the experience of death and the discourse of death is subtle, and at times the distinction can seem artificial. In funeral rites and in moments of sensitivity to death one is already dealing with the expression of a collective discourse, but one which is to a large degree unconscious. The repetition of the gestures and expressions of grief are all the more important for being involuntary. But beyond these manifestations of the unconscious the organized discourses of death which have evolved in time take shape. Like the positivists of the last century, we can schematize, in a rather caricatural way, the steps from a magical discourse to a religious one which was for a long time hegemonic, even unique. We can trace the progressive emergence of a secular discourse of death in its various scientific, philosophical and civic forms. Finally we could say that the modern era, from the end of the eighteenth century, has been characterized by the proliferation of a free literary discourse of death. Via a multiplicity of forms, right up to the contemporary mass media of television, comic strips and the like, the traditional framework in which the collective imagination was expressed has been exploded.

Through this discourse of death, and through a more indirect analysis of rituals and gestures, we can trace the evolution of representations of the next world which, for the majority of people, have extended and conditioned the global system of death and the hereafter.

A history of death on three levels – physical death, the experience of death and the discourse of death – undoubtedly entails certain immediate difficulties. An extremely subtle and complex analysis, cognisant of inertia and of rapid transitions, can only be written in the *longue durée*. Philippe Ariès, one of the first scholars to work on the theme, when trying to organize this enormous history, focused initially on the role of Christian death in order to bring its history up to the present.

Death in history

If it is now self-evident to state that death must be understood historically in the *longue durée*, it must be remembered that this has only recently been seen to be self-evident. Only twenty years ago, a group of scholars, theologians for the most part, investigated the theme of 'the mystery of death and its celebration' and discovered, not without some surprise, that they knew much more about early Christian and medieval forms of devotion to the dead than they did about modern and contemporary practices. Things have changed considerably since then and now the perspective of the *longue durée* is adopted by all scholars in the field.

But what is the history of death in the *longue durée*? Does it mean that we wish to find a death that is 'natural' or 'achronic' upstream of the great changes of the modern age? The *longue durée* in this sense runs the risk of becoming bogged down in the realm of the static and the intemporal. Nor is modern historiography immune from this temptation. More than one anthropologist, heir to the folklorists, has shown a tendency to believe in the existence of a stable, ancient system of death which hardly showed any sign of changing until relatively recently (in 1870 or even in 1914). Against the immobility of such a fixed concept of death certain scholars have sought to distinguish the major stages in the evolution of death. Even Philippe Ariès occupies an ambiguous place in this development in measuring the major stages in the evolution of death in the *longue durée* against a concept of achronic death, a death which was the same for a valiant medieval knight like Roland as for the Russian peasant in Tolstoy's *Ivan Illich*. The peasant, in turning his face to the wall to die when he decides that his time has come, is the image of a death which is accepted, the death which has been taken for granted since the earliest times and which still is today.

This idea of achronic death leaves me a little cold, as I believe that death has always been historical. In the *Song of Roland* one does indeed encounter the equivalent of the gesture of Tolstoy's peasant, but the character who employs it is Marsile, the Saracen king, when he learns of the death of the gigantic hero whom he has despatched against the armies of Charlemagne. Similarly, the character in medieval literature who immediately comes to mind in this context is Tristan, who turns his face to the wall to die when he is shown the black veil which tells him that Iseult is not going to come to his aid. What do Marsile and Tristan have in common in terms of a medieval sensibility? The answer is despair: they doubt God, they die a bad death. Yet that historical image of a bad death has now, in this century, become the image of a good death. All such representations of death are immersed in a cultural context which is properly the field of history.

Death as it is understood in the perspective of the *longue durée* is not achronic, but is part of the long processes of great secular and pluri-secular change. The appearance of stability is accentuated by the relative inertia of certain of the essential properties of the history of death. The traditional demographic pattern of death, with mortality rates above 30 per cent and its frequent and convulsive demographic crises is a case in point. Yet even this was not a wholly monolithic system. Right up to the nineteenth century it was affected by currents which, though they did not call the whole system of death into question, are nevertheless visible in the perspective of the *longue durée*.

Nor do the demographic facts explain everything. In the realm of behaviour, we also need to underline the astonishing obstinacy of ritual, of the whole system of deeply rooted gestures, reproduced even when they are no longer understood, as in the superstitious or magical rituals which are found in the rural response to death. Rather than speak of immobility in such cases, I would speak of gradual shifts, or of stratifications which ensure that, at one and the same time, traditional and innovative attitudes can coexist. We all give evidence, in our attitudes to death, of a collection of images and ways of behaviour which belong to different strata.

Thus, for example, in the second half of the eighteenth century, we can point to the account given by Mme de Genlis in her memoirs of the death of her friend M. de Puisieu, an aristocrat. Mme de Genlis, who is a fairly short-sighted and unimaginative witness, brings us right up to the deathbed, with three quite different readings of the final scene of just one man. The first – 'M. de Puisieu died in the greatest of sanctity' – is the image of a Christian death. On his body is found the hair shirt of mortification and among his papers the evidence of his charitable works. And the second? We read about them crossing the *salon* after leaving the bedroom and seeing a clock, surmounted by a figure of the three Fates, that Louis XV had given to M. de Puisieu, whereupon they are astonished: 'The thread of the Fates is broken.' So at the height of the Enlightenment, magical signs and portents of death persist in an aristocratic form. But, at the same time, Mme de Genlis describes one of the last scenes of M. de Puisieu's deathbed. A very famous doctor, Tronchin, one of the most fashionable doctors in Enlightenment *salons*, is treating the dying man. Through the doorway, Mme de Genlis sees Tronchin at the bedside of Puisieu, whose face is caught in a rictus of pain. Mme de Genlis is shocked and then chilled by Tronchin's reply: 'I have never seen such sardonic laughter, and I am happy to see it.' Here we see the impassibility of the *philosophes*, who reduced death to a collection of physical symptoms, and we see one death in three images which are as contradictory as they are simultaneous.

Not all examples are as graphic as this one. Yet if we look inside ourselves, at our own encounters with death, we find that we are heirs to a similar kind of stratification. One can see why Ariès, with whose interpretation I wholly agree, saw systems of death, not as successive phenomena, but as interleaved like rooftiles in a structure where different views coexist.

A convulsive history

In contrast to the inertia of its collective representations, the history of death is a convulsive history, marked by brutal stages. This has already been seen at the level of demographic history. We see this in levels of sensitivity towards death, which sometimes undergo great surges. This can be seen in the growth of the macabre in the late

Middle Ages; at the height of the Baroque between 1580 and 1660; and again in the return of darker images in the culture of the last decades of the eighteenth century, which saw the appearance of the Marquis de Sade's theatre of cruelty, the gothic novel and nostalgic interest in cemeteries, all within the framework of pre-Romanticism. Finally, this attraction to death can be found at the turn of the nineteenth and twentieth centuries, in the work of the Symbolists and Decadents.

Thus we can describe a curve, with stages of growth and decline, sometimes attributable to demographic factors and sometimes not. In order to conclude the theme of the periodicity of death, we can perhaps see that the central question of the inquiry might seem to be a naive one: does the history of death have a direction? Does it evolve in a given sense? Clearly we wish to know whether behind the spectacular phenomena of the story – the flaring-up of the macabre in the fifteenth century, the tensions of the Baroque – we can discern a continuous process in the history of collective representations of death.

In order to hazard some answers, we can, at least temporarily, forego opening (or half-opening) the door of the laboratory, to use Marc Bloch's famous image, and ask first about the ways in which this history can be written.

Silences

To begin with, the history of death, as we wish to write it, is full of difficulties in that it can seem to be a history of silences. The significance of such silences can be understood on two levels. The first is the common lot of all those who are engaged in social history and in the field of mentalities and who try to understand the anonymous masses as well as the wealthy and powerful. Despite the emphasis in older artistic treatment of death and in the *danses macabres* on death as a leveller of distinctions, there is nothing more unequal than the final passage. Among the evidence which survives, there are plenty of proofs and evidence about the rich, but much less for the anonymous mass of the poor. This is what makes us turn to different, non-traditional sources. Besides documentary sources, iconographic and archaeological sources – the archaeology of cemeteries, the iconography of frescoes and the decoration of tombs – occupy a place which is often as important as that of formal discourse.

But, particularly with the history of death, there is another kind of silence to complicate the task. This is what I shall call voluntary silence. When people are silent about death, the fact is as significant as when they construct a private discourse in order to domesticate it. Our own age has become aware, first in the United States and then in Western Europe, of a taboo which has made death a new category of obscenity. One thinks, among other things, of the hidden death of hospital wards and of private mourning. Such phenomena of rejection or concealment can already be seen in the earlier development of attitudes towards death, although naturally in very different ways. The literature of the eighteenth century, of the Enlightenment, especially as it was radicalized in the works of some of the spokesmen of the French Revolution, wanted to extirpate, to annihilate death; not, indeed, in the somewhat hypocritical terms of the American and Americanized civilizations of today, but in a heroic, Promethean form. The object was to expel death from human life.

One feels that the first problem facing us in the sources is that we wish to write a history of death and we are faced by silence. If this silence is heavy, it can also be as significant as the discourses themselves. I shall take, for example, one or two cases from the history of art. Why does the work of Delacroix appear as a bloody and murderous orgy, while, conversely, Ingres obstinately refused to represent death? Why did the Impressionists not deal with the subject of death (apart from Manet's *Death of Maximilian*, which is an early work)? It is because, as Odilon Redon said, they were 'low-brow' artists? The explanation seems too simple.

Few artists have explained their silences. One thinks of the extraordinary exception of Paul Klee who, stricken by the death of a friend in World War I, justified, in his diaries, his rejection of figurative expression in order to represent or transcribe his internal universe from then on.

One feels that the history of death is woven out of voluntary and involuntary silences. The list of tasks thus becomes inevitably longer.

Indicators and evidence

Fortunately, along with these silences there are sources in abundance; but they themselves pose specific problems. Initially, historical anthropology offers a tempting means for the reconstruction of the attitudes of the anonymous masses, out of the treasury of data which folklorists have been accumulating since the last century. In recording the characteristics of traditional civilization on the eve of its disappearance, they have emphasized the importance of death and of the actions which surround it, as the most important obligatory passage in human experience after birth and marriage. Historians, on reading the folklorists, cannot help being at once overwhelmed and troubled. Overwhelmed because they find there an enormous amount of information which gives them access to a mass of orally assembled evidence which no written source can ever furnish. A whole popular, rural practice of death is contained in gestures, a complete heritage can be exhumed in this way. Thus, as a counterpart to the official system of death, another system is revealed.

Yet the riches opened up by the folklorists are not without certain drawbacks. The folklorist systematically leaves to one side everything which is part of the official norm. The great folklorist Van Gennep, when he describes the funeral procession follows it carefully from the house to the door of the church, but as soon as it gets there, he abandons it, unless there is some detail which interests him – why, for example, the ritual knocking on one or other side of the church door in a Breton village? But as soon as the coffin has entered the building, it seems that here his zone of inquiry ends. Within such limits, the invaluable supply of knowledge from folklore leaves us dissatisfied with an 'ahistoric' knowledge which can only leave the historian hungry for more.

In order to find change and movement, there remains the option of relying on the indicators provided by another kind of research based on contemporary sources. Such evidence is undoubtedly poor and at the very least anonymous, but it is the essential for the study of gestures and attitudes. This, if I may be permitted to recall my own research, is true of the Provençal wills which I examined by the tens of thousands for eighteenth-century Provence. They show us, at a moment when people do not dice with death, the balance of collective attitudes for a period when a spiritual testament was an important element in the ritual of death.

Staying with the areas in which I have worked, we can turn to representations of the hereafter as I found them in Provence, in the company of Gaby Vovelle, on the altars to the soul in Purgatory, rushing from one country church to another to inventory the reredoses, the altars and the paintings left from the fifteenth to the twentieth century, until the time when monuments to the French dead of the Great War drove out the poor souls in Purgatory. Thus five centuries of collective images of life after death can be followed through the iconography of Purgatory.

Such delving into contemporary evidence still has a somewhat disconcerting quality, since it has the air of looking for history where one would least expect to find it. At the same time it has the advantage of continuity in time, in the *longue durée* to which we are committed. One important objection can be made to this kind of research, and it is an essential one, even though it can be raised against a whole field of historical research: what precisely does this kind of evidence reveal? Does it only give us access to practice, to external forms, or even to social convention, without showing anything of the naked anxiety of man in the face of death?

The objection is important, but it is not without an answer. The exhaustive handling of these anonymous sources does not diminish the value of the unique and highly significant document. Simply because one does not encounter a will opening with 'Joy, joy, tears of joy!', does not mean that Blaise Pascal's words lose their value as a moving spiritual testament. But, conversely, collective sources allow us to go more deeply into the unconscious attitudes of groups and masses, whom it surprises at a key moment, with all the indiscretion of a forced confession.

Prolix sources

If we move from sources which tell us about the gestures involved in death to the discourse surrounding it, we can get the impression that the silence or the scarcity of sources gives way to prolixity, to real riches. It can be summed up fairly briefly, however, since the discourse of death was, for a long time, stable, monolithic and unchanging. That of the Church, from the point at which it solidified during the Catholic Counter-Reformation, hardly changed until the end of the eighteenth century, or even well into the nineteenth. The discourse can be a testimony not of mobility but of the inertia of the systems in place. Yet, on the other hand, if the discourse itself was inert, some of its forms were particularly susceptible to change and mobility: as in literature and art, where death often occupied a disproportionately large place. One could say, as an extreme generalization, that the modern era, by freeing the collective imagination from the traditional framework in which it was contained, has been conducive to a proliferation of the ways in which death directly or indirectly figures in collective representations. Nowadays the free discourse of death must be sought in the more diversified sources of contemporary mass media: in popular songs, radio, television, film, best-selling novels, advertising and comic strips.

The historian of mentalities uses the evidence from these various genres as the basis for a wide-ranging inquiry. The question can be asked as to what this kind of evidence from literature and art tells us. Does it give evidence of collective attitudes – yours and mine – or does it give evidence of the irreducible personality of an author, an atypical and unclassifiable statement? What, for example, did the Symbolists and Decadents of the end of the nineteenth century express? An epidemic disease, the 'transient froth of time', an expression of the rejection of life by certain individuals or, more profoundly, the posing of a problem which ranged more widely than their own disillusionment with life?

Poor sources and prolix sources, both raise specific problems of reading and interpretation. History moves with justifiable caution through a forest of signs interrupted by silences. It is hazardous to suggest conclusions but I shall suggest them anyway. Such imprudence is necessary.

Demography?

What has changed in the history of death? How easy it would be to cut rudely to the heart of the matter and sum up the history of death as one simple process. One authority on the matter, Jean Fourastié, when he reviewed my work *Death in History*, confessed his annoyance with the contemporary interest in analysing the successive representations of the final passage. He saw all these details as being subordinate to one massive constant: the incontestable weight of the demographic cycle. In the past, up until the last two centuries, the Western family produced, in its conjugal history, an average of four children, of whom two survived their first twenty years to maintain the effective population. What is there to discuss? For Jean Fourastié, the real revolution in death is that which cut through this implacable noose in the modern era, and all the rest is literature.

One can agree thus far, that a fleeting glance shows a correlation between the periods of high sensitivity to death and the phases during which death tightened its grip. The end of the Middle Ages and the 'tragic seventeenth century' coincide demographically with eruptions of a macabre sensibility, but only up to a point and within certain limits. Similarly, and even more generally, the system of rituals and of folkloric gestures which surrounded death in the great rural world of traditional Western society lasted as long as the old demographic pattern. Yet it is clear that the field of collective representations of death cannot be reduced to this single aspect and that from a certain point (shall we place it in the eighteenth century?) this over-mechanical correlation becomes even more distorted. If we look at the period around 1900, and at the work of Thomas Mann, Roger Martin du Gard and others we can see that death occupied an essential, almost exaggerated place in post-Romantic and realist art. This contemporary, post-Romantic death, gave way to the taboo on death which emerged in America in the 1930s and in Europe in the 1950s, and we are currently involved in a rediscovery of death which has been under way since the 1960s. And all this has taken place within a demographic model which has been constant since the end of the nineteenth century in the continuous decline of mortality. It is clear that more complex mediating factors are involved.

Ideology

There is another temptation: to change tack completely and to make the human history of death into an ideological enterprise. Such an approach has impressive credentials. Without going too far back we can point to the *philosophes* of the eighteenth century, the theoreticians of the Enlightenment, who saw death as a system of exploitation, of economic exploitation in the trade in masses and indulgences and of political exploitation in the use of the rewards of the next life as a guarantee of order in the present, systems which were the fruit of the 'imposture of the priests', of 'superstition' and 'fanaticism'.

For the *philosophes*, the times of fear, of fanaticism and superstition had returned. The sleep of reason breeds monsters, as the famous engraving from Goya's *Capricciosos* had it, and it would be enough to wake the sleeper so that the monsters born of fear would vanish. Let us not be too dismissive about this voluntaristic optimism which saw a reformed pedagogy and the emancipation of humanity from material and spiritual shackles as a weapon in the fight against death. This is also our view of the matter. The nineteenth century transmitted the Enlightenment's belief in progress by associating it with the victories of science. The idealistic theory of the progress of reason was associated with the materialistic and mechanist theory of the triumph of science over death, and both formed a system which underlay scientistic ideology and biological philosophy. If I wished to be provocative, I could argue that the last echoes of Enlightenment optimism are to be found in our own times. I cannot read the last pages of Edgar Morin's famous essay on man and death, now more than twenty years old, without a certain emotion. He argued that, thanks to scientific progress, we were arriving, not at immortality but at an amortality characterized by a long life which ended voluntarily and without grief. If Bogometz's serum could be perfected then we could say farewell to death. This view should no more be dismissed than its predecessors. It testifies to a great spiritual project – the desacralization of death in the modern era.

The unconscious in human history

Are we thus taking neither one side nor the other, in a kind of bourgeois compromise? Contemporary fashion (and there are good fashions) is to emphasize neither the periodization imposed by demographic change nor that of the development of ideas as ideology but to dwell on the area between the two where a history of the unconscious can be written, the history which is made by people who do not know what they are making. This turns modern historians into anthropologists of the past in attempting to reconstitute the history of myth and of the workings of the collective imagination, going beyond the level of clear and formal thought. Such involuntary evidence is to some degree more reliable than the organized discourses of clerics and philosophers. Writers from Edgar Morin to Pierre Chaunu have described the trajectories of the major images of death and of the hereafter as they are present in history and geography. One can point to the spirit world where the dead, sometimes benevolent, more often hostile, wander through the world of the living, and must be appeased so that the living can be free of them. This is very like the image of death which we find in Montaillou. A relic of the ancient religions of the Mediterranean, and a recurrent element in medieval rural devotion, the spirit world had a rough passage before undergoing a contemporary resurgence, in different forms, if only as part of the apparently gratuitous games of a religious underground.

Parallel to this we can trace the progress of the theologies and eschatologies of resurrection which originated in the East and spread via the Mediterranean, those which spread through the mystery cults and those which accompanied the great expansion of Christianity. Between the two antagonistic systems of the spirit world and the eschatology of the resurrection there exists a whole dialectic of rivalries, contaminations and compromises across history. Popular religion and folk practices preserved the ancient model while, at the same sime, the Christian view was dominant between the thirteenth and the seventeenth centuries.

We can integrate the divisions proposed by Ariès into this primary global model without any contradiction. He traced the succession of medieval death, egotistic death (the death of the self emerging from the collective death of ancient times) to the death of the other, the romantic image of the loss of an irreplaceable individual, followed by the death taboo of the twentieth century. Such directive trends are at once satisfactory and unsatisfactory. To reduce it to its essentials, Philippe Ariès's argument stresses the progressive individualization of attitudes to death, a case which is hard to contradict, but which passes over more than one problem, particularly the problem of causes as modalities of the functioning of what he defines as the collective unconscious.

Ariès does not, of course, use this term in Jung's psychoanalytic sense, nor in that of Lévi-Strauss. He sees it as an autonomous development, not of mind, but of that level of consciousness which belongs to dreams and the imagination, the representations which spread them, the attitudes and gestures which express them and the rituals which structure them.

This is certainly to arrive at the area where the history of mentalities becomes particularly interesting. But one can nevertheless remain sceptical about the degree to which the collective unconscious can evolve without reference to the direct and indirect conditions which help to shape it.

I am, for my own part, aware of the limits of demographic factors. They were paramount in times of plague and epidemic under the traditional demographic model. But they were much less directly influential thereafter. Neither do I accept, as I have explained elsewhere in this book, the autonomous development of the collective imagination.

I see the image of death as belonging to what Marx called 'the general light, the particular ether which determines the specific value of all forms of existence', a deliberately vague formula which sees all human activity around death as a reflection of some of the most significant aspects of social life.

Let us take the example of 'baroque' death, as it appears in the first half of the seventeenth century, between, say, 1580 and 1650. If one reduces this model to a poor echo of the demographic problems of the period, the resulting view will be very distorted. Of course there were epidemics, and there was the Thirty Years' War, but there was also the 'affective mentality' of a period of tension and upheaval in the religious, social and political order. It was the time of Brémond's 'mystical invasion' haunted by constant references to the Last Things; it was the time in which the popular religion of death was being eradicated by the clergy, who saw it as superstition; it was the time of the burning of witches. Conversely, it was also the time when the impressive ceremonial of the death of the great came into being, when the hereafter was used more than ever as a guarantee of order and of the social hierarchy, with the stress on the abyss which separated the circle of the elect from the mass of sinners while still, at least in the Catholic world, leaving the door open for the purchase of time through the affirmation of the belief in Purgatory.

All these intersecting factors constitute a system of coordinates in which the social climate of a period and what Robert Mandrou called its 'vision of the world' are refracted in an indirect but very profound way. Death certainly gives us a privileged insight into this vision of the world.

One could say as much about the bourgeois image of death in the nineteenth century, whether one sees it fully structured and in place or, even better, in its constitutive phase from 1770 to 1820, when its characteristics were being formed, and later, in the profound crisis of bourgeois values which marked the twilight of the nineteenth century and the watershed of the years 1900 to 1914. Death emerges as a reflection of society, albeit an ambiguous reflection. The image of a Machiavellian hereafter, the invention of the mighty to ensure the docility of the weak as seen by the *philosophes* of the eighteenth century, was a poor expression of this determinism and adopted its contradictions. Counter-systems have also existed which used death to overturn symbolically the hierarchy of power. The medieval *danse macabre* is of this kind. Of course, death is not always revolutionary. Popular culture in the age of Rabelais used the comedy and satire of death to fight its last rearguard action. The French Revolution used the heroic sublimation of death to affirm the new morality of which it was the vehicle.

The question remains as to how the system of collective representations of death changes, following what rhythms and modalities. In this area, I maintain that such change occurs in the wide expanses of slow evolutionary change, in the history of the *longue durée*. Far from being static, the study of attitudes to death is an ideal basis for reflection on the idea of structure in the history of mentalities. Such structures are not at all rigid; we can see them gradually taking shape and decomposing across time. I do not believe that this implies that representations of death change imperceptibly, by constant retouching. Its history rather suggests a lurching progress occurring at the heart of crises of collective sensibility, taking the phrase in its broadest sense to mean those dynamic moments when everything comes together and crystallizes at times of global questioning. We have encountered episodes of this type at the origins of the Baroque, at the twilight of the Enlightenment, at the watershed of 1900 and maybe also in our own day, since the early 1960s.

These great shifts in collective sensibility do not only apply to the representation of death. Everything from the family to received value-systems is affected. Here again it would be easy to take the example of the great turning point of the second half of the eighteenth century, around 1760, when everything changed in Western mentality: attitudes to life, marriage, the family and the sacred. Such crises take place in the most profound and apparently deeply rooted structures of society. At the close of the Middle Ages it was the crisis of feudal and chivalric society as much as the Black Death which produced that general instability of which the eruption of the macabre was one aspect.

In a word, death, in all its manifestations, is the best metaphoric guide to the problems of life. Pierre Chaunu wrote that the collective and spiritual investment in death was 'a function of life expectancy'. I am inclined to add that systems of death are products of the aspiration to happiness. This is why we cannot avoid asking about the how and why of the rediscovery of death in our own times.

At the very moment when we are assimilating the image of the death taboo which we acquired from the United States, the rash of publications which deal with it and, more generally, the return of a morbid collective sensibility act like a dialectical negation. It is to the extent that we can understand and reinterpret both the taboo and the rediscovery of death in terms of the crises of society that we, the historians, can be of some use to present-day humanity.

Notes

This chapter has been adapted from papers read at San Diego (October 1978, Annual Congress of Historians of the Western United States), at Louvain (1979, Conference on Death in the Middle Ages; published Louvain, 1982) and at Montpellier (Centre Lacordaire, January 1979).

1   *Death in the West from 1300 to the Present* (Gallimard). The introduction, entitled 'The history of man in the mirror of death' amplifies the themes introduced here.

5

Popular Religion

The author of this synthesis must once again acknowledge the many contributions which have been used in this essay, which appeared as the introduction to a special number of Monde Alpin *on popular religion. The very wealth of the contributions surveyed, coming from all disciplines (history, ethnology, sociology . . .), called for a survey of the state of the problem. Popular culture and religion, indissociable until fairly recently, raise in a very direct way, from a study based on the Alpine and southern regions, the more general problem of the definition of the 'popular'.*

The theme of popular religion in traditional societies has been taken up by historians in recent years and several articles and books have been devoted to it. The theme has long been familiar to folklorists and ethnologists and the relative lateness (and loudness) of the historians' discovery may seem surprising. Yet it is possible that the popular religion which the historians are unearthing, and which forms a legitimate part of current approaches to popular culture, is unlike that dealt with by their predecessors in the field. It is important that a number of people add their voices to the chorus, and researchers, producing evidence of the validity, if not of the progress, of their approach to the subject, are at the same time looking for a definition of 'popular religion' which is acceptable to all.

A contested definition

Old, new, or simply revamped; so many definitions have now been proposed that one can step back from them and attempt to group them into families. In so doing, we do not pretend to innovation, in presenting the state of a problem which has already been examined in recent, useful syntheses.[1]

First of all there are those for whom popular religion has its own separate existence, unaffected by and independent of religion as it is taught and received. Thus Boglioni could distinguish between authentic popular religion and 'popularized' religion – that which emerged in the popular strata of the Christian message. There is a constant divide between religion as a product of popular spontaneity and that which is received by the people from outside, and Boglioni distinguishes between the 'history of popular religion' and 'the history of the religious life of the Christian population'.

Such a distinction is not far removed from a folkloric model, in which, traditionally, popular religion, reduced to a corpus of pagan survivals, superstitions and magical practices, perhaps affected by some characteristics of pagan–Christian syncretism, constituted another religion, but one seen as vestigial and static: a treasury in some measure, or the remains of one, which needed to be inventoried as quickly as possible.

Is it artificial to assimilate these static definitions, as Carlo Russo does, to those proposed by Meslin, on the basis of certain intangible structural characteristics? For Meslin, popular religion is anti-intellectual, pragmatic, emotional and defined in the following terms: 'a religious phenomenon is popular when it manifests hostility to any systematic objectivization of religious belief, since it is the explosion of subjective emotions and tends to bring the divine onto the horizon of daily life; it humanizes God in order to feel closer to him and in order to capture his power through the use of the techniques which it invents.' Can the historian of society or the sociologist unquestioningly accept a model in which the 'popular' is defined in terms of the purely structural characteristics of practice?

One doubts it, and current research has led many historians to ask questions about the very reality of popular religion. Can we not apply to it the stimulating questions which Julia, Revel and De Certeau have already asked about popular culture, of which it is, after all, a part, and ask whether the attractiveness of the concept owes something to the 'beauty of death' – whether the emergence of the term in the course of the last century in the work of positivist folklorists was not, in fact, due to the extinction of the civilization which contained these realities, a civilization which became the object of study and collection as it was destroyed? Can we say that popular religion is only an artefact, manufactured by nineteenth-century science?

Without taking responsibility for the whole debate, present-day
historians have become involved. The reduction of the question to a
dialectic of elite and popular seems to them to diminish the inquiry,
limiting it to a caricatural confrontation. They are also worried by the
immobility of popular religion when seen as something achronic, fully
constituted, incapable of enrichment and, what is more, of disintegration in the course of time. Robert Mandrou proposed a model of
of religious stratification in historical terms for the early-modern
period in 1961 which operated on three levels: an elite piety,
individualized and open to mystical experiments; a religion of urban
groups, narrowly defined and practically engulfed in religious practice, dominated in that period by the fear of death and by salvation;
thirdly, rural religion, a syncretic mixture of Christianity and of older
elements, often relics of paganism, which constitutes 'popular' religion as it has traditionally been defined.

In the wake of this approach, in an attempt to carry the analysis
further I proposed in *Baroque Piety and Dechristianization: attitudes
to death in eighteenth-century Provence*, a sociology of attitudes as a
function of social status. From the workshop to the shop counter,
among urban wage earners and domestic servants, in the maritime
world and the many groupings of peasant society I found well-
differentiated forms of behaviour in the face of a reality as important
as death. What then of popular religion?

One argument, of which I am well aware, that can be opposed to
such quantitive history is that it becomes immersed in pure sociography without having adequately defined its objectives. My quantification of the gestures of religious practice hardly possesses any validity
if the social practice of entire groups only reveals the socialization of
attitudes, if it leaves out the other religion, the submerged mass of the
iceberg of popular religion whose practices and rituals remain
invisible. Yet it must be asked, as many, including myself, have asked,
to what extent religion, even popular religion, survived as a living
thing at the height of the Catholic reconquest, without becoming in
large part integrated with the system of gestures of religious practice.

Another stage was reached with the arguments presented by Jean
Delumeau and other current students of the historically conceived
dialectic between Christianity and popular religion. Shall we be
accused of excessive annexationism if, stretching Russo's mere sug-
gestion to the limit, we state that such an approach is already to be
found in the very rich, but inevitably allusive, pages which Gramsci
devoted to the religious question and to folklore both in his *Prison
Notebooks* and in his 'Observations on folklore'?[2] At that early stage,

Gramsci saw popular and official religion as two cultural forces operating in a dialectical relationship, and he described in general terms the Church's oscillations between repression and compromise as part of a relationship of strength which contains echoes of other profound realities like the town–country relationship.

Jean Delumeau certainly did not start from the same methodological premises but his historical reconstruction, in the *longue durée*, also stresses some aspects of this secular trend. He sees the Church as having accepted, in the Middle Ages, the pagan–Christian syncretism which constituted the heart of popular religion as it was then elaborated. He also argues that the 'folkloric' character of peasant religion (if one can run the risk of anachronism) was not perceived as an obstacle to grace before the turning point of the fourteenth to fifteenth centuries. Things began to change with the foundation of the mendicant orders, whose pastoral mission was directed at the popular strata: the idea was being born among the religious elite that Western Christianity needed to be still further converted and Christianized. This consciousness reached its peak in the Renaissance: 'It seemed as if the elite and urban culture which was a product of the conjunction of Christianity, of the medieval discoveries and of humanism felt fragile and threatened in that period by an ocean of rural and oral culture whose immensity was much better known than before.'

One of the keystones of this pastoral mission common to 'both reformations', to use a concept dear to Delumeau, was the huge campaign of acculturation carried out among the popular, especially rural sections of society, to force them to get used to regular practice. Christian civilization, which in the course of centuries came to equate religion to a considerable extent with the gestures of practice, thus took up a central place in the sixteenth and seventeenth centuries, and dominated the following century. In its conquering phase the project of acculturation showed a repressive side of remarkable harshness: it presented a grim model, dominated by the fear of damnation, to the people, and typical of the eradication of popular beliefs carried out were the witch-hunts of the first half of the seventeenth century. It is clear that the apparent unanimity and homogeneity of practice hides a more complex reality. The post-Tridentine Church had to make compromises too, of which the most common, and also the most traditional, was the Christianization, to whatever depth, of traditional customs and feast days. Fighting on one side and compromising on the other, the activist pastoral mission succeeding in taking control of the parish church which it made into the centre of collective religious life, setting up altars to the new forms of devotion (the Blessed

Sacrament and the rosary) in the most prominent places, while relegating those of the traditional intercessory saints to the bottom of the church, or even further away in smaller chapels on the periphery of the parish. This process of conquest had its limits: popular religion found refuge on the periphery, only assimilating the new forms of devotion in modified versions which also conformed to traditional images, as with the Blessed Sacrament and the rosary.

Even so, the corpus of traditional beliefs disintegrated. One would like to prolong this long-range perspective into the nineteenth century, when the folklorists made popular religion a central theme in their work. But what do their discoveries, made between the end of the nineteenth century and our own day, and then fixed in the moment of transcription, really represent? Much more, it seems to me, than the remains of a treasure handed down from the earliest times, the ambiguous synthesis of an ancient residue stratified in the early-modern period and finally digested and 'popularized', becoming an integral part of the popular religion of the countryside just as the elite was turning away from religion, or rejecting its grim and meticulous aspects in favour of the purity of the 'good news'. In the meantime many newer categories of the popular lost contact both with the heritage of the *longue durée* and with religious practice. The residual, defensive attitude of rural popular religion was accentuated, and this development also raises the problem of the emergence of another 'popular' religion without roots, seeking its ways and modes of expression in the urban world of industrial society.

Does the application of historical methods to popular religion inevitably entail scepticism about the validity of a search for its origins? It remains the case that reformers on all sides in the sixteenth century were not fighting with shadows, and that a living and structured popular religion existed, and in a far more lively form between the thirteenth and sixteenth centuries than in the nineteenth, when the folklorists were studying it on its deathbed. How shall we define it?

We have seen the world of 'magism', of popular therapeutics, of fortune-telling, of magical actions, which is part of popular religion. These aspects have been described by Jean Delumeau and Keith Thomas. It is still important to reach agreement on the meaning of the word 'magic', even at the risk of being told by some authors, like Natalie Zemon Davis, that we are thereby unconsciously aligning ourselves with the restrictive and reductive position of official religion. Emmanuel Le Roy Ladurie, dissecting in *Montaillou* what he calls the 'five-legged sheep' of popular village religion at the beginning of the fourteenth century, argued that it was composed of one part pre-Christian heritage, one part Albigensianism, one part popular materialism and two parts Christianity (no doubt in order to get a round figure), insisting on the fact that magical practices, whether thaumaturgic or otherwise, only occupied a very restricted place, especially in view of the complex eschatology which occupied an apparently paramount position in the lives of the villagers and which was organized into one or even several constructs of the hereafter and of relations between the living and the dead. In Montaillou popular religion, for all its contradictions and incoherencies, contained a wealthy and abundant vision of the world.

To what extent can one extrapolate from a single glimpse of a place like Montaillou, which is still somewhat exceptional? Nowadays, in asking historians questions about this point, one is more often confronted with two models of early popular religion than with one.

The original 'other religion', fundamentally pre-Christian in its various forms, does exist. It is the type found by Gaignebet in his analysis of the phenomenon of the carnival based on folkloric and, to a much lesser extent, on historical sources. From Christmas to Easter, the carnival period allows us to see beyond the liturgical calendar and discover the lunar rhythm of the old religion, the key to which is the movement of souls first captivated and then freed by the Moon, before being finally drawn back to it, which is celebrated consciously and unconsciously by the festivity of carnival and by its popular mythology, from the Bear's breaking wind at the end of winter to the tribulations of the giant Gargantua.

By contrast with this model of a revived ancient popular religion we have, thanks to Bakhtine's important work on Rabelais and sixteenth-century popular religion, a very different view, albeit based on rather similar folkloric sources. For Bakhtine, popular culture does not consist of a corpus of magical and comical beliefs surviving (but in what a state!) into the dawn of the modern era. From the outset, Bakhtine warns us very appositely against the imperturbable seriousness of Gaignebet's interpretation. He sees popular religion rather as a collection of attitudes and modes of behaviour, in a word, as a dynamic, based on the inversion of values and hierarchies; the corrosive action of laughter and derision, whereby a spontaneous and constantly demystifying counter-system is opposed to the established order and the established religion. This is a provocative and abrasive thesis, even if it inevitably gives rise to hesitations and doubts. Is there not a risk that popular culture defined in this way may be just another imaginative creation, as unhistorical as that of the folklorists, equating popular culture with positive and anti-establishment attitudes from the outset? This would be aprioristically to reject popular fantasies born of the sleep of reason and all creations of popular fear and terror. One has only to think of the effects of the Black Death on mass sensibility at the time of the *danses macabres* . . . .

The most far-seeing among contemporary historians pick their way somewhere between Gaignebet's static model of an ancient popular religion and Bakhtine's dynamic of popular culture. Among works published in recent years we have no better examples than Carlo Ginzburg's two stimulating studies, *The Night Battles* and, more recently, *The Cheese and the Worms*. In the nocturnal world of the *benandanti*, the Friulian white witches whose story is preserved in the inquisition records of the sixteenth century, the men set off at night to fight the evil witches of the mountains in order to defend the prosperity of their villages by practising the ancient rites of the soil and also, significantly, to protect the migration of souls. Here we find ourselves in a world which takes us right to the heart of the ancient religion, the same, perhaps, as that of Gaignebet's model. The personality of the miller Menocchio, the tragic hero of *The Cheese and the Worms*, who is obstinate to the death, was taken by the same author from the same sources, and yet he is a hero of the Bakhtine type. A man of the people who was also literate, Menocchio worked out a private cosmogony which was spontaneously materialist, seeing the world as a great terraqueous cheese emerging from chaos, on which swarmed the worms, in the form of angels, while God himself, the worm of worms, was the product of spontaneous generation. This is an impressive example of popular creativity, even if the central character is exceptional in being very well informed and perhaps more representative of the intermediary 'demiurges' in society, about whom we are beginning to know more, than of an authentically oral culture.

We need not compare the *benandanti* and the Friulian miller, products of the same world and found in the same archive, point by point. There is no contradiction between the two studies. Rather, the cases tend to confirm a concept of popular religion as something quite plastic and undermine the notion of the masses as passive and conservative, or as the victims of a coercive, received message.

At the end of this preliminary discussion we have travelled quite far from our point of departure. The concept of popular religion which is being held up for examination is not one based on an unchanging reality, the hard core of which is the 'other religion' originating in paganism and preserved by the rural society, at least not uniquely so.

It also includes all forms of assimilation and contamination, and notably the view that popular post-Tridentine Christianity can be seen as a form of specifically popular creativity. And what, indeed, of the revolutionary cults of 1794? The definition as thus reformulated is certainly more subtle and, it seems, more likely to satisfy the historian. But it also entails a heavier list of tasks. In place of a treasure hunt we propose the search for a much more fluid and changing reality, in an area where techniques of research and exploitation pose a whole series of problems.

Problems of research

In approaching the subject of popular religion, the ethnologist and the folklorist use a whole series of tried and tested sources and methods, of which field work, largely based on oral evidence, is the core. The historian who wishes to embark on this kind of research quickly discovers the extent to which popular culture is shrouded in silence. Unable to rely on oral investigation, he is dependent on sources which shut out the direct voice of the subject and is forced to rely on the external, often hostile views, of those whose business it was to supervise and punish. His sources come primarily from the agents of repression, and are affected by all the distortions and omissions which such a role carried with it.

Under these circumstances it is necessary to change the rules and the historian initially does this by adopting a different or 'weighted' approach to traditional sources. This is how Chanaud used pastoral visitations drawn from the extensive archive of Mgr Le Camus in the diocese of Grenoble. Even better was the good fortune of Devos in discovering the papers prepared by the administrator before the visitations at Combloux in Savoy in 1733. One would like to know whether similar documents, found elsewhere in Savoy, are to be found in any quantity, as Devos hopes, in other dioceses. In Savoy, the visitation records sometimes make references of varying degrees of detail to popular practices under the heading of errors and infractions. The descriptions found here give a whole range of information about the object of devotions – in the chapels of the parish church and the countryside – and about the reasons for them – sickness, death, natural disasters. Of course the partial and prejudiced character of these sources, reflecting the views of priests from the towns, themselves impregnated by another culture and by a repressive view of parochial authority, only gives an external view of the people of the villages and the characteristics of a different system of behaviour and beliefs must be distilled from these negative and veiled impressions.

For this purpose, what we have called the 'different' use of traditional sources has much in common with the study of the sources of repression *per se*, illuminating situations of social cleavage and deviance, of the social pathology of a period. From the persecution of non-conformity via social, familial and sexual discipline, to the witch-hunts of the early seventeenth century, a whole range of sources is available which is familiar to French historiography from the work of Mandrou and Muchembled, in English in the work of Trevor-Roper and Keith Thomas and in Italian in the work of Romanello and Ginzburg. Leaving the kind of approach based on the perspectives of those who supervised and judged (e.g. Mandrou's *Judges and Witches*), we come to those who have taken the hazardous step of passing to the other side of the barricades and into the world of 'witchcraft, [which] seems to bear witness to a repressed and embattled world' (Pierre Chaunu) postulating 'an almost static world and a popular mentality based on magical beliefs . . .'. Even more than the former category, these sources entail certain dangers for our attempt to reconstruct the world as it was. After all, did not the inquisitors themselves create witches in the sixteenth century, by fantastically gathering the mass of spells, magical practices and innocent relics of the 'superstition' of paganism into a formula of diabolical ascendancy? Obviously, such a formula cannot be accepted uncritically.

There is a transition to secularism in this system of sources which becomes very perceptible in the second half of the eighteenth century when the elite of the Enlightenment – statisticians and travellers – began to cast a cold Stendhalian eye on the phenomena of popular religion, anticipating the perspectives of anthropologists and folklorists. Our periodization is, of necessity, exaggeratedly simplified. It would not be too difficult to find, in seventeenth-century humanists like Peiresc or Gassendi, the beginnings of a non-clerical and scientific outlook on popular customs and traditions. The seventeenth-century *savants* of Aix-en-Provence also fit this description in their investigations into the origins of the festivities of the *Fête-Dieu*. Conversely, clerical attitudes became progressively less strict and more accommodating in this period. We have, also from Provence, a marvellous little book on the local customs of Marseilles, published in 1685 by a local priest, Marchetti, which is a valuable description, within the limits of the author's ideological presuppositions, proving, for example, the truth of Christianity from the pagan heritage, in a kind of apology for the laxist method against the methods of the post-Tridentine terrorists. Yet urban popular religion also comes out of the shadows in a work of this kind, with its description of the processions of the housewives of Marseille, whose spells, green candles and festivals preserve the various layers of the Phocaean city's cultural heritage.

These, statistically, were the documents which preceded and heralded the changes of the Enlightenment, this period which saw the emergence of doctors like Achard, author of the *Dictionary of Provence* of 1787, essayists like Bérenger, author of *Provençal Evenings,* and, already, the appearance of erudite *savants* and government officials who began to tour France in search of archaeological and artistic treasures. Millin, the author of *Travels in the Departments of the South of France,* completed under the Empire between 1800 and 1810, was, for the Alpine and Provençal region, a typical representative of this period's curiosity in describing sacred and profane customs and practices. He saw them as reflections of the exoticism of a vanished age, without investing them with the beauty of death, though this change was not far off. Millin was typical of the consular and imperial prefects of statistics of the time of Chaptal who, along with their successors under the constitutional monarchy, were all cast in the same mould, reserving a special place for accounts of the local customs of their districts (see, for example, Delacroix in Drôme, or Ladoucette in the Hautes-Alpes). They did not strictly follow in the footsteps of their clerical post-Tridentine predecessors. Where the parish priests and ecclesiastical visitors of the Counter-Reformation fought with the devil, these men evinced a certain disdain for these dead phenomena, tempered by an interest which was to grow in the course of the nineteenth century into the erudite folklore of the period between 1860 and 1900. The latter period was characterized by collectors, who gathered up the remains of whatever survived in the rural culture of their own day. One thinks of Bérenger-Féraud's *Popular Reminiscences of Provence* for the south, but one could, without too much difficulty, find similar examples for practically every department in France. This generation saw the birth of contemporary folklore and the great collections, seen as the last gleanings of a dying civilization, were cited in the footnotes of one study after another. In this way, the 'treasury' of which we spoke earlier was formed: both an irreplaceable body of sources and, at the same time, an ageless corpus of material without any historical dimension, to the despair of the historian.

From the anathemas of the agents of the Counter-Reformation, via the cold, ironic stare of the *philosophes*, which persisted well into the nineteenth century, to the often nostalgic attachment of the folklorists of the late nineteenth century, was built up a large body of evidence of popular religion as seen from the outside by the representatives of the elite. This body of material is both precious and to some extent suspect, yet today it constitutes an essential source. Can one find other evidence which is more direct and therefore more authentic? Just because the common people, both townsmen and peasants, did not commit their religious views to paper, for very good reasons, does not mean that they are therefore lost in silence. It is necessary to turn to non-written sources to find this expression; to study what was done – belief expressed in actions; what was seen, through iconography and archaeology; and what was said and recorded in the oral tradition.

Can popular religion be caught in the act? It is easily said, but the programme leaves the problem of sources unresolved, since it requires either direct observation of surviving practices or the discovery of written evidence of former practices. Both methods are currently being used. As an example of the use of the first we can look at Professor Dupront's work on contemporary pilgrimages in Europe. This is an exemplary case of a regressive method using contemporary survivals of popular religious practice to go back in time and better understand its historic forms. Following the example of the study of pilgrimages, this method can be applied in other particularly massive and significant tests, as in the study of festivals such as contemporary votive or patron saints' days. This type of study presupposes a pluri-disciplinary and often comparative approach involving the collaboration of the ethnologist, the historian, the archaeologist and others. In static, conservative societies like the Mezzogiorno one can find the basis for a retrospective explanation of types of festivals and pilgrimages which have disappeared in our rural society but which existed at an earlier period. The work of Régis Bertrand on the pilgrimage to Notre-Dame des Oeufs at Gréoux in Provence, within the precise limits of a specialized monograph, is a good illustration of this method, starting from a contemporary study of the pilgrimage and proceeding to a regressive study in the *longue durée* based on archaeological findings, oral evidence and written documents.

We must acknowledge that the majority of the practices with which we are dealing survive only in a fossilized form. They need to be rediscovered in scattered writings where the attitudes and activities of the past are registered directly without the mediation of the elite. These are forced or involuntary confessions, but for that very reason they are of undoubted value.

My own work on the practice surrounding collective attitudes to death in Provence in the eighteenth century was just such a study. Based on clauses of wills, it was a serial study beginning with the triumph of the 'baroque' ritual of death among the people as well as the elite at its height in the period 1680–1720/30 and then tracing its decline in the second half of the century. I was aware, along the way, that I had seized on an important, and not merely formal, change in collective sensibility.

Research of this kind, based on registered practices, could be conducted on the basis of other 'indicators', as they are called nowadays. Anyone wishing to study familial attitudes to post-Tridentine Christian morality can study ratios of pregnancies and illegitimate births, abandoned children, demands for marriage dispensations for consanguinity and, in yet another direction, the respect for seasons when marriage and conception were forbidden, like Advent and Lent, along with the enforcement of baptism within three days of birth. This type of study has been carried out by Jean-Louis Flandrin, J.-M. Gouesse and others, based on the parish registers of the *ancien régime*. They provide a whole series of measurements of the degree to which the imposed discipline was observed and, by the same token, both the 'Christianization' of actions and the persistence of other systems which escaped the Church's control such as pre-marital liberties. This is not to say that groups scoring badly in the table of collective disciplines were less 'religious'. The sailors and fishermen of Marseille, for example, whose original and prolix devotions are known for that period, are nevertheless very badly placed in the 'hit parade' of demand for masses. They married in all seasons, especially Lent, since their spring departure 'on business' made it necessary for them to regulate their activities in the winter. Their religion simply did not conform to the official mode of expression.

The last example sets the limits of this procedure. The quantification of actions (when they are not actions of refusal or rejection) can give us an index of the extent of Christianization of popular attitudes and of the form it took. It can also show, but only in a negative way, the imprint of an older, pre-existing system.

We can expect another order of information from iconography and, in the longer term, from archaeology or the analysis of religious buildings and sacred space. Not that it is necessary to see in them the spontaneous products of popular creativity, directly expressed and translating its collective representations graphically. In the majority of cases a more subtle dialectic is visible. The 'popular' image is only popular in so far as the producers modelled their products according to the demands of a popular public; but they did so within a normative framework. The interior decoration of churches (pictures and reredoses) only show the evolution of collective representations via an intermediary and under the supervision of the priests in charge, and, indeed, through their initiative, as well as through the mediation of an artistic vocabulary. Even an ex voto, made on demand and in accordance with individual need, conformed to a codified expression. The image, the object and the place are thus more arenas of compromise and of conflict than direct representations. This applies, as we will see, to the interior decoration of the parish church, to country chapels and to cemeteries alike.

Thus we must not expect iconography and archaeology to show us popular religion in free expression – in the form, say, of the devil of Bessans. This example is too expressive to be ignored. A horned and grimacing devil was used by the makers of reredoses in Bessans in the baroque period, but it was represented as overwhelmed and chained up by the intercessory saints, an image both of the dangers of the mountains and the ancient pagan gods like Jupiter who had taken refuge there. Here we see the triumph of the Church over the solitude of the uplands, and the triumph of the pastoral mission over ancient fears. Next we see how this community of woodcarvers, chased out of the churches by Sulpician statuary in the nineteenth century could generate the ill-feeling which caused a grimacing statue of the devil to be left at the curé's window at night. This time, however, the devil had been 'laicized', no longer in chains but free as a kind of symbol of the other world which, having been emancipated from the Church, was rediscovering its old familiar demons. Yet the devil of Bessans, although it may be a metaphor for understanding the fortunes of popular religion, remains a curiosity which proves the rule stated above.

One can organize, in so far as is possible and in a very general way, the larger of the various series of popular religious iconography. To begin with, there are religious images which functioned as expressions of collective devotions, albeit for domestic and individual use. This is perhaps the most immediate object of research and several recent studies have emphasized Italian interest in the subject, for example A. Vecchi's *The Cult of Images in Popular Prints*. Systematic research on this subject has begun in France and which M. Mus's unpublished thesis (Aix, 1973) is a fine example. This remarkable work, tracing the production of central themes and imagery in the *longue durée*, from the painted images of the seventeenth century to the lithographs of the nineteenth, emphasizes the archaizing character of a medium which kept in touch with popular sensibility through simple representation of its hieratic saints; the astonishing importance of traditional devotions where the traditional Virgins and the saints of the countryside were more common than the Virgin of the Rosary, and finally the extraordinary stability of themes and characteristics into the heart of the nineteenth century, with the change from prints to lithographs having no impact on the continuity of the received models.

What part can be assigned to popular religion and to what Boglioni calls 'popularized religion' in the iconography and furnishing of churches, chapels and sacred places? One is tempted to argue for its importance in the case of objects of collective devotion for the use of the community which were set up by the Church for the edification of the faithful. This would be too hasty, however, as the pastoral visitations of the classical period show that considerable attention, and rarely benevolent at that, was paid to paintings and statues which were suspected of being 'indecent' according to both the modern and early sense of the term. Such responses show the persistent legacy of a less strictly controlled age, corresponding perhaps to Delumeau's expansive concept of the Middle Ages, in which a form of Christianity mixed with pagan survivals had its own, more spontaneous vigour.

The exploitation of this mine of iconographic information must be undertaken on several levels, which are stages in a process of discovery. The most elementary, in appearance, is the study of paintings, statues and reredoses in churches and chapels. This is the vein which I worked in collaboration with Gaby Vovelle in a thematic study, *The Image of Death and Salvation in Provence in Purgatory Altars, 1400–1900*. The same theme has been treated exhaustively for a very rich area by a team led by V.-L. Tapié working on baroque reredoses from Brittany.

What can one expect from such sources? I think we showed in *The Image of Death and Salvation in Provence* how the iconography of the reredos, although executed in accordance with orders from above, nevertheless shows changes in collective sensibility to life, death and the hereafter in the *longue durée*.

Current research focuses on another serial source, now being actively explored: the ex voto. Despite losses, theft and destruction, these documents survive in large numbers. B. Cousin had located

5000 of them in Provence and there are several thousand at Oropa in Piedmont. They offer the best hope of reconstructing the chronicle of accidents, illnesses, escapes from death and miracles in traditional society. By comparison with popular images, ex votos possess the originality of individual pieces of evidence, even if they conform to stereotyped formulae and are best analysed in the *longue durée*. Painted or illustrated ex votos, beginning in the seventeenth century (exceptionally in the sixteenth) and lasting until the present day, are most promising sources. But can the ex voto be regarded as evidence of 'popular' religiosity? We should not judge prematurely on the basis of a very noticeable popularization which took place in the nineteenth and twentieth centuries. The elites of the seventeenth century were not unwilling to use them. Without anticipating their conclusions, we can say that the studies carried out by Provençal scholars in recent years correspond to a general movement of interest in them in other regions, as shown by the work of M. Mollat on the maritime ex votos of western France. Two southern interpretations illustrate two complementary methods. Christian Loubet works on the Piedmontese shrine of Our Lady of Oropa near Biella, a place notable for its exceptional wealth of material in a relatively recent period during which anonymous marble plaques generally replaced illustrated ex votos in France. In his approach, the study of a sacred site on the basis of its ex votos is part of a diversified procedure which uses written sources (endowments, accounts of miracles) as well as oral sources, developing an experimental site using a range of complementary approaches. Bernard Cousin, on the other hand, is exploring in its entirety the massive corpus of 5000 ex votos which he has catalogued in Provence.

Systematic treatment of serial sources involves a recourse to methods of analysis which can only be provided by the computer. In the study of images, paintings, reredoses and ex votos, iconography is currently making contributions to the history of popular religion which together constitute a breakthrough in research. Will it appear mistaken or annexationist to insist on two further extensions to this area of research? The first involves an extension of the study of these objects beyond the traditional confines of iconography and archaeology into areas which are really the field of the historian of material life. Studies of Savoy, based on Combloux, Brison and Mont-Saxonnex, have shown in very different ways the role of the bell and of bells in popular religion, as a means of communication and as a magical object the sound of which keeps storms at bay and gets rid of demons. In this context, one can also mention recent research on the languages of the *glas* in south-eastern France by J.-C. Bouvier. The bell and belfry were claimed (or squatted) by the community for many different purposes which were denounced by the curé of Combloux. It shows the existence of popular complicity in taking part of the church out of the control of the clergy. The assertion that the bell was inalienable property was also at the heart of the struggle against 'revolutionary vandalism'. The bell retained the multiple and many-faceted value which Schiller, whom Aragon called the 'great poet of the people', ascribed to it.

What is true of an object can also be true of a place, and the example which comes to mind is that of the cemetery, which occupied a special place in the curé of Combloux's recriminations. The cemetery emerges as the locus of confrontation between the strict views of the post-Tridentine clergy, demanding decency and respect, and its collective appropriation by village culture, which remorselessly associated the world of the living and that of the dead. There are several studies of the cemetery in progress, ranging from the classical period to the nineteenth century (see, for example, M. Bée, 'The cemeteries of Calvados in 1801' in the special number of *Annales de Normandie* on religious life in the nineteenth century). One would like to see a systematic study of the forms of the secularized cult of the dead, centred on the cemetery, in the nineteenth century.

A study by J.-O. Majastre offers an example of such an approach, starting as a sociological study of a region (Isère) which combines a catalogue of archaeological remains of the nineteenth- and twentieth-century cult of the dead with an oral study of the collective attitudes which conditioned these visible expressions. This also entails a clarification of the contemporary discordance between the triumph of the cemetery, nowadays raked, swept and kept clean, and the slackening of familial and collective rituals surrounding death. Does the cemetery of today reflect the troubled conscience of a society which has lost its sense of being at ease with the dead?

This theme conveniently leads us into another aspect of current iconographical research which is increasingly taking account of the entire sacred space in the countryside. With the work of A. Dupront's pupils M.-H. Froeschlé-Chopard and L. Chatellier, taking up some earlier suggestions made by M. Agulhon in *Penitents and Freemasons*, the importance of networks of small country chapels, oratories and crosses has been realized, and not just in Provence, but also in Alsace and the Alps. These were places of stability and refuge for older popular devotions to the Virgin and to local intercessors during the rigour of the post-Tridentine period. The reordering which took place in the parish church in this period banished the 'saints of the church door' to the bottom of the church and affected the whole of the surrounding countryside, marginalizing the old popular religion which, in retreat, forged stronger links with the natural sites which had been places of worship since the era of paganism – forests, caves and springs. At Notre-Dame des Oeufs in the Alpine heights of Provence, the site of an ancient acropolis, a dried-up spring and a natural rock grotto occupy the same sacred site. The people of the mountains of Savoy, from Brison and Mont-Saxonnex, who have already been discussed, are outdoor people who practise their religion in the open air in a world populated with maleficent and benign presences. Iconography has brought us a long way from our starting point, to the archaeology of sacred places and, further still, where the sources are scanty, to a historical geography of beliefs which, as Philippe Joutard has reminded us, anchor themselves in a natural habitat and become rooted in a given landscape. In leaving oral evidence and the product of oral research until last in our list of sources we do not mean to set at a distance the researches of the ethnologist or the folklorist, but merely to see this kind of privileged source as part of a system of complementary approaches. Perhaps we also betray the historian's embarrassment when faced with sources which seemed particularly recalcitrant before Joutard used them. The very personal study which Arsène Bourgeaux, who works in this field, presented ('Religious interference in popular mentalities at Brison and Mont-Saxonnex in Faucigny') is so rich and abundant that it can be read on several levels. Arsène Bourgeaux is a storyteller as well as an expert and a scholar. The approach he adopts reflects the discourse which it contains, painstakingly gathered and richly digressive, picking up themes by association. From such research one can appreciate the potential of oral tradition as a source, with its stock of proverbs, stories, songs and rambling memories. Yet the author also has the wisdom not to exclude written evidence, the small change of stories in local newspapers and other documents which have preserved the oral source and on the basis of which oral tradition has enriched itself and developed. What is embryonic in the work of A. Bourgeaux is systematically handled in the studies of R.-C. Schüle, P. Joutard and C. Joisten, who all illustrate the techniques of current research in their different ways. Both R.-C. Schüle and P. Joutard presented thematic studies dealing respectively with stories about birth in an Alpine environment and 'superstition' in the Cévennes. In the first of these, two studies spaced over recent decades were able to grasp changes which took place in the very recent past, involving the destruction of a pluri-secular heritage. In this way, oral research allows history to be written within the short time scale of the recent past. Such an approach is not so easily applicable in Joutard's work on the wider time scale of the *longue durée*, investigating a process of persecution sustained over a period of four centuries, yet the combination of written historical evidence and oral testimony which he uses is a particularly fertile one. We can usefully conclude this review of current methods with Charles Joisten's work, demonstrating the complementary approach which is necessary in the use of oral evidence from collections of ethno-texts – indispensable elements in any future research. One ought to say that he was well served by his informant, Marie Vasserot of the village of Reotier in the upper Alps, who articulated a view of death which is very personal, at one level, but which also reflects the impact of tradition and of acquired views to such a degree that the inspired fantasies of the Embrunais region are embedded in an almost normal system of exchanges between the living and the dead, reflecting a long historical tradition.

For all its ambiguity, which is the price of its richness, the ethno-text emerges clearly as a basic element of all future research on oral evidence. It is one of the sources to which history must become accustomed.

It follows from this – and here the historian recovers all his critical acuity – that the use of oral evidence, more than any other kind of source material, demands an awareness of specific difficulties in the use of sources relating to popular religion which must be faced before its history can be written.

Cheating silence

In discussing the many aspects of the collection of sources we run the risk of forgetting the difficulties of interpetation. There is no easy way of reconstructing popular religion, and all interpretations must face the general and specific difficulties involved in the nature of the source material.

The most general problem, absent only in oral research, is the need to adopt an indirect approach to the characteristics of collective behaviour. This history is a history of silence, both the silence of those involved and the silence imposed by society. There is no shortage of examples to illustrate this theme. In the history of the festival, where religious elements are essential, one finds that surviving systems of ancient belief are kept at a distance or passed over in silence.

Similarly, unless one is exceptionally fortunate, it is practically impossible to write the history of the carnival from the records of its suppression. The anti-authoritarian Saturnalia of carnival are not unique in this respect. Secret pilgrimages and unorthodox games are rarely held up for public display. The Grassois, to take a rather lurid example, do not dwell on the details of the custom of the *jouvines* – a descendant of the ancient *juvenalia* – which was a curious rite of passage in which boys and girls competed to see who could produce the most impressive stream of urine.

It is not necessary to look for examples as lewd or incongruous as this one. On a more austere plane, it is by investigating a statement made by the Jansenist bishop of Senez, Mgr Soanen ('all evil takes place in the cemetery') that one discovers how the mountain folk of upper Provence were still, even in the last years of the seventeenth century, following the custom of repeatedly placing bread and wine on the tombs of those who had died that year. Likewise, but in this case in terms of attitudes to life, the custom of prenuptial liberties formed part of the category of 'dark secrets' which confessors denounced all the time, without ever revealing details.

The papers collected in this volume illustrate very clearly the difficulties involved in trying to penetrate silence, particularly in the case of the Cévennes. When Philippe Joutard began his work he came up against the standard interpretation which held that superstition no longer existed where the Reformation had driven out magic. Like Danilo Dolci working on the Mezzogiorno, who found zones of silence so disinherited that the people did not even sing, it seemed that there was nothing to be known from the silence of the Cévennes. Such standard interpretations contain an element of truth. We learn from Charles Joisten that there are regions with and without storytellers, but we also learn from him that even areas as silent as the upper Alps can be made to speak. Persistence can pay, however, as was shown by Joutard and Pelen who, having overcome the initial silence, demonstrated the existence of another system perpetuating magical thought in the casting and lifting of enchantments and through beliefs relating to death.

Whether one uses oral or written sources, the art of cheating silence necessitates a kind of reconstruction which is negative, or only visible in dim outlines, and is not without its dangers, given that the clues are often tenuous. The use of sources of repression makes us dependent on the perspectives, and often on the fantasies, of the inquisitor. Dare we admit that we are often more impressed than convinced by the ingenuity of scholarly explanations of the total system of the 'old religion' of the cult of the Moon and pagan deities as in Gaignebet's *Carnival*? If we do not wish to risk being carried away by such temptations, then we have to accommodate ourselves to the real weaknesses of the sources.

These sources are poor. When R. Chanaud presents the rather impressionistic corpus of Mgr Le Camus's pastoral visitations, he rightly insists that we should not expect too much from them. Having been carried out according to a precise understanding of the pastoral mission, these investigations were not conducted on our behalf and it is only on the margins of the parishes under scrutiny that one can even divine or catch a glimpse of the other world. This is a negative vision, or a vision of absences, to recall Dominique Julia's work. Yet Julia shows us how the traces of the other religion can be divined even within the sphere of official religion, both in the hit parade of the saints and in the persistence, alongside the new confraternities regulated from above such as the Rosary and the Blessed Sacrament, of the older confraternities such as that of the Holy Ghost which maintained the traditional sociability of the communal banquet.

If we pass from written documents to iconography, ex votos present a limited number of scenarios within a rigid framework and in an often stereotyped way: the image of the supplicant 'prostrate on the bed of sickness' or, externally, images like the overturned chariot, the drowned man, the fall or the millwheel. These documents present us with the task of deciphering fragile clues which show the links between the human world and the spiritual: prayer, adoration, a look or a ray of light, or simply the nature of the scene represented; we see the mother at the cradle and wonder whether the image represents a sick child, a successful confinement or a child conceived. Similarly, in an entirely different domain, demographic tests are often difficult to use and provide equivocal evidence of popular discipline or popular restraint in areas such as sexual abstinence, illegitimacy and obligatory early baptism. The elementary character of the message would be pointless were it not so masked and hard to perceive. I felt this about the subject of attitudes to death. One might say that the whole system of taboos and magic which surround the event contribute to its secrecy. In fact, I could only discern the profound changes in attitudes registered in wills and in the apparently fixed images of Purgatory in the time-frame of the *longue durée*.

One might think that oral research, which alone achieves the kind of direct contact vainly sought by the student of popular culture, would be free of these obstacles. Yet it is not, and in fact it seems to throw up new difficulties, the gravest of which is its tendency to accentuate to extremes the apparent immobility of popular religion. In the eyes of A. Bourgeaux's informants, as in other studies, we see a static world of great constants (Sunday, the curé, death) and seeming eternity. It is true that the scholar introduces history into this static discourse by focusing on the great crises of the French Revolution and the separation of Church and State. But this aspect of the study itself shows how collective memory acts as a reductive and simplifying function, sailing effortlessly from the earlier episode to the more recent. The memory of Labitte's mission of 1794 and that of the inventories of 1905 tend to blend into a single story. Given this, one can understand both the historian's annoyance and the injustice of his position from the point of view of the folklorist or ethnologist constructing a static or semi-static system. Yet one can also see the interest with which historians look at oral evidence in their search for change, either in the *longue durée*, as in Joutard's case, or in the short term, in that of R.-C. Schüle. Charles Joisten's informant still needs God (and how!), and she also needs the 'poor souls' of her departed family. But she has hardly any need for the devil and very little for the saints and one can see a whole process of change reflected in such absences.

Thus scholars seem to find themselves caught between two systems of inquiry as well as two systems of sources. One is based on oral research which gives direct contact with popular religion, but is deprived of a historical texture; the other commands a range of sophisticated procedures which place the facts in the context of the *longue durée*, but often impoverished and reduced to the state of bare indices.

A whole range of procedures is necessary, therefore, aspects of which have already emerged clearly. In the first place, we need an interdisciplinary approach. Régis Bertrand adopts one naturally in his specialized work on the pilgrimage of Gréoux, and Christian Loubet, working on an area with many similarities, and some differences, mobilizes a whole battery of convergent approaches around the sanctuary of Oropa. The same can be said about the majority of the authors here. Philippe Joutard combines historical documentation and ethnographic research for the Cévennes. Robert Chanaud, in studying Mgr Le Camus's pastoral visitations, has a kind of dialogue with Van Gennep and introduces a historical dimension to the so-called 'folkloric regions' of the twentieth century. Such an approach proves necessary in many cases. In order to analyse collective attitudes to death I have used iconography (see *The Image of Death and Salvation in Provence*), serial social history (in *Baroque*

Piety and Dechristianization) and every kind of source from demographic history to literature and painting in *Death in History*. Only a multi-faceted approach will answer the many questions raised by this kind of research.

The regressive method, which is also a comparative method, is demanded by the nature of a phenomenon, many of whose aspects we can still see around us; some in living form, others in a more residual way. When applied to pilgrimages, this method is one of the most fertile ways of overcoming the opposition between contemporary and historical sources which we have discussed above. In addition to this, the use of a quantitive, serial approach is as important in the task of reconstituting forgotten beliefs and practices as in any other field. This is the method used by Loubet and, even more systematically, by Cousin in his work on ex votos. Those who have worked on reredoses and popular art are in the same position as those who have worked on wills and parish registers. Such an approach certainly surpasses the inventory technique which has long dominated iconography, but it also goes much further in its objectives. It sets out to organize such involuntary sources, which contain many of the secrets of popular attitudes, into a statistical truth in the *longue durée*. The slow evolution of collective representations is registered in such series. The technique is easily combined with quantitive history, as long series of documents can be organized in time and also in space by the use of maps. This is not wholly new, given the existence of folklore atlases, but one can see its value in R.-C. Schüle's paper, where the shifting boundary between cabbages and storks in childbirth stories is shown to be far more complex than mere confessional or linguistic barriers. R. Chanaud in emphasizing the convergence of folklore characteristics within individual micro-regions also shows the value of the method and the way in which it elucidates the problems of cultural environments, which had hitherto been visualized in a much cruder way.

Is there any need to say that the triumph of quantitive method is in no sense totalitarian? A number of papers show that studies of individual cases are still indispensable. The old woman of the Embrunais who confided in Charles Joisten did not only speak for herself. Similarly Devos's precise monograph on Combloux, based on rich sources, and Chanaud's vast survey of the diocese of Grenoble, based on scanty archives, are complementary rather than contradictory. Philippe Joutard formulates some of the problems raised by this theme on the basis of his work on the Cévennes. He sees a quantitive approach as becoming increasingly essential if we are to go beyond easy generalizations; if we are to understand the quality of the silence and the value of the evidence which penetrates it.

Is it possible to arrive at some provisional assessment on the basis of these different approaches and even derive from them a system of popular religion?

A provisional assessment

In such an open field of research, one can posit several levels or several systems of 'popular religion'.

The first category is that of official or imposed religion, an external category of course, but by no means negligible. The presence of two religions – official religion and the religion of the community – emerges from the important Savoyard text used by R. Devos. The distance between the two is enhanced by circumstances since the curé comes from outside as the emissary of another hierarchy and another culture. Yet A. Bourgeaux describes the more ambiguous characteristics of the curé of 1900 (the type still remembered by old people in recent decades) who was both terrorist and complicitous. He was terrorist, because he was the man of the catechism and of Sunday observance, the opponent of dancing – as in the time of Paul-Louis Courrier. Perhaps he was also terrifying due to a magical fear, not born wholly of respect, which he evoked because of what he represented. He was complicitous, because the man of God was nevertheless countrified and integrated into the community of parishioners, some of whose less orthodox ideas he shared. Such a combination was also possible because the curé was not simply the agent of the repressive apparatus of authority, but was identified with the community in their common reaction against the separation of Church and State. Four basic elements emerge from the work of Devos and Bourgeaux as a kind of parallelogram of forces: authority, the curé, the community and the bell. The eighteenth-century curé is an agent of authority, vying with his parishioners for control of the bell and aware of its mysterious powers. In 1794 the community defends the bell against the state in the absence of the curé. In 1904 the community and the curé are allied in defence of their common interests against the tax collector and the police.

The model suggested by these two moments in the history of Savoy conceals a host of nuances. Mgr Le Camus's visitations from the late seventeenth century remind us of the existence of a great many priests who were only too well integrated into the local rural community, sharing its vices and superstitions before the advent of the generation of 'good priests' in the eighteenth century. Similarly, in the Protestant world, Joutard shows us a much more flexible kind of pastor than we might have expected. The pastor might warn against or refuse to participate in the rural compromise between religion and magical beliefs, but he could also close his eyes to, or even rationalize, the survival of elements of the old faith.

These factors tend to qualify the interpretation of official religion as something superficial imposed from outside. It certainly shows the importance of indiscipline and deviation operating almost as part of the system well into the eighteenth and early nineteenth century. The curé of Combloux knew his opponents, ranging from the confraternity of the Holy Name of Jesus to those who invaded the cemetery and occupied the belfry and young people visiting each other at night, just as the priests of Brison and Mont-Saxonnex knew theirs – unrepentant poachers, atheists and freemasons.

Given changes over time, the importance of indiscipline and violations of the code is easily seen. Far from showing the superficial or skin-deep character of official religion, it throws into relief its massive and insistent presence. Nor can one always sustain a Don Camillo image of the relationship between the priest and the local community. The kind of popular religion encountered by these scholars is a modified Catholicism, of course, but it is also one which is generally accepted. Its list of achievements is to be found in the number of its chapels, altars, images and holy places; its central place in people's attitudes is seen in the clauses of their wills at the moment of death. Even the confraternities, despite their ambiguities, ensured its place in village society. In the Protestant world of the Cévennes the profound success of the process of Christianization remains impressive, even given an awareness of the suspicious nature of its silence surrounding superstition. Even the universe of magical beliefs was reshaped and replaced in the popular consciousness in a way more in keeping with official religion. Thus, one is dealing with something far more than the concept of superficial disguise would suggest.

Of course, even at the heart of the official process of Christianization traces of the 'other religion' can still be found.

The 'other religion', which is truly popular, expresses itself firstly as a very direct and stratified relation to God. It is direct in that the parishioners, who are undisciplined as far as official practice is concerned, are looking to an immediate divine presence in their personal lives. The psychology of miracles as expressed in ex votos since the early-modern period shows considerable change. Cousin and Loubet have traced its evolution through the structure and composition of the ex votos and through the actions of the donors. At Oropa one is struck by the contrast between the older style of miracle, which was sought from a divinity or intercessor present on the site, and the automotive miracles of recent decades, enacted in a scene where the deity has departed and where the old-style panic sensibility is present in the spontaneity of the moment. Who is this deity? The persistence or re-emergence of older systems and traditions should not surprise us. At Gréoux-les-Bains, the site of an ancient pagan cult to a goddess of fertility, Notre-Dame des *Oeufs* is still venerated to this day and this is just one possible example.

The immediacy of divine intervention can be seen in the very direct evidence given to Charles Joisten by his informant Marie Vasserot. Although this is an extreme case by today's standards, it is probably normal in terms of traditional mentality. Like Pope Gregory, Marie Vasserot saw Christ at Mass at the elevation. Not the crucified Christ in agony, but a person, rather like a priest. Yet although the Virgin, and sometimes the saints, work for her, the pantheon of intercessors has become much smaller, almost residual.

God or the saints? We should not be surprised at the almost total absence of the crucifix in the village culture described by A. Bourgeaux. The attempts of the post-Tridentine Church to inculcate a religion based on the essential mysteries of the faith ran up against similar inertias. The Blessed Sacrament was accepted but the confraternity of the Holy Name of Jesus, with its annual *agape* feast remained influential among fathers of families. One can also ask whether the glorification of the Blessed Sacrament shown in the diocese of Vence by Froeschlé-Chopard was not assimilated in the popular mind to the traditional cults of relics and protective talismans. Statistics from the diocese of Grenoble for the late seventeenth century show the persistence of direct competition between the confraternities of the Holy Ghost and the Blessed Sacrament.

Wills and other sources show that there was recognition of the merits of the death and passion of Our Lord Jesus Christ, but also that it took second place to more immediate presences. It is not contradictory to state that a direct link with the deity was established by the existence of a whole pantheon of intercessors with the Virgin in first place. The Mariolatry which we saw established in the long series of representations of the souls in Purgatory and which triumphed in the classic age with the appearance of the Italianate image of the Madonna persisted into the nineteenth century. A protectrix in the hour of danger and of death, the Virgin was seen in two guises in post-Counter-Reformation period. Firstly she was the Virgin of the rosary, of the parish church and of sanctioned confraternities and processions. On the other hand she was also the traditional Virgin found in country chapels and ancient places of devotion: Our Lady of Pity, of Light, of Consolation, of Mercy, of the Angels, of Eggs. There is, of course, no absolute distinction between the two, but still we see the curé of Combloux trying, without much hope of success, to make his parishioners understand the mysteries of the rosary.

There were many other intercessors to pray to apart from the Virgin. Grenoble in the late seventeenth century had a whole constellation of mediators among whom the thaumaturgic saints (Anthony, Roch, Sebastian) were the most common. There was also a host of agrarian saints whose worship was often specific to localities, as well as protectors of fertility. Where the survey of a whole diocese reveals an enormous number of such saints, the study of a parish, like Combloux in the eighteenth century, shows about a dozen patrons and protectors on the altars of the churches and the countryside, among them apostles (Peter and Paul), traditional protectors (Felix, Maurice and Nicholas) or thaumaturgic figures, both for people and for animals. Innovation is also represented by the figure of St Francis de Sales who was prayed to in times of epidemics, yet always in association with St Roch. Thus we see a pantheon still populated by figures to be invoked in time of need. Changes in practice have to be seen in terms of the evolution of the use of space in the parish. The noble altars of the parish church were reserved for the new devotions like the rosary and the Blessed Sacrament while the traditional saints were gradually moved to the door of the church or even to country chapels. The redistribution of space shows the conflict that was taking place in the eighteenth century as do invocations in wills or the gradual decline of paintings of the souls in Purgatory.

Popular religion combined this kind of sacred mediation with a system of human solidarity based on the confraternities. The characteristic was not solely limited to the sphere of popular religion in the early-modern era but one can see how these forms of association lent themselves to the advent of new languages of devotion, like the Blessed Sacrament and the rosary, examples of which we saw in Grenoble and Combloux. They also remained centres of an essentially masculine form of sociability in confraternities such as the Name of Jesus in Combloux and the Holy Ghost in Dauphiné. Yet one can also trace the decline and disappearance of many traditional confraternities – St Sebastian, St Roche, St Joseph and even Our Lady of Carmel, supplanted, one suspects, by the rosary.

All of these things illuminate the process of Christianization in the countryside, but they do so more in terms of dialectic or conflict than in terms of a linear enterprise. One can appreciate in this way the artificiality of strictly juxtaposing, point by point, 'two religions' which were so intimately mixed together.

The other religion, however inseparably mixed, still has a palpable underground existence. Firstly, it can be characterized by magical actions. These are gestures which pay homage to an ancient code even though its original purpose may be forgotten. An example is the ritual of the sterile woman bringing two eggs with her on the pilgrimage to Our Lady of Gréoux; one of them she eats and the other is buried for a year in the sacred ground of the place. Nowadays we are left with the crumbs from the picnic, the last vestiges of an obscure ritual. A whole system of taboos existed concerning certain places, days, men and animals. Christian observance of Sunday was enforced in the nineteenth century by a series of immediate and deferred punishments, as of the sabbath-breaking hunter whose feet may bring him to places where he should not venture. Holy places or cursed places? Perhaps both at once, since these are the places where the forces of nature and the supernatural are at work. People are also affected in this way as enchanters and enchanted: the footsteps of the sacrilegious hunter are enough to dry up goats' milk, a bewitched calf can bring evil into the byre, and the priest himself can be a figure of fear. In the Cevennes, where the Protestant offensive went furthest in dismantling the existing system, the figure of the *enmaskaire* or enchanter is still one of the most irreducible manifestations of the magical universe, and he also has his benign counterpart in the figure of the healer.

A large number of exorcisms and spells were used to counteract such menacing forces. There was a code of behaviour determining what to do and what to avoid, presages which foretold evil and appropriate conduct and devices by which it could be avoided. The curé of Combloux, a contemporary of the learned Thiers, the curé of Vibray who had written on superstition thirty years before, doubted the legitimacy of ringing the bell against lightning and exorcising natural disasters, yet saw nothing in the manuals of the Church to stop him from following traditional practices, even when he suspected that they smacked of magic.

Can one see any systematic elements in these pre-rational practices which might reveal a conception of the world? A certain number of themes are worth considering, among them death, life, the relationship to the land, to space and to work.

In the first instance, life is reproduction, involving fertility rites and coupling, with clear indications, at Combloux, of a system of prenuptial liberties which tolerated frequent visits by the young men to the homes of young women at night without going as far as cohabitation before marriage. One can detect something similar in the Dauphiné through Mgr Le Camus's worries about anything which smacked of the mixing of the sexes including 'mixed' pilgrimages, wakes and winter games, things which seem innocent to us but were occasions of disorder for the stern bishop. And yet the carnal world of the prenuptial liberties is also the innocent paradise of childish secrets where another magical system operates for the use of children, where babies are brought by hermits or are found under heads of cabbage.

The isolated snapshots provided by the collection from which we are drawing this commentary show the ways in which we can attempt to reconstruct systems which have been the object of official scrutiny and are nevertheless very badly known. These range from the worried denunciations of surviving practices by the priests to the indirect evidence of the ex votos. The structures and concepts of the family emerge dimly from the stylized scenes of the ex votos. The great majority of the ex voto prayers were (and still are in the Piedmontese world of Oropa) made to obtain benefit for men. Children – the discovery of the eighteenth century – occupied an important, if strictly limited place in these prayers, as in prayers for a sick child or for a conception. Women, on the other hand, are here confined to the restricted role allotted to them within the family, even though they are the ones who are predominantly active in soliciting divine intervention through prayer, a role in which men play an increasingly insignificant role, a mark of their increasing indifference. In the wars of the twentieth century, as in its automated shrines, the male in Piedmont, and no doubt everywhere else, is the one for whom prayers are offered rather than the one who prays.

The theme of the family leads directly to that of death, which plays an important part in the surviving evidence. It has been said that death was domesticated in traditional societies, but it must be stressed that it was also feared, a fact which is attested in plain language by Marie Vasserot. The two aspects of death can coexist without contradiction. Domesticated death comes through in the words of the old people of Brison in Savoy: 'j'viendrais t'cri' or 't'vindrez m'cri' ('I will come and look for you' or 'you will come for me'). We also find it in the traditional cemetery which as a place of passage and pasture and as a meeting place symbolizes the coexistence of the living and the dead. The traditional cemetery was ill tended and not very well respected; it was the site of a number of different activities. As such, it was denounced by bishops and priests and is recalled by the sociologist J.-O. Majastre for whom, as we have seen, it gained very little for being better policed.

Yet the ex votos tell us of the fear of death, especially violent death, far from home, when one cannot put one's house in order. Against it was offered the prayer of the *Libera: De morte repentina libera nos domine*. From it spring the crosses planted on the mountain at Brison to exorcise the site of fatal accidents and murders. Its counterpart is the image of a placid death in wills, the figure 'prostrate on the bed of illness' in the ex voto, the model of which was the painting of the dying Joseph on the altar of the Good Death in parish churches. The placid model was not universally accepted. The coexistence of the living and the dead was not always peaceful. Following Pierre Chaunu's vast perspective which saw two major systems of the hereafter in the Indo-European tradition, one based on belief in a dual world of spirits who must be appeased and the other based on belief in the resurrection, it would seem that Savoy in 1900 as described by Bourgeaux was gripped by the fear of the dual world where wandering spirits, confused with the forces of nature, returned to seek the aid of the living – the disquieting presence of those who had not paid their debts and could only be freed with the help of the living. Not all such wandering spirits were tragic. In their most familiar form, as Marie Vasserot's memoirs depict them, the spirits of people we have known retain all their faults and idiosyncracies, their little mannerisms and fears. Some who were not good while they were alive have not improved, and yet they are still willing to lend a hand to help with the animals or the work of the fields. Such solidarity may also be a reflection of the new dialectic governing relations between the living and the dead which triumphed at the end of the nineteenth century in the doctrine of the souls in Purgatory, traces of which we have hitherto found in episodes from the childhood of St Teresa of Lisieux. The invisible family of the souls of the poor as it existed at the end of the nineteenth century shows the extraordinary impact of the process by which post-Tridentine Catholicism succeeded in Christianizing the spirit world by developing the doctrine of the souls in Purgatory. The possibility of reprieve, thanks to Masses, offerings and works, materialized the solidarity of the living and the dead and gave people the opportunity of banishing and at the same time freeing the restless souls of the dead. One can understand the minutiae of the system of annual Masses *de mortuis* on which the curé of Combloux spent much of his year and the inordinate importance of a ritual which, although it may have annoyed the curé, was one of the essential services which his parishioners expected of him.

Life, the family and death thus emerge as the major themes of popular religion. Ethnological studies show that the relationship with nature, space and work are equally important, if more diffuse. The space of the village is of primary importance, with its segregation of inhabited and uninhabited spaces, cultivated ground and wasteland around which is constructed a whole chronology of days and seasons and a geography of the sacred. The homogeneity of the spaces within which these forces work is established by their frontiers, although we should bear in mind the case of Combloux, which shared its confraternity with another village – something which shocked the curé. The contrast between town and country, which has always been important, hardened in Brison and Mont-Saxonnex during the French Revolution and later during the separation of Church and State. In La-Roche-sur-Foron, the terrorism of the Capuchins against popular religion gradually gave way to complicity, but lower down the mountains there was no possible compromise with the new urban world.

We also have to investigate the place of animals, of husbandry and of hunting which figure prominently in Bourgeaux's paper and the stories about them which form a kind of liturgy in competition with that of the village Mass. At the very least they flesh out the very strong links binding men, animals and objects. To conclude this section we can pose again the central question as to whether we are dealing with 'another religion' or with the *disjecta membra* of a once coherent system which has now deteriorated into a collection of disconnected memories. The several studies reviewed here do not pretend to give a panoramic view of such an elusive phenomenon. It could also be objected that the parts of the Alpine region studied here show a system in a far more advanced state of disintegration than other peripheral 'conserving' areas. One can point to the information presented about Mediterranean islands and peninsulas in the conference on Images of Death in the Mediterranean held at Bonifacio in the spring of 1976.

We have made clear our reluctance to accept elaborate theories like that of Gaignebet in his work on carnival, despite its many attractions. Can such a self-contained and elaborate system of popular religion ready for decipherment by the sociologist ever be found intact? Would it not be better to try to understand change in terms of a history that is somewhat less static?

Stasis or movement?

At this point we cannot evade the question posed at the beginning of
this review as to whether we are dealing with a stable religion or one
which is constantly changing, and if changing, whether it follows a
given rhythm of change.

The most striking thing in these papers is the evidence of the
persistence of some aspects of tradition. This is noticeable in the
system of attitudes to death in Brison up until fairly recently. One also
notes the extraordinary stability of formal structures and gestures in
the pilgrimage of Notre-Dame des Oeufs, even if the gestures
themselves are no longer understood. This still leaves us with
questions about the modalities of transmission.

One can of course ask whether the nature of oral evidence, by its
very intemporality, does not accentuate this impression of stasis, and
one can see how the transmission of memory contributes to the
abolition of the historical dimension.

Nevertheless the majority of these studies point more to change
than to stasis. The fact is particularly noticeable in Combloux in 1733
and in the pastoral visitations in the Dauphiné at the end of the
seventeenth century, all the more so because the very nature of the
documents as pictures drawn at a given date would seem to favour
immobility. The situation of conflict into which we are plunged by the
curé's account from Combloux shows us all the stratifications of
systems that are dead, dying and transplanted. Of the latter, we see
how some were accepted and others rejected in the course of a
determined offensive mounted to transform collective attitudes.

Serial studies, like those applied to Provençal and Piedmontese ex
votos, and elsewhere to wills, confirm the impression of movement.
They show changes in collective attitudes as a long process of
evolution in the *longue durée*. One can, of course, equally well ask in
reverse whether such serial studies of social practices do not tend to
accentuate change and ignore the submerged part of the iceberg – the
popular religion which is registered neither in texts nor in images.

Yet I am not preaching a bourgeois compromise, I hope, by coming
down on the side of plasticity in popular religion. In the early-modern
period we can see the imposition of a new compromise following the
destruction of an older equilibrium, one where old and new themes
coincide, but which can still only be viewed as a new incarnation in an
old adventure. The nineteenth century, which we can see through the
memories of old people, saw another phase in which the authoritarian

Christianization of the early-modern period was assimilated, digested and made part of folklore, a process marked by the transformation of the character of the curé who, despite certain residual terrorist aspects, was integrated into the life of the community. Meanwhile, the entire corpus of references to the other religion lives on in a crumbling state, while still continuing to impregnate certain attitudes. The stock which is currently being inventoried is residual and for the most part misunderstood. This does not mean that its history is finally over, as R.-C. Schüle shows in his study of systems which were still alive and well only twenty years ago, like the folklore of storks and hermits bringing newborn babies. Pregnancy care will probably still preserve the image of the stork even after the death of the old people who advise us to telephone for the hermit. One history ends and another begins, and J.-O. Majastre evokes this process in describing the present metamorphosis of the cemetery, which has been taken out of the hands of families and local communities and become the business of professionals.

We thus have an evolutionary process in which the dialectical relationship with the institutional Church partly conditions attitudes, but where other changes in the *longue durée*, especially in attitudes to life, also play an essential part, among them the changes in communities, in attitudes to marriage and to life and death. Such basic changes cannot fail to be reflected, both in the residual legacy of ancient beliefs as well as in the complex reality of Christianized popular religion since the early modern period.

Such processes are best observed in the *longue durée*. Yet shorter perspectives which emphasize events also play an important part in such a history. If the very functioning of collective memory has a tendency to blur the contours of change and even in certain circumstances, like the Revolution and the separation of Church and State, to annihilate them, it can also retain a certain vitality, as in Joutard's study of the Camisards. Then again, it also acts retroactively, as we can see in terms of the history of the festival, whose forms we studied in Provence from 1750 to 1820. The trauma of the Revolution, which was vividly felt in Provence and which lived on, in a sense, in the revolutionary festivals, was a major turning point in the history of the festival, if only by the irrevocable destruction of the traditional festive system. The restoration of old forms was only partly accepted.

This example also draws our attention to the ephemeral, 'emergency' creations of popular religion, examples of which can also be found in the French Revolution. Instantaneous creativity of this kind re-employed the language and forms of the old-style festival which was then proscribed and in retreat. Thus we find masquerades, iconoclastic processions and elements of carnival and charivari. But these phenomena are not so much the resurgence of an underground river as evidence of an unexpected plasticity in popular religion which has so often been imagined as something static.

The introduction of a diachronic dimension into the study of popular religion is more than just annexationism by a historian of mentalities. It provides a perspective which seems to attract a large consensus of opinion in interdisciplinary studies where a number of different approaches to the subject are combined.

It goes without saying that other methods are also necessary. One would like to see a more searching geography of the forms of popular religion, which has already been referred to in my discussion of the rituals of death in the Mediterranean region. Following from this, one would like to see a similar approach to the great problem of urban popular religion, not much dealt with historically, as well as to the town–country relationship, where the religious cleavage is one of the most expressive symptoms. All of this leads to a reformulation of the sociology of popular religion in more precise terms, a sociology which must go beyond the simplistic dichotomy of people and elite in order to penetrate the realities of social groupings; something which would also permit a more supple definition of the idea of 'popular' religion.

Clearly, popular religion is one of the most stimulating areas of interdisciplinary research at present, allowing the introduction of new sources and new perspectives, whether in the realm of iconography or of the oral tradition. It is already providing us with new views of a phenomenon which we thought we knew of old.

Notes

'La religion populaire, problèmes et méthodes', *Le Monde Alpin et Rhoda-nien*, vols I–IV (1977).

1 See Carlo Russo, *Società, chiesa e vita religiosa nell' 'Ancien Régime'* (*Society, Church and Religious life in the Ancien Régime*).
2 In *Literature and National Life*.

6

Cultural Intermediaries

This conference was organized in order to reopen the academic debate on popular and elite culture. The number and wealth of the contributions sent in response to the centre's invitation showed how well the idea was received and there were many contributions which questioned the status of the two cultures and which led to an investigation of the ambiguous concept of 'acculturation'.

The conference on cultural intermediaries met at Aix-en-Provence in June 1980 and was the third organized by the centre, following those on Oral Tradition and Collective Memory in 1975 and Iconography and the History of Mentalities in 1978.

Introduction

In adapting for publication the general introduction which I made to the conference, I do not wish it to act as a substitute for the participants' papers, especially not for the summary reports made at the end of each session. Presented now with the choice of anticipating or ignoring what was said I have chosen to confine this paper to its original purpose as an introduction in the strict sense of presenting the problem as it might appear to the members of the conference, given the fifty papers which were submitted to them for discussion.

These figures tell something about the character of the conference and of its success. The conference was meant to be open, bringing together a number of diverse approaches to the theme. Proposing a big theme like this one and waiting for the response is not without its dangers. There is a risk of disparateness, of scattering cohesion to the four winds. However, if one remains conscious of the central theme the open approach has its good points, not least of which is the appearance of the unexpected among the many contributions.

Because of the nature of the Centre méridional and of current trends in the history of mentalities, we expected a majority of modernists and certainly of historians. We were somewhat apprehensive of getting a collection of descriptive typologies, given the implicit focus on the standard intermediaries of traditional society: the parish priest, the doctor, the notary and the schoolmaster. Not that we wished to exclude them; they came and we were glad of them. But to confine ourselves within such limits would not, I fear, have been very productive.

The response to our request for contributions brought many more positive surprises than disappointments and led us into unexpected areas. The disappointments – or rather the silences – were themselves instructive. It was possibly a pure coincidence, although I doubt it, that the participants, the majority of whom were teachers, while dealing with doctors, priests and midwives, seemed to have had a sort of implicit taboo against writing about the figure of the schoolmaster. We also regretted that the sixteenth century and, a fortiori, the medieval period were not dealt with more fully, despite the special problems which they pose. This is a pioneering area with which those of our Italian, American and English colleagues who came, like Peter Burke and Carlo Ginzburg, seem to be more familiar nowadays than French historians.

Yet there were some notably pleasant surprises. Until recently, one would have said that contemporary historians were rather reluctant to embark on the study of mentalities and of cultural forms, with notable exceptions like Agulhon, despite the fact that early-modernists have long been working in this area. For this reason the high number of contributions on the nineteenth and twentieth centuries is particularly welcome and indicates that the questions posed were taken up and found to be useful. In addition, the expansion into contemporary history contributed greatly to avoiding the kind of static typology of traditional intermediaries which we wished to avoid and permitted a perspective in the *longue durée* from the sixteenth century to our own time.

Similarly, the generous participation of the non-historians – critics, art historians, sociologists and ethnologists, as well as professionals and present-day 'intermediaries' – was particularly illuminating and gratifying. An instance of this was the additional focus provided by the participation of social workers, who are an example of contemporary intermediaries. Halfway between satisfaction and regret we can also point to the pleasure we derived from some useful comparative soundings taken from different cultures, including intermediaries in the Muslim world, and regret both that there were not many more such studies and that the Third World, which nowadays offers a fantastic opportunity for a comparative approach in time and space, was not better represented.

All in all, the sum of all these varied contributions was far more than an anarchic proliferation of different approaches, but rather illustrated a process of collective inquiry which is more than just a fashionable preoccupation. The problematic of our approach was widened from the very beginning and one can safely trace an articulate programme of research from the beginning of the session by following the mature directions and hypotheses of the different contributions.

A wider problematic

It is useful to describe, without straying into the realm of pure anecdote, the basis on which the research team at the Centre méridional d'histoire sociale came to research into the subject which was finally defined as 'cultural intermediaries'. One of the first approaches, for which I must acknowledge a personal responsibility, focused on the group which we classified as 'demiurges of the social world', a provisional label which I had used to describe the auto-didact self-made man Joseph Sec, whose career I wrote about in *The Irresistible Rise of Joseph Sec, Citizen of Aix*. Joseph Sec, the anonymous hero only rescued from oblivion by a curious Jacobin, masonic sepulchral monument erected to him in 1792, illustrates the socio-cultural position of the group of cultural 'half-castes' who no longer belonged to the popular world but who never really became part of the elite, forging their own world of representations and thus acceding to the status of 'inspirés', to use André Breton's now fashionable surrealist term.[1] In replacing the term 'naive' with that of 'inspiré' Breton both discarded the negative connotations of the former term and re-evaluated the dynamic which led these cultural mercenaries to seek a form of expression appropriate to their internal universe, be it painting, sculpture or composite works of which the *Palace* of Cheval, a postman, is probably the best-known example, although similar examples are not hard to find. Whether 'naive' or 'inspiré', 'demiurges of the social world' or 'cultural half-castes', they confront us with a multitude of possible labels for themselves, which is a reflection of the riches and complexity of the subject.[2] On inspection, these marginal figures, often rather odd and seemingly locked up in a secret personal adventure, can offer evidence about much larger social groups, since they stand in the no man's land between the culture of the elite and that of the popular classes.

In these circumstances, it is not surprising that we can follow a natural course from the marginality of the 'inspirés' to a more far-ranging study of the current dialectic of elite and popular culture.

This two-edged subject is currently being intensively researched in France, following the pioneering work of Mandrou and Bollème, nowadays being continued by Muchembled and others, including a large number of scholars of popular culture in other countries such as Natalie Zemon Davis, Peter Burke, Keith Thomas and Carlo Ginzburg. Meanwhile, approaches to elite culture have also matured and become established, following the pathfinding work edited by A. Dupront and F. Furet in *Livre et Societés* and Daniel Roche's masterpiece on provincial academies in the eighteenth century. Yet if each of these two approaches has much to offer by itself, I am not alone in wishing to escape from a rather summary dualism which can be limiting. A vacuum exists between the world of the illiterate and the semi-literate, nowadays investigated using ever more sophisticated techniques arising out of Maggiolo's literacy maps of the late nineteenth century, and the other world of 'elites', defined by their experience of secondary education, access to the humanist classics, academies and the theatre, and this vacuum needs to be filled.

It would be simplistic and facile to think that this vacuum reflects nothing at all. As examples of the area between the two worlds we can nominate artisans and village traders, as well as independent urban producers in workshops and specialist crafts, to mention but a few examples. Thanks to Albert Soboul's meticulous work we now know a great deal about the socio-cultural world of the Parisian sans-culottes, and we can ask how this group fits into our current problematic. Are we dealing with popular culture? Certainly not in the sense of a culture dominated by oral transmission and anchored in tradition. Are we then seeing an elite culture, transmitting the main ideas of bourgeois culture and the Enlightenment in ways which have yet to be analysed in detail? Such views are also limiting, reducing original and autonomous expressions to reflections of something else. We therefore need to leave the rather sterile symmetry of popular versus elite culture if we are to make progress.

Another naive response to the task would be to produce an

unsatisfactory bourgeois compromise whereby we leave the existing two levels and invent a third which would be occupied by the intermediaries, passing, if I can be forgiven the trivial metaphor, from a two-scoop icecream cone to a Neapolitan slice. With this fear in mind, I was aggressive, with the best intentions, in my response to some of the papers, including J. P. Poitou's 'A History in Layers' and J. Molino's 'How many Cultures?'. It is not anticipating the valuable discussion to say that the organizers of the conference were well aware of the danger of setting up factitious structures and were also wary of reifying cultural intermediaries by fixing them in a static position at the crossroads between two cultures.

This reflection leads on to a final point in the account of why we began our programme of investigation, namely the definition of the cultural intermediary. To provide an elaborate definition at the outset would limit the debate, and we will be careful not to do this. The question must be taken up at the end of the session, in the summary reports and discussions. What I can say to begin with is that it seems to me that the cultural intermediary has to be seen in dynamic terms, as the name suggests. Cultural intermediaries, in their various forms, are like traffic police, if I can be forgiven another dubious metaphor. Situated between the world of the powerful and the world of the powerless, the intermediary has an exceptional and privileged position, but it is also an ambiguous one, since we variously discover him as the guard dog of prevailing ideologies and the spokesman of revolutionary ideas. On another level, he can also passively reflect the various influences which combine in his identity, always ready, if circumstances permit, to become what Barthes called (in the spirit of Breton) a *logothete*, forging a language for himself which is the expression of a unique world.

Faced with the many options open to us, many of them apparently contradictory, we cannot judge prematurely or lock ourselves into an aprioristic definition. This is why I did not want to begin by embracing any of the models which are available and which must be discussed, as many contributors did. These range from the Gramscian 'organic intellectual' to which some papers referred and Lévi-Strauss's 'handyman' (*bricoleur*) mentioned by others.

The most legitimate and non-limiting way of proceeding, on the basis of the various papers given, seemed to be to identify the various groupings which emerged in the course of the debate and to suggest a nomenclature which would not be rigid, in that it places the different and contradictory faces of cultural intermediaries in a historical dimension.

A model and models: the many contradictory faces of the cultural intermediary

It is both useful and legitimate to begin with the old-style model of the cultural intermediary, as we see it in the early-modern era. Its most evident form is as an agent of downward vertical diffusion of a dominant knowledge and ideology, terms which mean the same thing for many.

Much time has been devoted to the function of the intermediary in the role of messenger, from the parish priest to the notary and agents of justice, omitting the schoolmaster, as we saw, and dealing also with the doctor and the midwife.

Such people are always present, constantly appearing in new guises, bearing new modes of instruction. Thus we can compare Pierre Larousse whose *Dictionary* was a massive force in the acculturation process of the nineteenth century with broadcasters in our own day, who derive their enormous influence from their medium.

Between intermediaries who function as pathways or transmitters of culture and knowledge and those who are popular spokesmen, there are a number of transitional types, beginning with those who are outside the law like quack doctors, who cheat the official channels of communication of elite knowledge and are content to mimic its external trappings. Yet because of this they maintain a more direct contact with the popular universe which provides them with a public.

Then, on a very different level, there are those groups of 'functional' intermediaries whose position places them somewhere between the two worlds of the masters and the governed. Domestic servants belong to this category, since their behaviour and even dress partake of both worlds. Marivaux's servants ape their masters and mimic the group on which they are dependent. Conversely, of course, it is via the servant, or the nurse, that the elite maintains contact with the small change of popular culture, even if it sometimes meant cheerfully slumming it in eighteenth-century France and Spain. Although unequal, such exchanges are nevertheless bilateral.

Let us look at the other side, at the Promethean group who act as the spokesmen for the other culture of the popular world. These types need not necessarily be revolutionaries. Many papers presented tranquil representatives of the 'other culture', a popular culture which had not yet been marginalized or driven underground and in which the intermediary officiates like a priest or notary. A typical case is the *armier* in Languedoc – the messenger of souls – present in the South of France in medieval and modern times and acting as an intermediary between the living and the dead. Rather than being simply tolerated, he is a constitutive and integral part of rural society.

There is a gradual process whereby the demiurge or shaman of the old magical world developed into a popular intermediary who was seen as subversive without necessarily being revolutionary. Such a figure is the innkeeper of eighteenth-century Savoy, who also turns up in Balzac, at the Sign of the Letter 'I'. He is certainly an agent of contact and of circulation, but he is rightly suspect in the eyes of the powers that be.

Via this figure, as well as others, there is a transition to the real popular spokesmen, involved in popular revolts, like the heroic figures of the Renaissance Papal States described by Carlo Ginzburg, or the French Revolutionary *Septembriseurs* of 1792, important from the point of view of gesture more than of discourse. We are led by this route to the militant workers, socialists and utopians of the twentieth century, described here in a few silhouettes and some significant case studies.

The intermediary can thus be the agent of diffusion of knowledge and power on the one hand, and a Promethean hero on the other. Things would be so much easier if they always appeared in such linear clarity. It is sufficient, nevertheless, to be at the crossroads of both worlds to be involved, willy-nilly, in both systems and also to reveal the functions that are thereby assumed. Babeuf, a feudal landlord who became the spokesman of the landless peasant, typifies the radical ambiguity of the cultural intermediary.

Forced to make his own way amidst the confluence of cultural influences of which he is the receptacle, this social type is often an autodidact, fashioning his culture in his own way, with greater or lesser degrees of success, by contrast with the priest and the doctor, who are the bearers of an already codified message. The results are also very different in different cases. By contrast with the revolutionary or the popular hero we can find, in practically the same group, the 'inspiré' who pursues his personal satisfaction within a world which he has built for himself. This is a non-functional intermediary in direct contrast to the personalities we described at the start.

There are in fact many transitions between the messianic zealot who dreams of changing the world by becoming the spokesman of the crowd and the quiet egocentric dreamer cooped up in his suburban dream-home. The examples which have been offered and those which spring to mind abound with conscious and unconscious mystifiers, like the Saint-Simonian prophetess Marie de Saint-Rémy, who devoted herself to soothing the disappointment of the rejects of society, a vector of the cultures of consolation which multiplied in the nineteenth century. In all 'inspirés', there is a slumbering prophet. Joseph Sec or Cheval the postman sent a message to the world from their ridiculous pedestals, monuments, palaces or soapboxes.

A collage of the different faces of cultural intermediaries, presented in this broad way without any historical reference, runs the risk of seeing differences as static, hiding a real continuity and being ultimately misleading. To take just one example, there is often very little between a functional intermediary, placed in a position of authority in the service of a dominant ideology, and one whose programming suddenly breaks down, transforming him into the prophet of a small marginal sect. The Jansenist curé of the sixteenth century, whose career was described at the conference, is a marvellous illustration of the continuities which upset the simple categories which I have just outlined for the sake of explanation.

The necessary historical dimension

It is necessary to turn to history in order to escape from these ambiguities. There have always, of course, been cultural intermediaries, following an obvious social need. But it is possible, on the basis of the studies assembled here, to distinguish one or more profound and significant processes which reflect secular changes in the *longue durée*.

Before the early-modern era, say the end of the seventeenth century, the very fragmentary studies which we have at our disposal nevertheless contain some suggestive starting points. In the late Middle Ages, when medicine had not yet placed itself in strict opposition to the legacy of folk recipes, even though it had its own learned code of reference, we encounter, in the work of D. Fabre and E. Le Roy Ladurie (in *Montaillou*) functional intermediaries at peace with popular culture, mediators of the world of the living and the dead.

The papers of Peter Burke and Carlo Ginzburg show, as do their other works (I am thinking particularly in Ginzburg's case of *The Cheese and the Worms*, his amazing evocation of the mental landscape of a heterodox Friulian miller of around 1580), an active and continuous exchange between popular and elite cultures at the heart of the sixteenth century – an idea familiar to us from the work of Bakhtine on Rabelais and the popular culture of his age, but which needs to be pursued in greater depth. In the tragic adventure of the

'Conjura di un buffone' (the trial and death of a popular agitator in early seventeenth-century Bologna), Carlo Ginzburg shows the beginning of the persecution of the intermediary – the popular spokesman, already, at an early stage in the Counter-Reformation, assuming a baroque theatricality.

The second stage would seem to be pivoted on the early-modern era, but an era so broadly defined that I see no difficulty in finding its characteristics among the schoolmasters of the educational conquest of the nineteenth century. Another global model seems to prevail at this stage. In a world still dominated by the traditional structures of rural society, a codified and structured system of intermediaries came to the fore whose typology can easily be listed: the priest, schoolmaster, midwife and barber-surgeon and even, in an open-ended list, the sacristan. In this structure, the spirit which attacks, or dutifully suspects, the pedlar and the innkeeper, not to mention the prostitute, fulfils a function of descending acculturation.

From the nineteenth century on, the relatively stable picture becomes blurred under the pressure of a social as much as a cultural evolution which profoundly modifies the given elements of the whole. We can see an accelerated rhythm characterized by a considerable spread of books, then, thanks to the press and mass media, of the means of ideological diffusion and/or domestication; at the same time, perhaps, as a relative depersonalization of contacts which become less direct – despite what has been said about radio personalities and new forms of complicity at a distance.

In such a context, traditional cultural intermediaries, incapable of recycling themselves, show their age and their tiredness, while the development of urban society, rightly stressed by many of the contributors, breaks the personal and codified contacts of village society and also produces new cultural forms of which the 'interstitial culture' of the suburbs, also dealt with, are an eloquent testimony. A host of intermediaries of new, principally urban social status, of which the recluse is neither the least important nor the least expected, embark on new cultural adventures.

It is necessary to recall the effects of growing literacy, the diffusion of primary education and of books which stimulate the production of the autodidact as a type and, on another level, the birth of working-class movements which could be seen as a powerful school of acculturation of a new kind?

We therefore see an explosion which can, at the risk of excessive simplification be traced to the French Revolution and the spokesmen of the massacres of 1792 who were at once both anchored in older languages of revolt and heralds of a new style of relations and of exchange.

A whole new range of intermediaries has been described in the papers devoted to the nineteenth and twentieth centuries. The old model still exists, far from being completely extinct, and in this context a whole series of related contributions clarified the exemplary figure of the social worker, a type that is at once both contemporary and traditional. Yet we also have the totally contemporary figure of the media presenter, the product of a technical revolution in communications which was studied through the figure of radio personalities. The figure of the spokesman is one of those to have undergone the most profound changes, from the primitive rebel to the contemporary militant, certainly acculturated but possessing a specific working-class culture – another essential frontier of research.

Finally we have the tangential group of the 'inspirés'. Have they not always existed and is their comparatively recent emergence not an optical illusion, the result of the way in which reinforced concrete and breeze blocks can give the domestic handyman the ability to construct his private universe? On a more profound level, I think that such proliferation is a product of a real multiplication of hitherto unknown personal and social types, from the lower middle class to the trades of the tertiary sector, where such an intermediary culture finds a natural habitat.

We can see that such secular changes give rise to more than an enriched typology which can integrate new categories of people. A more profound revolution is being studied here, and the very nature of the topics cannot but reflect these new realities.

From mediators to mediations

What I have called the depersonalization which began in the nineteenth century could be used to introduce a paper which was not presented at the conference called 'The death of the cultural intermediary in the modern factory', but the theme exists in the other papers in the growing importance of the study of aids for direct human contact with the passing of traditional oral culture. It would be wrong, of course, to extrapolate from the other papers in a way which only suited my own perspective. Some approaches showed the richness of traditional mediations, when there was still a functioning exchange between elite and popular culture, as in Peter Burke's study of the theatre, the drama, the 'happening' of carnival in Elizabethan

Europe. But clearly the study of the contemporary period focuses our attention on the role of media, techniques and aids, leading us from the door-to-door peddling of books in the nineteenth century to the adventure of Pierre Larousse's *Dictionary* and of the *Petit Journal* and on to the radio station and the arts centres of the present.

Amid such a proliferation of instruments, props and structures has the cultural intermediary become an obsolete and almost suspect character?

The intermediary as an expert witness

Roger Cornu, one of the contributors, warned us against the ambiguities to which the status of expert witness gives rise, and we accept this warning with all the attention it deserves. We do not want to incur the reproach made to some Africanists – ethnologists and indeed historians – who believed it essential to be mystified by the native shaman in order to give their work the seal of authenticity. Yet we can accept the challenge conscious of all the dangers involved.

Demiurge of the social world, 'inspiré', cultural half-caste, in repeating the litany with which we began, we ask for whom the cultural intermediary speaks.

Breton's 'inspirés' can be sociologically situated, within the chronological confines of his original definition of the group, on the frontier between the wage-earning class, who were sparsely represented, and the cultivated middle class. There is no longer, as there was in the fantastic world of the lord of Bomarzo, an Italian prince sufficiently independent to give free rein to the products of his imagination.

What can we say nowadays about the 'inspirés'? Autodidacts and handymen who say, like Piquassiette, the gravedigger from Chartres, 'I worked on a small scale, within my own limits.' It helps if we seek the support of certain specific sources such as autobiographies, ex votos, sepulchral monuments and suburban dream homes, and peculiar forms of expression like graphomania, proselytism, naive pedagogy and a messianism which can lead to a cosmic or eschatological world-view.

If we accept these constraints as being rich in themselves, we must nevertheless remember that it is not enough to be in an intermediary position to be an 'inspiré'. As long as we can develop a sympathy with their world without being mystified by it, these individuals in situations of rupture or of instability can be very good witnesses, given the amount of information they can supply to us for the history of dreams and fantasies and of an imagination which is not unique to them.

One culture, two cultures, or more?

From such an abundance of contributions and suggestions I come away with the impression, not of a confused jumble of ideas, but with the idea that we cannot avoid completely reassessing the sterile dialectic of popular and elite culture. We seem to have left a war of attrition for one of movement which corresponds to the 'dynamic and pluralist' approach called for by Jean Molino in his paper 'How many Cultures?'. If this paper has helped to achieve this, it will have served its purpose.

Notes

Introduction to *Les Intermédiares culturels*, the proceedings of a conference organized in June 1978 by the Centre méridional d'histoire sociale, des mentalités et des cultures.

1   See André Breton's *The Inspirés and their Houses*, with photographs by Gilles Ehrmann.
2   See the appendix 'Keys for the understanding of the *naifs*' in *Joseph Sec*.

7

The *Longue Durée*

Originally a contribution to The New History, *this paper is more than a stylistic exercise on a theme which has lost none of its sharpness since Fernand Braudel's famous article of 1958.[1] Since then, however, the problematic has been enriched by many reflections provoked by new kinds of research.*

When Fernand Braudel published his famous article 'The *longue durée*' in 1958, the text, in the tradition of *Annales*, was like a proclamation, or even a profession of faith. There were not a great many historical reference points from which to work. Although Braudel could refer to his own methods in *The Mediterranean and the Mediterranean World in the Age of Philip II*, which was an exemplary demonstration of continuity in time and space, and one could also nominate Marc Bloch's *French Rural History: an essay on its basic characteristics* or Ernest Labrousse's *Outlines of Wage and Price Movements in the Eighteenth Century*, there was a distinct lack of notable examples, although Pierre Chaunu's work *Seville and the Atlantic, 1504–1650* was then in the course of publication. It was in the years immediately after the publication of Braudel's article that a series of monographs appeared which were firmly situated in the time-frame of a century or more. Among them we should mention Pierre Goubert's *Beauvaisis* of 1960 and R. Baehrel and E. Baratier's *Provence* of 1961. From this point the number of examples multiplied and the very idea of a longer time-frame expanded, covering four centuries in Emmanuel Le Roy Ladurie's work on the total social history of the peasants of Languedoc between the fourteenth and eighteenth centuries.

It is not at all facile to begin with Braudel's essay so as to ask, twenty years later, just what has happened to the longer time-frame, which was novel in the 1960s and is now triumphant, commonplace and sometimes contested. It is not enough to say that Braudel was fighting on two fronts, internal and external to history; he was actually fighting on at least three or four. In the field of historical theory, he wrote against the background which now seems fairly distant, of a 'historizing' or event-orientated history which had been criticized by the first leaders of the *Annales* school. He condemned 'the explosive, newly-sounding event . . . [whose] delusive smoke fills the minds of its contemporaries'. For Braudel, the event had, in its ultimate manifestation as 'the short term – the most capricious and misleading of time-frames', dominated political history for a century. But the recent successes of economic history, which Braudel greeted with mixed feelings, did not mark the end of the process. He saw in Kondratiev's 'recitative of conjuncture, cycle and inter-cycle', the danger that a new event-oriented history would emerge in which a 'new-style pathetic fallacy' of the economic short term would indirectly revert to a 'very old-style pathetic fallacy', of which Labrousse's famous model of 'three crises, three revolutions' seemed to him to be an example. These references help us to place Braudel in a definite historical conjuncture and might also allow us retrospectively to see that his initiative contained a certain amount of 'teasing', as Pierre Vilar said.

But the initiative went far beyond the elaboration of a position which is now historically dated. By announcing his project with reference to developments in the other human sciences, which were annexationist and apparently victorious at the time, Braudel sought to give history an option for the future. If he reserved the possibility of stronger contacts with anthropology and ethnography, once temporary misunderstandings were overcome, he was extremely hard on the short time-frame of the sociologists. In the programme which he outlined for future historical writing, under the banner of the *longue durée*, many key ideas emerged which now serve as a leitmotif. Firstly, these involved the idea of structure which was then coming to the fore and of which Philippe Ariès had already become the champion in his essay 'The times of history', and the idea of a model, borrowed from qualtitative mathematics and already in use in the other human sciences. These were so many means, offered with a mixture of daring and caution, for better grasping the time or times appropriate to history – not the near intemporality of myths, or the unchanging elements of human behaviour, but the 'moderately' *longue durée* of a social history which can be defined as unconscious, in the sense in which Marx wrote that 'men make history, but they do not know what they are making'. Unconscious history, for Braudel, was precisely that history which took place in the *longue durée*, beneath a crust of all-too obvious events, and which could legitimately be organized into successive structures where the complementary elements of a system interact. This is socioeconomic history, but it involves more than the movements and breakthroughs which had been hitherto emphasized. It is the history of 'economic civilizations' in their persistence; 'layers of slow history' moving with the semi-immobility of slow motion. In addition to this, perhaps even more so, it includes cultural history or the history of mentalities, which he defined as a vital field of study in the longer time-frame, because he saw it as a history of 'inertias' and of 'prisons of the *longue durée*'. This was a theme on which Braudel and Labrousse were at one. Labrousse opened the Saint-Cloud conference on social history in 1965 by urging historians to investigate the 'third level' – the history of mentalities – defined as the history of 'resistance to change'.

In this mixture of calculated imprudence and cautious initiatives, Braudel's profession of faith, even if it has aged somewhat, should be an invaluable instrument for evaluating the course of events since 1958. Ambiguities have been removed and problems have settled down. The structuralist invasion has passed, and history is still very much alive. Indeed, without any premeditation, and generally without preliminary consultation, historians have got heavily involved in many of the fields which it opened up. The history of the *longue durée*, as a description of its areas of research shows twenty years on, is not unfaithful to the model which was provided for it, even if its development has often led to unforeseen results.

Some of the conflicts discussed in 1958 are now very much behind us. Not to dwell on the point, one can say that the death of a certain kind of historizing history is now an accomplished fact. For all this, has the 'event' which Braudel criticized entirely disappeared from the historical scene? Yes and no. Yes, if one considers the extent to which massive events like the French Revolution, the supreme example of what Braudel called 'emotional incongruity', have become discredited for at least one section of French historiography. No, of course, because events have a long life span and, to use an argument which is itself conjunctural and event-orientated, it only took a small wave, like that of May 1968, to revive a whole outbreak of belief in the short term, and not just as a response to a momentary fashion. But this is not the only reason.

If some themes seem to be governed by the considerations of twenty years ago, some former hopes have themselves become things of the past. Braudel and other early leaders of the *Annales* school wanted to root the return to the longer time-frame in geo-history, a project which reflected a time of fertile contact between history and geography. It was Pierre Chaunu, one of the best qualified to speak, who showed how the great studies of vast ethnic or geographical personalities like the Mediterranean and the Atlantic have since diminished in scale to the more accommodating dimensions of the regional monograph. Studies in the *longue durée* do not absolutely require very wide contexts. The Mediterranean is almost contained within the bounds of Montaillou, which does not represent 'Occitania' except in one of those extensions of which publishers are so fond. Yet for all that it does not lose any of its demonstrative value. Taking account of these and some other variations, it cannot be denied that, in general, the tendency which was announced in 1958 has been followed. It is as well, at a primary, purely descriptive level, to begin with an account of the victories of the longer time-frame.

The victory of the long time-frame: a change in historical focus

This victory was the product of a number of essential causes which I shall attempt to sum up along two lines: the change in historical focus and the change in methods and techniques. These two elements are constantly connected.

A change in historical focus? I remember, nearly ten years ago in 1970, after I had finished *Baroque Piety and Dechristianization*, a discussion with Emmanuel Le Roy Ladurie in which we spoke of the third level, which I classically called the level of ideological superstructure, and of the movement which had led a whole section of French social historians 'from the cellar to the loft', as we put it — from economy to mentalities. Le Roy Ladurie affirmed that he was still attached to 'the cellar'. I wonder if he remembers that statement now, after having shown, in *Montaillou*, his mastery of the whole building, from the cellar to the loft, from the structure of land tenure to the most complex forms of the collective mental life of the village?

From the cellar to the loft could be the theme of a survey of one specific area of the victory of the longer time-frame. The time-frame of various kinds of history which, for the sake of simplicity, we can call 'classical', has been modified. Even political history, in more than one area, has abandoned the framework of events to formulate problems which can only be conceived of in a longer time-frame —

essentially the time-frame of the state, an all-encompassing structure which should not be confused with the academic realities dealt with by traditional institutional history, which is a catalogue bogged down in its own categories. The change is even more obvious in religious history which is increasingly feeling the pressure – or help – of religious sociology and the history of mentalities. Theses are no longer written with titles like 'The bull *Unigenitus* in the dioceses of ...'. Current interest focuses on a number of topics like popular religion, from the pre-Christian animist heritage which so deeply impregnated medieval and early-modern Christianity, to the forms of Christianized popular religion which emerged in the twelfth and thirteenth centuries, right up to the triumph of the Catholic reconquest in the classical period, and all of these are studied in the *longue durée* over a number of centuries. Where we once believed in the existence of a state of 'Christianity' in France on the eve of the Revolution, we now ask with Jean Delumeau (who took up a subject first broached by Gabriel Le Bras) whether a whole section of rural France was ever thoroughly Christianized. All these phenomena can only be observed by casting the net deliberately widely over several centuries.

Economic history, formerly the methodological 'locomotive', and still going strong, shows the most profound change of perspective. It earned its credentials as the history of change and conjuncture. The French school, from Simiand to Ernest Labrousse, established the economists' three interlocking times as an accepted truth: the short term of the decennial cycle with its convulsive paroxysms of periodic crisis, the medium term of the intermediate cycle and the longer time-frame, even if progressively shortened, of secular change in the *longue durée* from the Middle Ages to the present. These are Simiand's classic A, B and C phases. The temporal dialectic of price history, constructed from long series of records such as price lists of grain or manufactured goods, was the first great triumph of quantitive history, which was then still part and parcel of serial history. If we want briefly to summarize this process, with all the inevitable risk of caricature, it is useful to recall the changes which have taken place in the last twenty years which have altered the profile of the subject. Quantitive econometrics, in the wake of the 'New Economic History', has tendentially moved away from economic history, following its own criteria and extending its speculations on conjuncture into the contemporary arena. In the historical field, economic history has, without repudiating its established procedures, moved out of the domain of the history of prices, which emphasized sudden change, conjunctural phenomena and crises. In turning, wherever possible, towards a history of production and growth it necessarily opens onto a much longer time-frame. This is because massive series, which are less subtle and more intermittent, accentuate the trend from a deliberately quantitive research to serial history.

This transition has not taken place without some resentment and gnashing of teeth. And if it is nowadays fashionable to sneer at the patient scholars of former days who laboured to correlate fertility series, adjusted back nine months from birth curves, with graphs of grain prices adjusted to harvest years, we should also recall the difficulties and incomprehension which greeted the new, sometimes aggressively stated ideas of Baehrel in his attempt to replace a history of prices with a history of growth and production. Nowadays the affair is settled; new ideas have been assimilated and the lines of difference have blurred. We can also take as examples of new developments works which have been deliberately formulated in the long time-frame of the secular fluctuations of the landscape, coordinating historical geography in the Braudelian tradition with the movements and migrations of people and their social and productive relationships. In this area Emmanuel Le Roy Ladurie's *Peasants of Languedoc* is exemplary.

Le Roy Ladurie went right back to the heart of the Middle Ages, to the turn of the fourteenth century, to study a province still dominated by the agrarian economy. This dual foundation doubtless explains the emergence of a world which, generally speaking, was 'immobile' in terms of the measurements of its agrarian economy over a very long period. Yet specific, exemplary monographic studies of the kind which have become fashionable once again in their new form as a total approach to the microcosm of the village, also lend themselves to this kind of demonstration. One might say that *Montaillou*, another innovative experiment by the same author, a searching autopsy of an 'Occitan' village in the first decades of the fourteenth century based on an invaluable inquisition document, hardly advances our case, since it illuminates a specific moment in time. Yet, in this context, one thinks of G. Bouchard's concept of the 'immobile village', of the kind he discovered in Sologne (which is not, of course, unique!), the monolithic structures of which he analysed for the classical period. In what Ernest Labrousse taught us to call the traditional economy, lasting right up to the first half of the eighteenth century, we can see how the model of an 'immobile history' can take shape over a period of four centuries (from the fourteenth to the eighteenth century), which Le Roy Ladurie affirms in a provocative way. This model is not, moreover, limited to the economic sphere. It combines the various levels of total history within a global structure.

But before taking this aspect into account – which needs particular attention – we must, in this investigation, be aware of the new pathways opened up in the material history of people and in the conditions of their lives. Not to multiply examples, we can point to the study of habitat, of the house, in the permanent realities of the *longue durée*, conducted in Normandy and Paris by Pierre Chaunu and his team. This is not a history of inertia. Medievalists in Poland, England and Italy have taught us to follow long-term phases of growth and decline in the countryside, the slow ebb and flow of the rural habitat, as inscribed in the archaeology of abandoned villages.

This history of the very slow evolutions of material culture can become a history of humanity approached in its biological and anthropological forms. Here again Le Roy Ladurie has shown the way in his anthropology of the French conscript, based on the conscription records of the nineteenth century. But sophisticated techniques, as used in the study of kinship groups in certain valuable sites, can be used to construct this paradoxical history which is at once human and yet beyond the grasp of deliberate human consciousness – at least at first sight.

Once embarked on this course there is no reason to stop. Nonhuman history, the history of physical conditions, biological or geological, has been one of the great gains of recent times, although one can find some precedents. The history of diseases, their appearance, decline and eradication, their changes and also their relationship to the ecosystem, is one branch of study which is at a formative stage. We have begun to discover the history of earthquakes and, of course, thanks to Le Roy Ladurie, the history of climate, as he has summarized it since the year 1000, has become an independent discipline, based on sources as varied as the dates of grape harvests, the advance or retreat of glaciers or the study of tree rings. It is much more than an ancillary science or a marginal curiosity, even if it does not really unlock the ultimate secrets of movements in agricultural prosperity and decline in the *longue durée*. In this kind of history we are dealing with another kind of time, which is quite different from human time, even though human beings have some leverage on the physical and biological conditions which affect them. From the time of the pastoral revolution, the eco-history of diseases came under human control to a considerable degree. But rhythms were established which were specific and to a large extent went beyond the human time-frame which they helped to shape.

From social change to social structures

In the field of social history, the study of structures – systems in the *longue durée* as they are seen by historians – has been one of the great advances of recent decades. Not that it is necessary to make a choice between an approach which involves structures and one involving social dynamics, giving pride of place to one or other emphasis. Current social history began as the study of 'social movements', especially the labour movement, a term which is nowadays somewhat dated. The study of the labour movement in the nineteenth and twentieth centuries has led to a regressive approach, spearheaded by some pioneering works on revolts prior to the industrial revolution – jacqueries, tumults, outbursts of anger as some historians significantly call them. It was in this area, where ideological investment is most apparent, that the clash between different interpretations was most severe in the study of what I choose to call the forms of class struggle in precapitalist society. The controversy between Roland Mousnier and Boris Porchnev on popular revolts in France in the first half of the seventeenth century shows this. There is a strong temptation to see these popular explosions as a semi-constant in the context of a society which was for the most part immobile, in which popular revolts transferred the periodic crises of traditional society to the social level, and also to see them as vehicles of an inevitably backward-looking ideology for which continuities can be traced between the period of the League and the French Revolution.

In this interpretation, the study of social dynamics, at least on the level of the masses, important as it is in some works (again, see the *Peasants of Languedoc*), fades away before the study of structures. It is certainly true that historians have been studying structures in the *longue durée* in this area since the 1960s, following the programme outlined by Ernest Labrousse to the Congress of Historical Sciences in Rome in 1955 entitled 'New ways towards a history of the bourgeoisie in the West'. The history of social structures was not invented in this area. It was already alive in the study of rural society, based on a solid tradition dating back to the work of Loutchisky in the heroic age of such scholarship around 1900. This tradition was represented in the 1930s by Georges Lefebvre's thesis 'The peasants of the North and the French Revolution' and continued without interruption from then on in a series of monographs, including Roupnel and Saint-Jacob on Burgundy, right up to great modern works of synthesis like those of Goubert and Agulhon which have renewed the genre. Labrousse's revolution of the 1960s was most clearly felt in the area of urban societies which had been neglected up to that point. To avoid an excess of examples we can nominate, among the urban studies which range over a century or more, M. Garden's anatomy of eighteenth-century Lyon and P. Deyon's study of Amiens in the seventeenth century.

The history of social structures, both urban and rural, is part of the new history of the *longue durée* and, until recently, of the history of continuities which contradicted the mobility of official history. But I believe that the recent development which has most directly contributed to bringing the new social history into the longer time-frame has been the process drawing it closer and closer to the history of mentalities.

Mentalities: the privileged field of the *longue durée*

As a historian of mentalities aware of his responsibilities, I am one of those for whom the field, far from being seen as a counterpoint to social history, is its cutting edge and culmination, the level at which social phenomena register as collective attitudes and representations. It is true that the 'third level' was considered, on the basis of strong assumptions, to be the domain of the 'prisons of the *longue durée*', in Braudel's phrase, or of 'resistances' according to Labrousse. We were called on to investigate the 'force of inertia' of mental structures. It seemed at the outset that these processes could only be dealt with in the perspective of the secular time-frames in which they took place – at least for a historiography which seemed to have forgotten that one of the neglected masterpieces of what could be called the history of mentalities *avant la lettre* was Georges Lefebvre's *The Great Fear*, a detective-like reconstruction of the wave of panic which crisscrossed rural France in 1789 and whose effects toppled the agrarian structures of the *ancien régime* in less than three weeks.

Yet it seems that it was cultural history rather than the history of collective attitudes which made the most striking breakthrough in the longer time-frame of traditional society under the *ancien régime*. Robert Mandrou was the first to discover the main characteristics of French popular culture in the eighteenth century on the basis of a study, in the *longue durée*, of the little blue pamphlets of the *Bibliothèque de Troyes*, reprinted *ne varietur* over the centuries. The story of this literature sold by pedlars stretches out, often with only minuscule changes, from the dawn of the modern period down to its demise in the middle of the nineteenth century. It is true that at this initial level of the history of mentalities – cultural history – there are some preliminary questions which cannot be avoided. To simplify matters, these involve a dual time-frame: that of popular culture, which is an area of inertia and tradition, and that of 'elite' culture, which is one of provocation and innovation. Elite and popular culture: another major dialectic which is the theme of current research.

Things are doubtless not as simple as we might have thought. In order to illustrate the 'prisons of the *longue durée*' of the collective mental universe, Fernand Braudel, twenty years ago, used Lucien Febvre's extraordinary work *The Problem of Unbelief in the Six-teenth Century: the religion of Rabelais*, which provided him with an image of an 'all-encompassing' structure, a vision of the world articulated at every level and a means of banishing the anachronistic interpretations of positivist historiography. No, said Febvre to Abel Lefranc, Rabelais could not have been the freethinker you wanted him to be, in a world where religion was the framework of collective life. Can we still defend this totalizing (dare we say totalitarian?) view of mental structures today, when Febvre's work in its turn appears to be historically dated? Anyone who has discovered Rabelais as the spokesman of a still vital popular culture in the work of Mikhail Bakhtine, and who has read the papers of Carlo Ginzburg and Natalie Zemon Davis, both of whom show us a sixteenth century riven with tensions, conflicts and contradictions and containing a dialectical exchange between elite and popular culture which was neither dormant nor unique, cannot accept Febvre's vision without some reservations, a vision which is limiting in its structure and in its one-dimensional view of the realities.

It is clear, if we pass from the history of cultures or of clear thought to the new field of the history of mentalities, which deals with the domain of attitudes, behaviour and what some scholars call 'the collective unconscious' (Philippe Ariès), that the longer time-frame is undeniably necessary.

There are no struggles nor even, strictly speaking, sudden changes or events in the traditional sense in the history of the family, of attitudes to childhood, collective sociability or death, to list almost haphazardly the new fields which have been opened up. Philippe Ariès, one of the originators of this kind of history in the fields of childhood, the family and death, asserts strongly that it proceeds by secret evolutions in the *longue durée*, processes which are, in addi-tion, unconscious because they are not seen by those who are experiencing them. The image which he gives us, notably in his recent history of death, is not that of an 'immobile' history, although he does reserve a place for a subterranean, achronic history associated with traditional societies. Ariès's vision is of wide stretches of history, a succession of structures or models of behaviour which, rather than replace each other, overlap and are enmeshed like slates on a roof. Thus, he leads us from 'tamed', achronic death, which is the same for Ivan Illich as for the valiant Roland, to the first awakening of consciousness of the tragedy of individual death, from the Middle Ages to the classical period, to its transfer to the death of the other, the love object, in the Romantic period, right up to the emergence of the death taboo of our own time. The passage from one structure to another takes place in wide historical frameworks where imperceptible changes are far more important than visible processes such as the sense of the macabre at the end of the Middle Ages (an epiphenomenon?) or perceptible turning points like the end of the eighteenth century which mark the passage from one structure to another.

Although it is one of the most systematic and attractive achievements of the present day, Ariès's reconstruction of attitudes towards death and childhood is not unique. Historians of the family – another theme dear to contemporary scholars (yet are studies of childhood and the family not just different aspects of the same adventure?) – also refer us to models in the *longue durée*, the 'European pattern' established in Western Europe at the end of the sixteenth century, which lasted until the end of the eighteenth, characterized by the emergence of the nuclear family and late marriage as a form of spontaneous Malthusianism before Malthus. Can such a history tolerate 'revolutions'? The long discussion on the origins of contraception in the eighteenth century, taking up Shorter's controversial notion of a 'sexual revolution' in this period, calls attention to a problem which needs to be looked at again.

It would be bad grace on my part to declare war on this slow-moving history of collective mentalities. Have I not – modestly – preached by example in studying changes in the representation of the hereafter based on a valuable iconographic series of altars to the souls in Purgatory in the South of France, from the appearance of images of Purgatory in the fifteenth century to their disappearance at the beginning of the twentieth – a study which can only be conceived in terms of the *longue durée*? This example is far from unique nowadays, but it should encourage us to ask questions about the current victory of the longer time-frame from another perspective. Up to now we have been looking at the consequences of the expansion of the field of research; the opening up of new territory where the traditional norms of the measurement of historical time have proved inadequate. In order to be thorough, this explanation needs to go further.

Technical explanations: a new conception of the sources

Can this modification of historical time, or times, be seen, on the whole, as the result of a change in the very notion of the historical source? Given that every age chooses the sources which respond to its own needs, this preliminary question cannot be left unexamined. It allows us, once we have dealt with the idea of different histories, to see more generally on what level the change has taken place.

One can say, somewhat naively, that the emergence of the *longue durée* is both the result of the discovery and use of new sources and the price to be paid for the difficulties encountered when working in a field where the silence of the documents forces us to expand our chronological horizons. These two statements, one optimistic, the other less so, are only apparently contradictory.

It is true, in the first instance, that we now use documentary series in the *longue durée* which we would not have dreamed of heretofore. However blasé we might have become, we can only admire the way Peter Laslett has produced a continuous graph of legitimacy in England over a period of four centuries, from 1550 to the present, giving us an indicator of attitudes to the family which goes far beyond the anecdotal approach. To leap from subject to subject, statistics on climatic variations, demographic statistics – now become even more familiar – and data on prices and production present us, nowadays, with a whole range of sources which touch on the most varied aspects of the human adventure.

At the heart of this revolution was, of course, the emergence of new sources for studying normal, everyday life, touching on the lives of the anonymous masses in a historical continuum. Lists of grain prices and the civil records of traditional society – baptisms, marriages and burials – were the first sources exploited, and this kind of work gave us the principles and philosophy of serial history as it is now practised. But the degree of analysis of the past which is possible through these sources is limited by technical factors. Despite some exceptions, the sixteenth century is a boundary beyond which it is practically impossible to go in most areas of investigation. The eighteenth century constitutes another such boundary, introducing progressive stages towards modern conditions between the first third

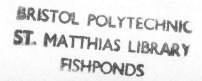

of the century, in which parish registers become generally reliable in all areas, and the first third of the nineteenth century, which saw the general extension of the gathering of statistics into the most varied areas of life.

With these sources, new processes of sophistication and 'banalization' took place. The pioneering field of social history discovered new extensive sources in the *longue durée*. The realization of the potential value of notarial sources, for example, including contracts, leases, wills and inventories, was something which only became obvious after it had happened. This development also did a great deal to abolish traditional frontiers in history. From the twelfth and thirteenth centuries, or at least the fourteenth, when the practice of making wills first became widespread, right up to the end of the eighteenth century and even (why not!) up to the present day, wills provide a homogenous, formal resource for the study of social and mental attitudes towards death. Thus, an obstinate barrier between medieval and modern historians disappeared; both had the feeling, which was more than just a feeling, that they were working towards the same objective.

The discovery of new written sources, capable of being organized serially in the *longue durée*, was the result of the recognition of the value of dormant masses of anonymous documents which had hitherto meant nothing. This discovery was both essential and limited. One could give a host of examples. Fiscal records, for instance, going back to the heart of the Middle Ages, can sometimes compensate for the absence of other civil records, as in the listing of hearths in cadastral surveys in Provence or Italy, just as the 'humdrum' judicial archives of lay or ecclesiastical courts can allow us to trace back the long history of the dialectic between repression and protest. But there are limits and they are well known. The exploitation of every facet of the everyday documents of the past stops at the point where no written document exists.

Here we are helped out by different kinds of sources, by their very nature requiring a much wider interpretation. Under such circumstances, writing loses its privileged status while archaeology acquires a very high status, along with iconography and even oral research, in the context of historical ethnology. A whole section of current research, from work on material life to the different fields of culture and popular mentalities thus appears as a kind of obstinate attempt to cheat the silence of the sources, using methods which would once have been considered irrelevant. The archaeology of the house or the living space leads onto the study of material culture; iconographic series lead onto the history of mentalities. An inventory or analysis of the religious furnishings of the sacred space of the church, or, more widely, of the parish, from the Middle Ages to the modern era, can thus constitute a resource for the analysis of the successive forms of popular religion.

Without wishing to multiply examples, let us choose ex votos, which are currently being catalogued for the whole of France, and elsewhere. This is a series in the *longue durée*. In the South of France, the oldest visual ex votos date back to the sixteenth century, the most recent are contemporary in areas where traditional forms have not been displaced by anonymous marble votive plaques. This source is rich and poor at once. It is rich in the multiplicity of possible applications and uses – from the history of material life or of customs to that of disease and death, attitudes to the family and religious feeling – experienced as a means of obtaining a miracle, or of obtaining grace. Yet the document itself is poor, most often difficult to date except within wide chronological limits; its images appearing with inertia in the *longue durée* of representations which change but little. Such sources emphasize continuity, and only register change slowly. Likewise, popular imagery preserved the static silhouettes of saints' images, which derive from fifteenth-century reredoses, right through the classical period (and even into the nineteenth century). More than one such series of sources leaves us with the impression of a muffled, sluggish time without sudden changes or shifts. This impression does not just derive from the imprecision of the sources, nor from the fact that they lack the clarity of written sources; it derives, rather, from the fact that they are a direct reflection of slow processes which are objectively registered in a slower time-frame.

The stability of objects in a traditional civilization, like the house and its furnishings, echoes and confirms the ideas suggested by iconographic representations. What is true of the visual object holds true, a fortiori, for the oral source. A very special kind of time emerges from the studies of those who, like Philippe Joutard, have undertaken, on the basis of direct research, using ethnological methods, to reconstitute the various elements of collective memory around a given theme – in Joutard's case the memory of the Camisard War. The folk memory is impoverished, but at the same time creative, sometimes assimilating different events into one memory, but also capable of enriching a memory at several stages through contact with written culture. Oral research, moreover, puts historians into contact with the time-frame of the folklorist or the ethnographer, which they no longer refuse to take into account as something outside the scope of their own research. Yet they approach it with the urge to stamp it with the seal of history, dating as precisely as possible phenomena which have hovered in an irritating intemporality, in a time-frame which is an essential element in the understanding of traditional civilizations.

One is left with an ambiguous impression after looking at the views of time dictated by this diversity of sources. Beyond the technical difficulties of precise dating, one has the impression of having grasped the rhythms, the breathing, of the great masses who have made history, and of an important part of the forces which shaped their lives. One can better understand why a whole section of French historiography, starting with Braudel and Chaunu, was tempted to replace the expression 'quantitive history' – too 'economistic' no doubt – with the more accommodating notion of serial history, which involves the organization in time of the successive images provided by the same source. These do not have to be strictly commensurable in their intensity. We can find series of images of the family in requests from dispensations from marriage ordinances; of images of miracles based on ex votos; of the hereafter in the reredoses to the souls in Purgatory; of gestures of rejection or repression in judicial records. All of these are part of an ideal which, without rejecting quantification, opens up into the area of the new history of mentalities, allowing us to follow the story in the *longue durée*.

Are we seeing, through this new jurisprudence, the establishment of a new interpretation of historical time?

Time in the *longue durée*

It will be useful, in order to appreciate this reappraisal of historical time, to begin with the traditional outlook: the short time-frame of events in the traditional history of politics or of battles, focusing on dates like 1610 or 1815. It goes without saying (perhaps?) that no one would like to see a return to this outlook, which is only concerned with a small, superficial crust of human history. True history, like real life, lies elsewhere. So be it. Economic history performed the invaluable task of imposing its own tripartite modality (of the short-term crisis, the medium-term intercycle and long-term change in the *longue durée*) onto the impoverished sequence of historical events with their linear causalities. This system is operative in its own sphere, but Braudel's question, posed nearly twenty years ago, as to whether such a model of interlocking times can be transposed to other areas of history, beginning with social history, never received a definite answer. Indeed, it seems that this schema is too mechanical for scholars working on slow-moving histories, and is therefore of little use to them.

It seems, therefore, that we are engaged in a process of multiplying the varieties of time, in anticipation of the 'interlacing' of historical times of which Althusser spoke. Time, in economic history, in social history and in the history of mental structures does not move at the same speed. When Ernest Labrousse spoke of the history of resistances to change, to be found in the history of mentalities, he implicitly presupposed the existence of different rhythms; at the same time he preserved the idea of a single rhythm which is progressively obscured, starting with an initial material or infrastructural impulse followed by the emergence of conservative social structures and culminating in the prisons of the mental universe in the *longue durée*. This interpretation, referring too explicitly to the Marxist dialectic between base and superstructure, is no longer fashionable in mainstream historiography, where we smile at the very idea of succumbing to what our American friends call 'vulgar Marxism'. We almost prefer, without always making it explicit, to return to a hardly less simplistic interpretation based on the dialectic between time as it affects the mass of the people, which is practically static, and that of the 'elites', which is nervous changing, creative. The latter is no doubt a superficial crust, but it is a good one – the crust of a bread which has been leavened by historical change. A large part of the present-day *Annales* school in France could be said to reflect this tension, or perhaps this division of roles. Some, like François Furet and Denis Richet, stress the mobility of elite time; others, like Le Roy Ladurie, stress the immobility of ethnographic history.

But it is not saying very much to state that historical times have multiplied. They also overlap, which is another aspect of the interlacing of times of which we spoke earlier. Take the example of Philippe Ariès's history of death in which different time-frames are stratified like tiles on a roof, as we previously said. The static, achronic time of tamed death, as it was accepted in traditional societies, has not disappeared, of course, and we can see it re-emerge in the course of everyday life. But other historically rooted attitudes, such as the 'death of the self', or its sublimation in the person of the loved one (the 'death of the other') and the subsequent modern taboo surrounding death all exist within geographical, social, religious and even individual parameters. In the light of these studies there emerges the idea of the independence of historical times which are 'symphonic' in that the different rhythms which can be identified become intermingled in the whole or, conversely, shoot off on their divergent courses. This might well provide a definition of 'conjuncture', reformulated in terms which extend beyond the narrow confines of the economic sphere.

Is this still standard practice for contemporary historians? It might be said that I am being unfair to Philippe Ariès, whose work is very close to my own and who certainly merits this interest by virtue of the originality and representative character of his own contributions. In his eyes, of course, a history as important as that of collective attitudes towards death in the *longue durée* has a very real autonomy with regard to demographic pressures, social structures and social representations and, even more curiously, with regard to ideological, religious and philosophical structures. Ariès follows the autonomous processes of a 'collective unconscious', which is animated by its own internal dialectic, in the *longue durée*.

Is Philippe Ariès an extreme or exceptional case? I believe not. He has the great merit of clearly expressing what is often left unformulated elsewhere. Yet one has little difficulty in finding interpretations very close to his own, as in the field of the history of the family, which is currently opening up. Historical ethnology, too, and the history of material life, which are working hard to introduce a subtle historical movement into their time-frames, are very much tempted to assume the existence of a very long time-frame which is, of course, specific to each subject.

We can see where all this is leading, and can summarize it in two connected themes. The first concerns the problem of a history which is avowedly static. The second involves the reappraisal of the idea of change and sudden transformation in history – in a word, the idea of revolution.

The first perspective (I will not say the first danger) did not escape Braudel who was, it is true, writing at a time when the conquering pressure of the human sciences was at its height. We can leave the task of describing this internal debate to Pierre Vilar, who witnessed this stage of the process, with his own very discreet sense of humour: 'Braudel wanted to let himself be seduced. These new ideas went in the same direction as his own – the direction of resistance to change. But he also liked his job. The historian certainly wanted the longer time-frame; but if there was no longer any time-frame at all, then the historian would have to disappear.' Saved by a moral, not to say corporate, reflex, did Braudel definitely banish the idea of immobile time – an expression which we can find in his own work? It seems not, to judge by the extent to which Le Roy Ladurie drew on him in his brilliant inaugural lecture at the Collége de France in 1975 entitled 'Immobile history'. I do not wish to put words into the mouth of the historian of Languedoc: his history is not definitively fixed. There are long stretches of immobility, perhaps from the sixteenth century to the beginning of the eighteenth, certainly towards 1720. But from this point things do change, and the indicators used – land ownership, habitat, production, demography, material and mental equipment – indisputably shift and become mobile. Then again, within this long, pluri-secular semi-stability we see any number of oscillations around the mean, sometimes slow, but often convulsive, whether involving human migration, family size or the outbreak of popular revolts. Yet it is also true that even though Le Roy Ladurie adapts Braudel's notion of 'structure' in this way, defining it as 'an assemblage, an architecture, but, even more, a reality with which time deals harshly and which it changes very slowly', in a compromise which preserves historical change *in extremis*, he has not gone as far as some others in this respect.

Are there, Braudel asked, when writing about ethnography, elementary characteristics of behaviour which persist in the *longue durée*, such as the incest taboo; characteristics which are fixed in a real intemporality, or in such distant origins that they might as well be? Can we, provocatively coining neologisms to express our mean-ing, speak of 'gustemes' and 'mythemes'? We certainly have a strong impression that mythemes exist and that we have encountered them in the work of historical anthropologists. Claude Gaignebet's work on the carnival shows us a structure of inversion, a hidden eruption of popular Saturnalia from prehistory to our own time which redeploys or rediscovers images and attitudes as old as the world, or at least as old as the ancient pre-Christian agrarian religion, in the service of its own cathartic progress. Charivaris, festivals of fools, Valentin and Ourson's backstreet dances lead us on a merry dance back to the origins and beyond! Rabelais would have agreed. Do these gestures, or fragments of myths, carried on by the centuries into the pages of the folklorists (but in what a state!) offer the key to the secrets of behaviour or of formal structures void of real meaning and content? We can leave present-day Panurges to wear themselves out decipher-ing the words and gestures frozen in the antediluvian ice of the Singing Isle and we can profit from their results. If, at the end of their journey they succeed, like Panurge, in seeing the Sibyl's cave then much good may it do them!

The complement, indeed the reverse, of this descent into the quest for origins and constants is, as we said, the reinterpretation not just of dangerous events, but of every rapid change, every catastrophic 'mutation' (to use a term which Braudel rightly disliked). It is not clear how we can emerge from closed and tightly bunched structures, and the new history runs the risk of being as much afraid of change as the traditional history was afraid of resistance. Admittedly, the theme 'one crisis; one revolution' derives from a mechanistic interpretation of historical causality (this was not at all Labrousse's view, however, who pointed out, with apparent innocence, that, although there are decennial crises, there are not decennial revolutions). Yet it has become tempting, for the kind of historiography which makes no distinction between 'vulgar' Marxism, and Marxism pure and simple, to throw out the unwanted revolutionary baby with the bathwater.

During a conference on the origins of the French Revolution, held at Göttingen in 1974, the question was raised in some of the discussions as to whether the French Revolution ever happened. The Revolution, it was argued, was a myth, and the historical interpretation which saw it as a major turning point in modern history, dividing the nation's destiny in two, was part of an 'ideology legacy' (F. Furet). In the work of François Furet, Denis Richet and their pupils (like G. Chaussinand-Nogaret), where new interpretations of the Revolution have been developed, the real Revolution represented by the Enlightenment and by the formation of a homogenous 'elite' combining members of the nobility and the bourgeoisie in the earliest stages of modernization, had already taken place by 1789. The event itself only served to distort the healthy perspectives of history as it ought to have been, by introducing the incongruous and backward-looking intervention of the mass of the people, with their outdated ideologies. The true destiny of French society was thus deflected (thereby incidentally providing an oxygen mask for the poor French peasantry for more than a century) and, by the same token, the event, or the intrusion of the short time-frame, if not wholly futile, is nonetheless out of keeping with the direct line of historical development as it should have taken place. This is the tendency of interpretations like the 'hijacking' of the French Revolution put forward by Furet and Richet, which have been a source of polemic for the past fifteen years.

Not to rake over the coals, there are plenty of other examples to hand which are less polemical and therefore less suspect. If we want to choose a massive perspective, we can take a great turning point like the Black Death in 1348. In the traditional interpretation, the Black Death cut the Middle Ages into two main phases: one of expansion and then a declining phase lasting until the middle of the fifteenth century. Another interpretation, which is not at all traditional, has validated the idea of a major turning point brought about by that dramatic event. Millard Meiss, analysing Florentine and Sienese painting of the mid-fourteenth century, has very subtly analysed the symptoms of a trauma in the collective mentality of this period.

Since then, without going into too much detail, we can see how the Black Death has been pushed backwards in time. The real turning point took place before 1348 (sometimes in 1315, or even at the end of the thirteenth century). It was not the Black Death which heralded the demographic turning point, but the recurrence of earlier plagues. In Italy, and sometimes elsewhere, demographic recovery was rapid and the great depression of the late Middle Ages did not exist. The result of all these precisions and nuances is that the Black Death has been refined out of existence. Ariès practically conjures it out of existence in his work, which admits of no sudden changes in the model of the *longue durée*, and he makes do as well as he can – in my view rather worse than better – by emphasizing the incongruity of the macabre at the end of the Middle Ages.[2]

Do we not need to move forward, if not by rediscovering the event, by defining a new dialectic of the shorter and longer time-frame in history?

A new dialectic of the short and long time-frame

It must be stated that current paths of discovery in historical research do not only follow the trails of the longer time-frame. Likewise, we can see the forceful emergence of a new inquiry into change in both its brutal and gradual forms. If we want to classify new developments in this area also, then it will be useful to begin with the new role attributed to the event in more than one field of study.

When M. Crubellier presented an apologia for the event to the 1965 social history conference in Saint-Cloud it was, to exaggerate slightly, a plea for a lost cause. When Pierre Nora, ten years later, announced the return of the event in a collective work entitled *Making History*, it was to register, as a contemporary historian, the violence and potential of specific facts which create their own importance. No doubt, such events are blown up by the emphasis placed on them by the media, but they are perfect illustrations of the power of key ideas which are transformed into material realities when they penetrate the masses, to follow Marx's famous statement. Pierre Nora's 'rehabilitation', however convincing it may be, runs the risk of remaining ambiguous in one respect. Taken superficially, by a strict interpretation, it can be seen as a variation on the old theme of historical acceleration. In this theory, contemporary history is characterized by the mobility and agitation found in events whereas previous periods are characterized by long stretches of immobility or of slow change. Here we can find a compromise even with the historian of immobile history, Emmanuel Le Roy Ladurie, for whom history begins to change around 1720, after four centuries of oscillation around a semi-constant mean, and also with ethnologists. For Varagnac, for example, as for the folklorists, the structures of a practically monolithic traditional society only began to dissolve relatively recently – it matters little whether we nominate 1870 or 1914–18 as the turning point – from which point we can trace the disintegration of a very old system.

I believe that we must go beyond this very important stage, in that we can assert that the event, or, to avoid any ambiguity, sudden change, is far from being the prerogative of contemporary history, and that a whole series of studies over the past twenty years have been polarized by the dialectic of the longer and shorter time-frame – the interaction of the event and the *longue durée*. Some examples come to mind which show the different ways in which this historical problematic has been handled. Paul Bois's thesis, *The Peasants of the West*, moved from structure in the *longue durée* to the event. One can also find a development from events to the *longue durée* by means of a regressive history in the work of Maurice Agulhon or in my own work on death and the festival. Paul Bois's work, which appeared in 1960 but the methodological importance of which has only since been recognized, is almost an exemplary case. He began, apparently very classically, with a portrait of one department in western France – La Sarthe – at the end of the nineteenth century. The situation he found there revealed little that was new. It reflected the ideas of André Siegfried's famous *Political Portrait of Western France under the Third Republic*: characteristics reflecting the short and long time-frames of sociology; structural realities inherited in the *longue durée* which constituted a series of almost ageless determinants, including the *bocage* landscape, dispersed habitats and the dual domination of the church and the chateau. Yet Bois's research quickly showed that this history was only apparently immobile.

In La Sarthe a frontier divides the peasantry in two: royalist and *Chouan* in the west, republican in the east. In seeking to explain this frontier, the factors mentioned above – the *bocage*, the parish priest, 'the master' – offered no conclusive explanation for the division. The author looked for it in history, going back to the precise moment when the split came about, the French Revolution. The two peasantries, which differed in their structure, their dynamism and their aggressiveness, chose their lasting collective options at that point in time.

We can see, even from such a brief summary, how this kind of exemplary study conveys a rich and ambiguous message. On the one hand, it justifies study in the *longue durée*, the delving into the pluri-secular past in which the lasting characteristics of behaviour are handed on with real inertia, even after their initial conditions have disappeared. But, conversely or complementarily, the shorter time-frame reasserts its importance here as that of the initial trauma of a truly revolutionary rupture on the basis of which some became *Chouans* and others Jacobins, both separated by a frontier which is perpetuated in modern electoral geography. This combination of the long and short time-frames is not a bourgeois compromise. It places each one in its proper place and banishes at least one of the forms of the *longue durée* – the old theory of a timeless determinism – in order to stress what Pierre Vilar called the 'moderately long' time-frame. This phrase, despite its lack of elegance, possibly best expresses the time-frame in which the historian feels most at home.

It could be said that Paul Bois failed to answer one of the questions raised by his work, which concerns the modalities in which attitudes, not to say messages, are transmitted. In his work we see the culminating point, but we also need to go back to the starting point. Between the two lies the field of collective memory, conscious or unconscious, which is another problem. In undertaking to study this area, Philippe Joutard working on written sources and via direct oral research in the present into the current manifestations of a deeply rooted memory (the traumatic event of the revolt of the Camisards in the Cévennes), approached the same problematic from another direction. Yet he too tried to weigh the significance, in time, of an event, which marked an important turning point in history.

Paul Bois started with a structure and discovered the event. Without any contradiction others start with the event and rediscover a structure. Maurice Agulhon, in a series of articulate writings based on his research on eastern Provence, seems to start from the very specific event of the Provençal revolt in defence of the Republic in 1851 – the unexpected emergence, if you like, of the enduring 'Red South' which appeared as a counterpoint to the 'White South' of the first half of the nineteenth century. From his thorough study of the sociology of these urbanized villages we will, for simplicity's sake,

choose just one aspect. He showed how the *chambrées* (the republican secret societies) of the South could be linked to the structures of
sociability under the *ancien régime* which he had studied, working
backwards through the revolutionary clubs of the First Republic to
highlight the multiplicity of male associations which existed in the
eighteenth century, of which penitent confraternities were only the
most spectacular expression. But this stable formal structure in fact
covers a real mobility. In his masterly work *Penitents and Freemasons*, Agulhon showed how the Provençal elites deserted the confraternities in the second half of the eighteenth century to join the
masonic lodges, which were more suited to their new aspirations. The
dialectic of the long and short time-frame is particularly rich here.
Starting from a regressive study in the (moderately) *longue durée*,
research indicates the existence of a process of slow change. The
constant here is perhaps the characteristic of 'sociability', the importance of which the author points out, but he also stresses the limits of
its use as a formal support for a history of change.

The procedures which I applied in my analysis of the phenomenon
of dechristianization from the classical period to the French Revolution were not all that different. In this case the specific fact was the
spectacular dechristianizing outburst of the Year II, the principal
features of which were analysed and mapped for the whole of
south-eastern France. This is a prime example of an event which is
not just 'emotional' but scandalous, to the point where an entire
historiography chose to ignore what it saw as an unfortunate
historical mistake. The determinism of the short-term revolutionary
time-frame – general politics and the local initiatives of revolutionary
officials or clubs – were insufficient to explain the contrasts and
structures of the evidence. I sought a solution in a wider study
covering the century of the Enlightenment, using a rich and valuable
indicator: thousands of Provençal wills. This source enabled me to
trace the apogee, destructuring and eventual disintegration of the
system of 'baroque' practice and religiosity in the South of France. On
this basis, I was also able to identify a turning point around 1750
which affected collective sensibility, starting with attitudes towards
death.

The model tried out in Provence proved to be workable, but it
lacked any comparison with other regions. This has now been
possible following the work of Pierre Chaunu and his team on death
in Paris. Furthermore, my own work only followed the descending
curve of the baroque funerary system, from around 1680, whereas
the Paris project has gone much further and shown how it was

established in the second half of the sixteenth century and continued into the middle of the eighteenth. The idea of structure, as it is used by social historians and historians of mentalities, loses all sense of rigidity and monolithism. It expresses a grouping of characteristics, of course, which form a coherent system, but it does so in the context of an equilibrium which is constantly being reappraised and of a system which is truly historical.

I hope I will not seem conceited if I take another example from my own work to illustrate the dialectical procedure which can unite the long and short time-frames. Yet it was, on the whole, just such a question which led to my study of the metamorphoses of the featival in Provence from 1780 to 1820. More precisely, it was an attempt to understand the connection between an established festive system which was popular, widespread, vibrant and 'folkloric' *avant la lettre*, and the revolutionary festival, which was national and civic and required a very different process of decoding. Was there cross-fertilization, coexistence or mutual rejection between these two systems? The balance sheet is varied. The revolutionary festival provided an opportunity, especially at a local level, for the expression of an ancient and repressed festive heritage – the festive carnival which dominated the great masquerades of the Year II. My conclusions were not at all opposed to those of Mona Ozouf in her book *The Revolutionary Festival*. The revolutionary liturgies were a cross-roads of past and future which saw the emergence of, and experiments with, a new form of the sacred which was to dominate the structures of civic and patriotic religiosity in the nineteenth century. At this point in the discussion, we cannot avoid the objection which Braudel foresaw in his pioneering article. Given that rapid change and explosive events do occur, are they really creative? Do they not simply sanction and highlight the results of a muffled process of change in the *longue durée*? Mona Ozouf's book may, on a very specific subject, provide an answer to the question. Is there a phenomenon more incongruous than the revolutionary festival – 'which has neither past nor future', like the Supreme Being in the revolutionary hymn? Nevertheless, we can see that it was the all-important vehicle which carried a whole ideological discourse into the future. Apart from the idea of the event as a catalyst or a mere echo, is there a creativity born out of the heat of the moment? I recall in this context the debate (which was more than just academic) between myself and Albert Soboul when I presented the first results of my approach to dechrist-ianization in the *longue durée* of the eighteenth century. The Jacobin historian countered with examples of the spontaneous creativity of revolutionary religiosity – patriot saints, martyrs for liberty, heartfelt litanies – all of which were occurrences which, even though they had no successors, were more than just momentary curiosities. Which of us was right? Neither, certainly, was wrong.

To conclude, however, on this essential dialectic of the long and the short time-frame, I hope I will be permitted, before closing the door on my own researches, to recall an old acquaintance: the history of death. Death is a good test for the history of the *longue durée* since we can say, without too much black humour, that it is an ideal constant. I think I touched on an essential aspect of the problem when I became (amicably) irritated at finding those long smooth stretches of change happening without incident in the pages of Philippe Ariès's work. Just as the sense of the macabre in the late Middle Ages was ruled out, so too was the baroque preoccupation with death between 1580 and 1630 and also the return of morbid ideas and the poetry of the tomb at the twilight of the Enlightenment. As for the tragic turning point of what is known as the *belle époque*, Ariès once wrote that its sense of the macabre was only a curiosity found in the work of a few Belgian and German artists. To call it a mere curiosity seems strange when speaking of the age of the Symbolists and Decadents, of Huysmans, Munch, Ibsen, d'Annunzio or Thomas Mann! For my part, I am struck by the importance of these great crises of collective sensibility – which are not merely literary curiosities and which, in fact, show the turbulent, convulsive rhythms of the various stages of a history of sensibilities which is not at all immobile. Death is just one example; one part of a larger whole. In a recent essay, 'The prerevolutionary sensibility', I posed the apparently naive question, what happened around 1750? This is an old question, to which classical literary history long ago gave its own answer, but it has been recently revived from the perspectives of serial history, based on a heartening variety of statistics dealing with illegitimacy, prenuptial conception, delinquency, trends in bookselling, demand for masses and ordinations to the priesthood. All of these indicators suggest that people's views of the world changed in France in the 1750s, and not just in the case of the elite. A rhythm can be detected here which has peaks and troughs of crises, in the widest sense of the term, which were not at all the result of a contemporary acceleration of history, no more than they are the superficial froth of a history which is for the most part immobile. I think we need to redefine the dialectic of the long and short time-frame. This is an exercise which is already familiar to the economic or demographic historian, but it is one which the student of social history and the history of mentalities has to face up to. Is the current impasse – no doubt temporary – not a result of the difficulties involved in finding a concordance of times between the various fields of research?

At the heart of the problem: the concordance of times

In reality, I believe that the problem of the dialectic of the long and short time-frame will soon seem a thing of the past, and will be historically dated. It will seem as dated as a certain kind of Jacobin voluntarism and certainly as dated as the current revisionism which has tried to banish the 'antiquated' image of the Revolution (Furet's 'ideological legacy'). The solution will not be found in a bourgeois compromise but in a dialectical progression. For all that, if this dialogue might shortly appear to have been a stylistic exercise, it must be agreed, on the basis of the examples we have looked at, that it has been stimulating, allowing us to raise a whole new series of questions.

It will be much more difficult, I think, to reach agreement on what I have somewhat simplistically called the 'concordance' of times or, if you will, what Althusser called the 'interlacing of times'.

Like Pierre Vilar, I am drawn towards a comment of Althusser's, which is relevant to the theoretical limitations of 'empirical' historians: 'Historians have begun to ask questions, but they are satisfied with stating that there are long, medium and short time-frames, and with seeing interventions as products of the interaction of these times rather than as products of the totality which governs them – the mode of production.'

The historians' caution, which is certainly blameworthy, especially on the part of those who claim to be inspired by Marxism, is perhaps a product of the fact that the current explosion, in all directions, of the historical sciences ('from the cellar to the loft') has often resulted in their being locked in the prison (in the *longue durée*!) of what has been branded as vulgar Marxism, where a mechanical dialectic links ideological superstructures with infrastructures in the most simplistic way. Such an approach, which is easily refuted as new areas of research reveal the greater complexity of historical time, was made possible, perhaps, by Marxist historians' reluctance, up to very recently, to apply a historical approach to that 'third level' of explanation which had previously been reserved for other, more 'informed' specialists. At this stage of historiographical change we can appreciate the foresight of Labrousse's call to historians in 1965 to take up the study of the third level, which we have come to call the 'history of mentalities'. At this level, Paul Bois's thesis (*The Peasants of the West*) is the first, and so far the only study to undertake a total investigation of socioeconomic structures in relation to collective attitudes and their dialectic in time. Labrousse's definition of this relationship as a 'history of resistances' or of 'inertia' can nowadays seem a somewhat impoverished view of interactions which take place in the context of what might be called, following Althusser, the 'determining totality' of the mode of production.

But here, Pierre Vilar reminded us how Marx (who is much less dogmatic than his interpreters make him) showed historians what their responsibilities were by defining the mode of production (in what is not, he admits, stylistically the 'best Marx') as 'the general lighting, the specific ether which determines the specific weight of all forms of existence to which it gives rise'. This clearly leaves a certain latitude within the 'determining totality', while at the same time imposing a real duty of precision and invention in the recognition of the complex links which hierarchically unite the various levels.

If historiography rejects the worksheet prescribed by the Marxist method, there are other promptings available. These no longer involve the search for the universal panacea of one or other determining historical thread, whether it lie in Peruvian mines or the sunspots, but are to be found in the facility of a longer time-frame, registered in an immobile history, or an ethnography which is less and less historical, becoming the repository of a multiplicity or specificity of times in which every history proceeds at its own pace. This temptation is heady, but it is a ship of fools. Philippe Ariès makes the development of attitudes towards death move along on a cushion of air as a function of the specific dynamic of the 'collective unconscious' which is not otherwise defined . . . .

Nobody need fear that I want to replace the ship of fools with a 'great contraction', locking current expansion within a narrow framework. This is why I think Pierre Chaunu (if I may be forgiven for citing him in such a paradoxical way), in putting forward his hypothesis of the evolution of attitudes towards death in the *longue durée* as 'a product of life expectancy', reduces a very complex phenomenon, involving both inertia and fantastic creativity, to dimensions which are too strictly demographic. My solution when confronted with this proliferation of historical times, of the serial studies in the *longue durée* which now confront us, is to correlate them, contrast them, range them in hierarchies. In this way, the *longue durée* need not be a lure, nor a hiding place, nor an abdication, but very much a means for affirming a better understanding of historical time.

For the rest, there are few causes for pessimism. As we said before, since Braudel's article appeared the structuralist invasion has come and gone and history is very much alive. Moreover, the fear of dependence on the other human sciences reflected in Braudel's article has given way to real confidence. The consciousness of the *longue durée* as an idea which has yet to be fully mastered, but which we have tried to analyse in its various ambiguous forms, is not at all unrelated to this recovery of confidence by the historical sciences in all their specificity.

Notes

1 'The *longue durée*', English translation in F. Braudel, *On History* (Chicago, 1980), pp. 25–62.
2 See his 'Huizinga and the theme of the macabre' and, following this, *The Hour of Our Death*.

8

History of Mentalities, History of Resistances, or the Prisons of the *Longue Durée*

The conference held at Aix in 1980, at which this paper was delivered, took place under the twin shadows of Ernest Labrousse and Fernand Braudel, from whom the components of the title of the paper have been borrowed. But these two prophetic formulas were applied to a very current preoccupation. I was trying to tackle the question, which I posed to the conference in this opening address, of the role of change in the context of resistance or inertia.

The Centre Méridional d'Histoire Sociale, des Mentalités et des Cultures decided, in 1978, to deal with the subject of 'cultural intermediaries', meaning those people in the no man's land between two cultures by whom change is effected and by whom, sometimes, scandals are provoked. In formulating the question, we wanted to get away from the now sterile dialogue which confronts popular and elite culture, moving away from a war of position which polarizes them in order to reintroduce the notion of interaction and dynamics.

In raising, today, the question of the history of mentalities as a 'history of resistances', it might seem that we are returning to just such a war of position. But this is not really the case. In the title of this paper, which at first sight might seem esoteric, I am actually asking what constitutes resistance in the history of mentalities, what are the forces which act as a brake – sometimes called the 'force of inertia' of mental structures, a term which, I feel, runs the risk of offering no more than a verbal explanation. In looking at the how and why of resistances we are, of course, posing one of the essential questions for the definition of the methods and perspectives of what has come to be called 'the new history' of mentalities.

The emergence of an idea

The idea is not totally new and, if we wish to date it precisely, then we can say that the history of mentalities is at least partly bound up in the history of resistances, as it emerged in the heroic era of the new history in the late 1950s and early 1960s. Fernand Braudel, in his famous article on the *longue durée* in 1958, first defined the history of mentalities as the important locus of slow change and inertias, describing mentalities as 'prisons of the *longue durée*'. But, not long afterwards, Ernest Labrousse concluded the 1964 social history conference held at the École Normale Superieure at Saint-Cloud by calling for more studies in the history of mentalities, which he explicitly defined as the 'history of resistances'. These two professions of faith were made in a historical context where new, often stimulating, research was beginning to discover, or rediscover, the idea in the course of research. It was around then that we read with fascination Eric Hobsbawm's work on *Primitive Rebels* in modern Europe. These people in revolt, if not revolutionaries, were nevertheless characterized by being opposed to, or at least on the margins of what has come to be called 'the march of history'. Therefore, in the historical conjuncture to which we are referring, one can see the emergence of a new idea of historical time, different from that inherited from the Enlightenment, which was characterized by progress and an indefinitely forward-moving trend, and also different from what is now fashionable to call 'vulgar Marxism'.

This discovery, which led to the formulation of a certain number of theories, such as 'the force of inertia of mental structures', coincided with the emergence of a number of new procedures or ways forward. In Ernest Labrousse's case, this came out of the study of movements in modern society, particularly the labour movement, and led to an interest in the history of the forces which acted as a brake on those movements – the history of the obstacles which they came up against. In Fernand Braudel's case, on the other hand, the discovery was rooted in a consciousness of geographical conditioning, legacies of the *longue durée*, and was enriched by interdisciplinary contact with ethnography and sociology, of which his article on the *longue durée* was an ambiguous reflection.

These discourses were somewhat abstract, even though they were the product of specific reflections. Beyond them, a certain number of monographs and specific studies, which proliferated in their wake, demonstrated the potential of the themes which confronted scholars. I think it is significant that it was in this period that we began to see studies appear on the Counter-Revolution, which developed out of research on the French Revolution. In this period, Paul Bois, in his thesis on the peasants of the West, formulated the problem of discovering not just why change occurred but also why there was resistance to change, based on his identification of an enduring political frontier in the *bocage* landscape of the Sarthe region of rural France. In this period, too, we saw the emergence of studies of the Vendée in Tilly's work. Throughout these works, despite differences of approach, the common idea emerged that, in order to understand change, we need to take an essential detour and begin by understanding those things which do not change.

In parallel with this trend in social history, a similar problematic arose in other areas of history and sociology. I am thinking, without trying to multiply examples, of the field of religious sociology, in the tradition of Gabriel Le Bras, which went beyond the perspective of pastoral voluntarism to produce some new assertions. The results, as presented and formulated by historians like Perouas in his thesis on the diocese of La Rochelle in the seventeenth century, or of sociologists like Canon Boulard, showed the importance of the legacies of the *longue durée* and of inertia which at first sight were incomprehensible. Analysing the results obtained by these scholars, Pierre Chaunu asked about the reasons for the existence of such deep-rooted frontiers, and was tempted at this stage of research to ask if there were traditions which were as permanent as geological formations if, to use his expression, 'the cold plainsman' and 'the fiery *bocain*' were tangible personas, not just in terms of religious history but also in the history of collective temperaments. Canon Boulard, whose works are still extremely suggestive in this area, as in his reflections on the notion of 'cultural regions', developed this very line of inquiry.

From these specific questions, formulated on the basis of particular historical work between 1960 and 1965, the subsequent development of the methods and problems of the history of mentalities has reinforced the importance of this line of questioning. In moving gradually from the history of elites to the history of the common people, and in passing from the history of ideas and the history of cultures to a history of collective attitudes, historians of mentalities have inevitably found themselves going from a history of movement and change to a history of inertias. In some cases, particular emphasis has been placed on this notion of inertia or tradition as factors in a history conceived as a continuation of older gestures. In their book on the French Revolution published in this period, François Furet and

Denis Richet did not hesitate to present the popular movement of mass attitudes as a practically unchanged repetition of backward-looking impulses which, if they did not go back into the mists of time, were at least repeated almost without change from the revolts of the League and the Fronde.

The very notion of an 'outburst of anger', which was the phrase used by Roland Mousnier to describe popular upheavals in the period prior to the Industrial Revolution, is evidence of a perspective in which history is seen as a continuum. On the whole, we can say that Emmanuel Le Roy Ladurie's picture of popular revolts or upheavals in Languedoc fits in with this general interpretation. At the root of this, we can see a conscious or unconscious challenge to the idea of 'revolution', the relevance of which was then being disputed by a whole section of French and international historiography.

At the same time as the study of the history of mentalities was coming into being, the triumph of the *longue durée* gave rise to an impression of slow change, even immobility, and this impression was accentuated by contact with (and contamination by) the time-frames of other human sciences like anthropology, to the extent that the history of mentalities established itself with particular vitality, not just in the contemporary historiography of the eighteenth and nineteenth centuries, but also in those parts of modern history where traditional attitudes and behaviour were still prevalent. One can see why Robert Mandrou could define the sense of time in the history of mentalities as a 'longer time-frame', finding common ground with Braudel and many others on this level.

Having thus situated this idea in a definite historical context, it is our task, having access to more information, to inquire into its relevance and significance. To do this, it may be best to begin, very simply, with some observations.

Some observations

I hope I may be permitted, in opening the debate, to present a series of maps which will help us to see the phenomenon of inertia or resistance *in situ*, at its geographical roots. The maps which we can call on today are the product of time-consuming, persistent and sometimes relatively recent historical research, and, at first sight, they are excitingly varied. The first map (p. 158) was the work of Canon Boulard and it illustrates zones of religious practice in twentieth-century France. This map is historically dated, being based on direct

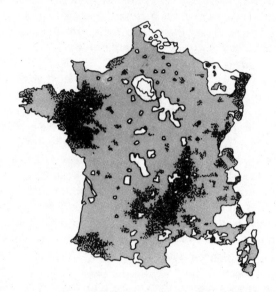

Easter religious observance in rural France in the twentieth
century (from the work of F. Boulard)

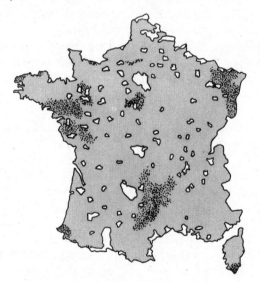

The right-wing vote in the 1962 elections
(maps taken from J. Dupleix, *Atlas of Rural France* (Paris, 1968))

'Conservatories' of religious loyalties and conservatism in politics.

or indirect research in religious sociology carried out in the 1950s. Now that the practice of recording attendance at Mass has been discontinued, such research would probably be impossible. The results provide a monumental record of French religious practice at a moment in time in the middle of the twentieth century which has not yet ceased to pose a whole series of questions about the realities of 'collective temperament' in the *longue durée*, which it also reflects. Boulard, who dealt with both the rural and urban world in his work on cultural environments, demonstrated the existence of a process of imitation between urban and rural societies. The map reveals very strong structural patterns, identifying zones of strong religious practice in western and north-eastern France and in the south-eastern part of the Massif Central, as a counterpoint to areas of dechristianization. This poses some very direct questions, all the more so because it is not without equivalents in other areas. It has been noticed – and it is now naive, although perhaps useful, to recall it – that this map has a great deal in common with maps of electoral sociology based on electoral statistics from the end of the nineteenth century to the present (maps pp. 158, 160). The same distribution of conservative areas and of regions which show support for change is found in these maps. Such similarities, or sympathies, lead us to ask just how far back we have to go to find the causes of this partition of the French countryside, and some recent studies do seem to testify to the great antiquity of this chequered landscape. To cite just a few examples, I can point to the map I myself presented in my work on the dechristianization of Year II of the First Republic (1793–4), showing the successes and failures of revolutionary toponymy in changing place names during the French Revolution (map p. 160). The extraordinary cohesion of the map is striking, showing the contrast between areas where the Revolution was accepted and implemented, where changes were multiple and significant, and areas where there were very few such changes, indicating a collective rejection of the Revolution. These geographical divisions, when compared with the two maps of religious practice and electoral sociology, show sufficient similarities to raise a fundamental question. The areas which opposed the Revolution – the west, the north-east and the south-eastern part of the Massif Central – stand out in striking contrast to the horseshoe of rural Jacobinism and also of early dechristianization which surrounds the Massif Central and its borders, from Morvan to the Nivernais, from Berry to the Limousin, reaching down into south-western Aquitaine and even extending into parts of Languedoc and Provence. Equivalents can be found for this map of revolutionary

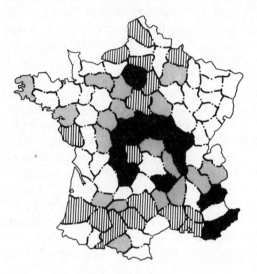

Revolutionary toponymy in the Year II (darker shading represents
the successes of this process)

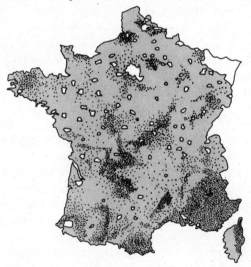

The left-wing vote in the 1962 elections
(maps taken from J. Dupleix, *Atlas of Rural France* (Paris, 1968))

A changing France . . . or another system of loyalties? The
continuity between rural Jacobinism and the left-wing vote in the
twentieth century.

toponymy, in a very global and general, but suggestive way, in other areas of the expression of collective mentalities in the *ancien régime*. I am thinking, in particular, of Brancolini and Bouissy's map of the diffusion of semi-popular reprints of books, based on the statistics of provincial book production in the eighteenth century. The contrasting maps of profane and devotional literature also anticipate those showing twentieth-century religious practice and political allegiance.

We should not expect to see these macroscopic approaches, which reflect global realities, precisely reflected in a mechanical way in microscopic studies of districts or cantons. They reflect the global sum of attitudes, and from them it is useful to pass on to the idea of the frontier. Paul Bois's thesis formulated the problem of frontiers of collective temperaments in his analysis of the limits dividing republican attitudes from areas of *Chouannerie* and conservative loyalists in the rural department of La Sarthe in western France. Such frontiers are not just political. One can think of other tests and other approaches in this context, and in particular of the idea of 'sociability' proposed by Maurice Agulhon in his work on eastern Provence.

In developing the problematic proposed by Agulhon, I asked what the limits of such southern sociability might be, and I tried to explain it in terms of a number of indicators, such as maps showing the distribution of popular societies and clubs during the French Revolution, or the distribution of masonic lodges at the end of the eighteenth century. This kind of research provides us with a series of representations *in situ* showing the roots, the continuity or, even more simply, the reality of collective temperaments.

It is useful, however, to compare this first system or first set of maps with another set which, apparently, show other realities, and where the collective landscape is quite different, no doubt as a function of other determinants. In this context one thinks (to avoid too many examples) of the literacy maps derived from the application of modern techniques to the work of Maggiolo, which have shown a massive contrast between two Frances: the 'educated' France, covering the north-eastern part of the country, bounded by a line stretching from Mont-St-Michel to Geneva, on the one hand, and the other, 'ignorant' France, covering the south and west of the country. There is possibly another dual France, if we are to believe the complex arguments of a recent study which purports to show that south-eastern France, from the Alps to Provence, has been undergoing a process of recovery since the end of the eighteenth century, while the Atlantic seaboard to the west has been caught in a spiral of continuous decline. We can also add to this game of comparisons the

maps which Emmanuel Le Roy Ladurie has given us in his monograph on the French conscript in the nineteenth century. The list does
not stop here if we add, for example, the maps of family structures
which have been prepared by American scholars at Ann Arbor, which
show the marked contrast between the France of nuclear families and
the France of extended families in the middle of the nineteenth
century. Whether we look at the stem families of south-eastern France
or at the big families of some of the mountain regions of central
France, we discover a landscape which sometimes also reflects the
boundaries of religious sociology and of political beliefs in a system of
harmonies which raises profound questions.

At first glance we come away with an impression of perplexity from
trying to superimpose these various elements and make comparisons
between them. Perplexity shows through in Canon Boulard's work
when he asks why someone born at Angers should have three or four
times more likelihood of going to Mass than someone born in
Marseille. A very similar perplexity was expressed in different terms
by Peter Laslett in the course of his study of the geographical patterns
of illegitimacy in the *longue durée* in England from the sixteenth
century to the present day, when he revealed the obstinate reality of
certain regions – certain villages even – which remain persistently
deviant or heterodox. From this initial impression of perplexity we
can pass on to the formulation of a question. Can we suggest
explanations for these facts? Explanations are certainly not lacking at
first sight, but they confront us with different, often contradictory,
systems.

The first explanatory series reverts to social or socioeconomic
determinism as the ultimate justification for the patterns visible in the
landscape as a whole. This deterministic element, which is of course
essential, is given pride of place by many scholars. Many, however,
have found that there is no purely mechanical linkage. Collective
attitudes, as they are found *in situ*, do not automatically follow on
from socioeconomic forces in a large number of cases. Other scholars
are hardly less blunt in their search for a material determinant. I am
thinking of the kind of explanations, which have had their heyday,
which explained religious temperament as a function of the geological
divisions of the landscape between igneous and sedimentary formations, a theory based on an impoverished, even magical determinism,
even if such a frontier, as in Maine-et-Loire or every other region of
western France, evidently exists. Geographical determinism does
exist, and we do not mean to underestimate it. If the argument did not
concern the duality of limestone and granite, it would invoke the

dualism of the plains and the mountains, the importance of communications and so on.

Anyone who has worked on the characteristics of either stability or
change in collective attitudes cannot fail to have been struck by the
importance of conservative groups – generally communities which
are isolated in terms of the possibilities of contact or communication.
Thus, in studying religious practice in the eighteenth century on the
basis of wills, I was able to stress the importance of such sanctuaries
or 'museums' of baroque practices and gestures in the Alpine valleys
of Ubaye in La Vallouise and in other areas. But we also know that
this simple contrast between open regions in the plains and closed
regions in the mountains is not absolute. In my book on dechristianization in the Year II, the maps clearly show that there are radical
and Jacobin mountain regions, just as there are lowlands which are
profoundly resistant to change. Here again, if we can apply geographical determinism to explain the data, we cannot thereby discover the ultimate key to the problem. One might also propose taking
account of intellectual determinism or fatalisms which reflect a rooted
temperament. The notion of a 'cultural region', as used by Canon
Boulard, comes under this heading. One is aware from the outset,
moreover, that such explanations, which are essential in that they
reflect indisputable results, can also contain elements of the magical
or the mystical, or simply of the purely verbal. All in all, they explain
nothing; certainly hardly more than the idea of the 'force of inertia of
mental structures' to which we have already alluded.

To rise above these contradictions, scholars have been led to
suggest other factors, which stress the role of history, the weight of
tradition in history. I am thinking in particular of the notion of what
can, simplistically, be termed 'historical traumatism', which is registered at a given moment in the collective mentalities of a region, and
is subsequently perpetuated well beyond any clear awareness of it
which people may preserve. This notion has been brilliantly and
clearly illustrated in Paul Bois's thesis on the peasants of the west,
when he diametrically reversed the stereotypes which had been
accepted since the appearance of Siegfried's work. Bois showed that
the sociological determinism which was poorly registered both in the
short-term perspective of the sociologists and in the intemporality of
long-standing tradition, based on the double presence of the aristocracy ('the master') and the Church (through the influence of the
parish priest), explained none of the realities of the frontiers of
political beliefs which are to be found in the landscape. By the same
token, he showed the necessity of proceeding by a regressive

approach, to the historical moment when the split took place – in this case during the French Revolution – when an antagonism which was both deeply felt and differently formulated in the various regions, was inscribed in the collective memory, at the same time as the social structures generated by prior developments tended to solidify these contrasts.

The method which Bois used in *The Peasants of the West* can be applied to other frames of reference and to other constitutive or original events. One thinks in this respect of the importance of the confessional and religious split in explaining collective temperaments in the South of France, and especially in Languedoc. This kind of explanation seems, on reflection, to be a kind of compromise between a mechanistic explanation based on socioeconomic conditions to the extent that they impose their weight at a given moment, and what I would call an idealistic explanation which registers the survival of collective representations in the *longue durée* beyond the immediate conditions which give rise to the emergence of such attitudes. Such a procedure raises its own questions. How far does collective memory extend? To take one example, how long will the reality of the Red South, which came into being around 1848 in a remarkable inversion of the political patterns of the first half of the nineteenth century, survive the erosion evident in maps of recent electoral sociology, which is the fruit of contemporary socioeconomic change? This process is mirrored in the desertion of the countryside by the migration of the traditional peasantry and the repopulation of the villages by a very different pattern of migration. To take one example, Lawrence Wylie, whose monographs on Roussillon portrayed the typical southern French village, now finds himself confronted with a very different kind of settlement, where the hotelier has become the mayor and where the inhabitants are people from northern France or the Benelux countries with second homes in the area. How long will memory, as expressed in collective options, survive the erosion of history?

Geography has offered us a series of explicit approaches to the study of attitudes but these have tended to become over-generalized, because of a globalizing approach to phenomena which are much more diverse in detail. By the same token, the macroscopic geographical approach can lead to stimulating, but often mystifying, suggestions. We need to go further and consider the reality of social groupings behind the contrasts inscribed in the landscape itself. Here too we can find groups which offer resistance to change, and we might usefully establish a transition from isolated geographical communities to isolated social communities. This can be seen in urban districts which contain homogenous and 'resistant' groupings, whether based on ethnicity, professional status or simply endogamy. To avoid multiplying examples, and drawing on my own research, I can cite, in this context, the position of Italians in eighteenth-century Marseille, already a great cosmopolitan city in this period. This community, composed partly of Piedmontese and partly of Ligurians originating in Genoa or its hinterland, formed a structural unit which was closed in its traditions and collective attitudes. Likewise, in the same city, we can also point to the porters in the eighteenth century, thousands of people united by the structures of an organized trade which guarded its traditions, and in which a firm social cohesion was maintained by endogamy and by the quasi-hereditary transmission of work. The porters also maintained their traditions by processes of conservation, even though they could become the agents of violent change, as during the Revolution. Yet the Restoration image of the porter as a reactionary or legitimist is very suggestive of the profile of the group as a whole. To continue with this perspective, it would seem that the prime example of a social grouping, in the widest sense of the term, functioning as a refuge for resistance to change can be found in the rural world. The image is certainly mythical, since it springs from too wide a combination of multiple social realities. Yet this accepted image of the peasantry, which possibly stems from the experience of 1848 and of the peasant vote, when the peasantry was seen as a conservative group, is doubtless the prototype of the collective image of the peasantry as the embodiment and the guardian of traditional civilization.

At the other end of the social ladder, it is tempting to discuss the conservatism of the higher groupings, the aristocrats rather than the 'elites', the term used in social history to distinguish mobile elites, open to change, from conservative aristocracies – doubtless express- ive of a strongly felt contrast. It is true that it was in aristocratic circles, from the classical period to the present, that a whole range of traditions, gestures and defensive attitudes was maintained. Furth- ermore, the very notion of aristocracy needs to be relativized, since it does not only apply to the caste of the nobility. In the world of the peasantry, too, it was what we call the 'peasant aristocracy', the great *laboureurs* of northern France, and the stewards of the south, which best maintained its traditions and its resistance to change.

Starting from this second series of observations, extending those derived from geographical studies, we can pass on to a second series of explanatory hypotheses. Here, too, there is no shortage of ideas and suggestions. We can say that conservative groups explain themselves by reference to what can be called the dynamic or direction of history. These are groups which are losing ground, adopting defensive positions in the face of developments which pass them by as they become traditionalists. This assimilation or extrapolation, however simplistic and caricatural it may seem, does not lack confirmation or examples. The aristocratic nobility provides more than one, as does the peasantry, if we are to believe a number of authors. François Furet, for example, describes the peasantry of the French Revolutionary period as being very loyal to its own concepts, but even more loyal to its gestures, attitudes and backward-looking forms of sensibility. More precisely, it is not difficult, when analysing a concrete environment, whether urban or rural, to see in the traditionalism of certain groups the symptoms of a decline affecting their structures and vitality. The porters of Marseille, mentioned above, became all the more intransigent in their traditionalism when, in the course of the nineteenth century, they found themselves faced with competition from the reserve army of dockers, the *robeyrols* as they were called in southern dialect, who had existed from the seventeenth century to the first half of the nineteenth century as a proletariat of unskilled workers which rivalled the labour aristocracy of the porters and eventually triumphed over them after 1860. This was a bitter triumph, of course, since, materially, it meant the increased exploitation of a labour force of unskilled manual workers. Yet we can understand the totality of defensive attitudes and modes of behaviour in which the organized porters took refuge when faced with competition from this reserve army of unskilled labour.

In the same geographical area, it is not difficult, either, to point to the example of the local master-fishermen, governed by their own tribunals, who ranged their own strong cohesiveness and their institutional, social, religious and even familial traditions against competition from newcomers such as the Catalan immigrants, the squatters of the labour market. This explanation in terms of social dynamics is certainly very convincing. But there is another explanatory system which does not run counter to it and which complements it, based on socio-demographic analysis. The endogamy of groupings which are closed in on themselves, dependent on one system of production, can be contrasted with the mobility and exogamy of the newcomers. Such mobility and exogamy is met with at both ends of the social ladder, at the most vulnerable level of urban wage labour and at the level of merchants, wholesalers or members of the liberal professions and people involved in tertiary activities like bureaucrats and others who were the most open and flexible groups in the eighteenth-century city, even more so in the nineteenth and twentieth centuries.

I hope I will be permitted to take another example, in this context, from the South of France. In current demographic and sociological studies of Provençal communities, the groups which show the greatest tendency to marry outside their own circle are the agricultural labourers, on the one hand, and the artisans and retailers on the other. By contrast, the rocks of stability, which were to become the guardians of tradition in the age of Mistral, are to be found among the stewards and the traditional 'bourgeoisie' of this society of urbanized villages.

The contrast between mobility and exogamy on the one hand and endogamy on the other is also quite convincing as an explanatory model. But it does not exclude another system of explanatory factors which essentially derive from cultural realities. There are powerful elements of resistance to change and to what is called acculturation in cultural or ideological traditions. Popular religion, 'magic' as it is sometimes rather simplistically called, persisted despite the offensives of the Counter-Reformation and the acculturation of the nineteenth century, right up to the death throes of the folkloric system which accompanied the demise of the traditional society. Even conventional religion, as opposed to popular religion, has been seen, on the basis of some strong assumptions, as an element favourable to traditionalism and continuity. The 'sanctuaries' of western France, for example, or of certain mountain regions, are at once centres of very strong religious practice and persistence, and also centres of traditionalism. I might be accused of being deliberately paradoxical if I take as another example – which is apparently more contrived – the link between illiteracy and a certain tradition of rural Jacobinism, which current historical maps indicate exists in central France from Morvan to the Limousin. In this region, a delay in the acculturation process accompanying the spread of literacy was generally accompanied by a tradition of rural Jacobinism which, in its own way, might be an expression of the defensive attitudes of a vulnerable peasantry.

Taking all these references into account, we can see how and for what reasons historians of mentalities and demography now attribute so much importance to the family. Canon Boulard, in his work on cultural regions, saw the family as the vital centre for the direct transmission of belief, and as the crucible in which historical continuities involving religion were shaped – or, indeed, in which traditions of rejection were perpetuated. Boulard's observation in the religious field is corroborated in other spheres, as in the areas of sexuality, marital customs and collective behaviour. Thus Laslett, in his studies of illegitimacy in England from the pre-industrial period to the present, stresses not just continuity in localities which seem predisposed to certain types of attitudes, but also the importance of direct familial continuities. One has little difficulty in appreciating the importance of the family, both as a vital centre of acculturation and also as an area of resistance to compulsory acculturations. We are tempted to extrapolate from what we know from the study of the family to other similar ideas which have recently been taken up by the history of mentalities. I am thinking in particular of the idea of the sociability which has recently been so happily rediscovered by Maurice Agulhon. Is sociability, as we find it in the South of France and elsewhere, part of change or continuity? Studies carried out in Provence and elsewhere show the ambiguity of the idea in terms of our current problematic. Sociability can at one and the same time represent an ideal non-variable and a formal buttress of realities which have undergone profound change over time. In the transition from confraternities of penitents to freemasonry and thence to the social democrats of 1848, based on the framework of the Republican clubs, sociability offers both a structure of collective resistance and, at the same time, an element which is capable of absorbing new ideas and of providing a means for their diffusion.

Having established the persistence of formal structures like sociability through successive manifestations in the pluri-secular time-frame of the *longue durée*, we are further tempted to take another step up the ladder of this type of study and ask whether the study of these resistances of collective mentality does not ultimately lead us to a recognition of the 'invariables', the constants which history has long refused to adopt from structuralist anthropology.

At the end of the search for resistance, the historian comes up against a system which, some say, does not change and will never change: the buffers of the *longue durée*, the constants of human history. Fernand Braudel, in his famous article on the *longue durée*, discussed, with a certain amount of humour, what he called 'mythemes' and 'gustemes', cultural realities which are present throughout human history. This might have seemed like a stylistic sally in Braudel's writing, but was, in fact, the product of interdisciplinary contacts which made him aware of the value of structuralist anthropology; it has become increasingly important in the current preoccupations of the new history of mentalities. Nowadays, we can see that historians are no longer hostile or inattentive to the persistent memories and fragmentary ideologies which they encounter in a discipline which has come to have more and more in common with historical ethnography. Historians have a right to ask how they are to cope with such characteristics when they come across them, not just in the work of folklorists, but in the historically rooted documents with which they are concerned. To take just a few examples, when historians come across a detail, in the ordinary course of research, or in the work of a folklorist like Van Gennep, such as the ritual knocking on the church door which takes place during funeral processions in a whole series of Breton communes, with some variations from one place to another, but reproduced without change right up to the present, they can justifiably ask what these details signify. Are they insignificant? And if not, how should they be interpreted?

Another example, among the myriad possibilities, occurs when the traveller to an English town in early November runs into crowds of children wheeling around the grotesque figure of the guy. We are struck both by the persistence of a memory over several centuries and can, at the same time, justifiably ask what the image of the guy means to these children who take up the game in order to earn a few pennies. How many of them, whether they be English or Jamaican, could explain that the guy is a reminder of the Gunpowder Plot, of the Popish menace, and is a debased form of an old historical memory? Yet this is just the first level of interpretation of a historical phenomenon which needs to be situated in an even wider context. Historians of mentalities are nowadays tempted to compare the grotesque and comic dummy of the guy with the Halloween celebrations taking place around the same time in Scotland or in English-speaking North America. Guys in English cities, like the grotesque figures, masks and ghosts of Halloween, are all, to our eyes, clear examples of the image of 'dual death', the legacy of traditional popular religion, which was exorcised by the Reformation in Protestant countries as part of the attempt to abolish the Catholic belief in Purgatory. Yet the Reformation did not wholly succeed in taming or naturalizing the hostile spirits. In this way the guy represents the extremely long memory of a tradition which goes back far beyond the Gunpowder Plot. But, of course, it would be pointless nowadays to ask the majority of English and American adults, much less the children at street corners, to understand such distant references, which require a profound process of decoding.

We need to inquire into the meaning and significance of these fragmentary ideologies. This is to be found, of course, in collective attitudes and behaviour, in the shaping of resistances with which I am concerned in this paper, the weight of memories which lie heavily, even though unconsciously, on people. Thus, for example, we can see how the political frontiers of contemporary France reflect a past which is far from being embodied in the traditions which derive from it. How many people in western France are consciously aware of the heritage of revolutionary upheaval which still continues to shape their political habits? How many people from the Provençal Vendée, between Aix and Arles, who traditionally vote for the right or the far right, are aware of the historical conditions in which such divisions came into being during the French Revolution? These unconscious memories are certainly one of the most obscure and, at the same time, most deeply rooted of the facts we are trying to grasp. Collective mentality thus appears to be composed of unconscious layers of memory, unconscious but operative. To move to another field, it was at the level of what he called the 'collective unconscious' (a term which merits further discussion) that Philippe Ariès, among others, studied collective attitudes towards death, which he explained independent of any reference to a constructed, controlled, even objectified discourse, and yet a discourse which was no less essential for all that. We can even ask whether there are gestures which are quite devoid of meaning – as if any gesture can be meaningless for the historian. Yet by this I mean gestures whose meanings are so obscure that they are completely incomprehensible. One thinks of the Halloween celebrations mentioned above and of the carnival, the incongruous forms of whose heritage the anthropologist Claude Gaignebet has tried to decipher in the *longue durée*. Halloween or the carnival, which are nowadays reduced to derisory or infantilized celebrations are nevertheless a reflection, not just of the persistence of memory, but of an unconscious presence and a collective need.

At the end of this road, we are in danger of running into the theme of 'immobile history', which has recently emerged in Emmanuel Le Roy Ladurie's works, and of finding ourselves as the point at which historical and anthropological time merge, so as to incorporate ideas which run, unchanged, right through history: the 'invariables' which Lévi-Strauss illustrated in concepts such as the incest taboo. I believe we should not baulk at the challenge which structuralist anthropology is proposing to history but, instead, should try to apply a historical approach to these phenomena. This has been brilliantly done by Georges Duby in his recent work on the imaginary universe of feudalism, which deals with the tripartite division of feudal society both in its historical context and in its paradoxical durability. Indeed,

I feel that a whole series of studies which are currently dealing with the delicate problem of popular culture have to face up to this kind of reflection. Popular culture is doubtless the most complex, but also the strongest expression of resistance to change as a process of acculturation imposed by elites. Such a culture can only be defined by a corpus of beliefs which are buried and lie underground, but which are capable of re-emerging in unexpected forms. Many are now discovering that popular culture contains a system of representations, including the theme of the world turned upside down, inversion, laughter and derision, all of which constitute a series of defensive and subversive mechanisms fighting against the mutilating and mystifying forces of acculturation. From Bakhtine to Ginzburg and Natalie Zemon Davis, new historians are analysing the structures and processes of rejection which have obstinately persisted throughout history. Such interpretations can, as in Gaignebet's case, lead to interpretations where history is hard put to find a role. Yet they need not inspire our distrust. In all cases, they help us to try to analyse, or merely suggest, the mechanisms, forms and strategies of resistance to change.

To try to survey the specific difficulties of a subject of this kind is to try to go beyond accommodating but mystifying verbal explanations such as 'the force of inertia of mental structures'. The inertia is very real, but it derives from a hidden quality which we need to explain. In the search for an explanation, historians find themselves faced with a certain number of problems, and I shall attempt to describe some of them, without claiming to be exhaustive.

The first characteristic, or the first difficulty, doubtless involves coming to terms with mentalities which appear to be buried and stratified, the objects of a history in stages, as it were. This is as true of collective attitudes as of the individual sensibilities of each one of us. How can a person be Catholic and Polish? How can someone be Italian, Communist and a believer? Such objective contradictions exist, and not just in the very simple examples given here. Mentalities, at the level of collective attitudes rather than clear thought, present this image of seeming to overlap like the slates on a roof in ways which Philippe Ariès's work on death had brought to our attention. In commenting on the different kinds of attitudes whose development he studied in the *longue durée*, Ariès did well to insist on the coexistence of different forms of collective representation and on the overlapping of different sensibilities. It is doubtless such a characteristic which explains, in some measure, the viscosity evident in changes in mentalities which makes it one of the sectors most resistant to sudden change, even though the possibility ought not to be ruled out.

The second characteristic which seems worthy of note is the need to look for the explanation, or the secret, of resistances in sources which lead us away from the habitual expressions of the dominant culture or acculturation, which may be hegemonic at a given period. This is why in this area, as in many other areas of the history of mentalities, classical written sources cease to be predominant, and it is more necessary than ever to attempt the difficult task of investigating the silence of majorities which are . . . silent, by analysing their apparently insignificant gestures, the products of oral research and the unconscious evidence contained in iconography or in the objects of material civilization. Another way of cheating the deep silence of these resistances is, of course, to concentrate, as more and more scholars are doing, on the history of marginal groups, the history of rejection which is currently fashionable – and there are good fashions.

This is all very well for research into deep-rooted resistances – resistances 'at rest' so to speak – but it goes without saying that rejection can be expressed in an explosive way, and not just in the small change of various forms of marginalization, but in the vocabularies of revolt. At this level, we must look at the forms of protests, of revolts, and particularly those which go against the grain of history. In a word, we need to expand the study of the 'primitive rebels' who were brought to light by the ever valuable work of Eric Hobsbawm.

The result of such an inquiry might confront us with ideas which history has disparaged, such as concepts of 'temperament' or of 'collective personality'. These are hateful words, I agree, and to use a term which has been applied to dechristianization, are 'false clarities', ideas which are misleading by their haziness or vagueness. Yet, at the same time, anyone who neglects these realities runs the risk of allowing important facts to go unnoticed. I hope I will be forgiven for using some very contemporary examples in this context, since I find them very expressive. I believe, for example, that the French Left has underestimated the importance of regional factors for far too long, seeing in them only meaningless realities or futile memories, and that the current revival of these phenomena as key ideas capable of mobilizing opinion shows the importance of historic memories in that they are rooted in a definite socio-historical context. Not to stick within the limits of France, there is a great deal of very hard thinking to be done about the importance of a phenomenon like Islam, or of its revival in a certain number of contemporary liberation movements. The example of Iran in 1979 is the one which most immediately comes to mind. The best way, it seems to me, of getting rid of the fuzziness or vagueness of concepts of collective temperament is to analyse its component parts very precisely: the forms of its historical emergence and, eventually, of its revitalization. In this way, a history of resistances seems inevitably to change – by an unavoidable shift – into an inquiry into the history of movement and change.

The history of resistances leads back to the history of movement

In order to understand how the idea of 'movement' has been conceived, it may be useful to see it from a hereditary or historical perspective. This heritage might be seen as deriving from the Enlightenment, but it is also derived from the post-Tridentine Catholic reconquest; from absolutist centralism as much as from enlightened despotism. This perspective offers a triumphant process of acculturation as a counterpoint to a system of resistances successively defined in Manichean terms as superstition, fanaticism or lack of cultivation – the lack of cultivation which was thought to be characteristic of the rural masses and the popular urban groupings.

Along with a series of ideologies characterized by hegemonic pretensions, including those of the Counter-Reformation, the Enlightenment and the triumphant bourgeois ideology of the nineteenth century, there emerged a negative image of the resistances of collective mentalities and, conversely, an ideal stressing the continuous progress of the human spirit and the cultural maturation of the masses. We can find certain common characteristics in the successive forms of this outlook, including the idea of a progressive erosion of a very ancient system of myths, beliefs and magical practices, which was violently rejected only to be re-evaluated, at the end of the nineteenth century, as part of the rediscovery of folklore. This linear view of the struggles between resistance and the accepted idea of progress in each period, has given rise to a certain number of explanatory schemes which describe how ancient beliefs are eroded. Thus, some theorists, borrowing from sociology or anthropology, speak of processes of descending imitation, whereby collective representations which were once associated with the elite took refuge in lower social groups; I am thinking here of the forms of sociability in the South of France analysed by Maurice Agulhon. There are also discussions of the process of 'infantilization' of traditions, for which there is no shortage of examples from both folklore and history – such as the wandering Halloween ghosts of the English-speaking world.

The idea of movement is not, therefore, obsolete, and we can see that it corresponds to quite a number of interpretations which are currently accepted. It seems, moreover, that in the course of history a much more dialectical and dynamic picture is gradually being established. If the French Revolution saw itself as being an essential stage in the war against obstacles to progress, in its offensive against dialects and its struggles with the Church – characteristics which show it to have been a real cultural revolution – the history of the revolutionary period shows how the Revolution produced its own dialectical opposite in the Counter-Revolution. The history of this process shows how resistance could assume a form which was not merely latent, passive or underground, but a vehicle for real dynamism. All in all, the subsequent history of the nineteenth century showed the ambiguous character of the idea of resistance, which was often revalued in terms of the discovery or defence of tradition. Aristocratic traditionalists developed a body of doctrine in this period, and the development of nationalism in all its forms (of which the discovery of folklore was not the least important) caused a resurgence of an awareness of tradition as a positive thing. Such resistances to change thus appear to have an ambiguous meaning. They could be backward-looking, and therefore seen as dangerous, but they could also be revalued as a defence of a threatened heritage. We could also add, jumping to the present, that the current emergence of the concept of popular culture in contemporary historiography reflects the ambiguity of a very complex legacy and also says something about contemporary sensibilities.

For many of those who study it, popular culture is the image of a positive defence of an underground way of life which should no longer be treated with the contempt which it was afforded during the Enlightenment and the Counter-Reformation, when it was seen to deny any rights to an autonomous personality. This recognition of the existence of other systems which are not completely devoid of culture is one of the characteristics of the developments which concern us here and, in a way, it justifies our problematic. But such an investigation into the significance of change at the opposite extreme of the resistances of collective mentalities does not obviate the need for an investigation of the dialectic between the long and the short timeframe in the history of mentalities. This is a vast theme which requires separate treatment, but I shall deal with it here to the extent to which it directly concerns us. Are there, in these attitudes and forms of behaviour – in collective mentalities – possibilities for leaps forward, sudden change and even revolutions? The question has received a series of different answers and we can see how contemporary historians are beginning to move away from recent 'revisionist' attitudes, as in the work of Le Roy Ladurie and François Furet, which repudiated the very notion of sudden change in the history of mentalities. Current interpretations are rediscovering the idea of revolution as something more creative than imitative, which brutally gives birth to a new system of values. This is the theory of the transfer of sacrality which Mona Ozouf develops in her book on revolutionary festivals, and might also be the theory of the 'transfer of legitimacy' which was the keystone of François Furet's recent essay on the Revolution, *Thinking the French Revolution.*

This investigation is of direct interest to us to the extent that the dialectic of the short and long time-frame implicit in the possibility of a 'revolution of manners', as it was once called, leads to the possibility of a cultural revolution which could both modify the collective landscape of allegiance and reactivate forms of open resistance. In this way, we move into another fundamental problematic involving the question of the unity or plurality of historical time, especially in the history of mentalities. It is clear that the resistances of collective mentality express the discordance between the time-frame of the 'elites', the hegemonic social groups, and the time-frame of an important part of the mass of the people.

Between the different levels of consciousness or self-consciousness there is a latent period which is very real. I tried to study just such a discordance in my work on southern French wills in the baroque period. Brémond, in his famous *Literary History of Religious Feeling* spoke of the 'mystical invasion' which took place between 1620 and 1640, the period of great French religious figures such as Bérulle, Arnaud, Saint-Cyran and Vincent de Paul. I felt that I had grasped, not the mystical invasion, but what I called the 'devotional invasion' which was the small change of the former process, between 1650 or 1680 and 1720, the period in which the baroque system of practices and attitudes towards death reached its height in Provence. Fifty years of latency or inertia allow us negatively to measure the weight or force of resistance, based on the slow progress of change. Such latent periods can be registered in different terms, not as resistance to a conquest, but as resistance to the destructuring of a system. Daniel Roche, for example, in his recent article on the literature of death, which dealt with *artes moriendi* produced in France in the seventeenth and eighteenth centuries, saw the sustained growth in the production of such works peak around 1700, leading to a long period in the eighteenth century which lacked any of the creativity of the preceding century and which he called 'the century of reprints'. Roche presents a graph of attitudes towards death which anticipates by about fifty years the turning point which I saw taking place in Provence on the basis of wills – in the realm, that is, of common thought, if not of popular thought. Here we have an example of resistance cushioning the process of decline registered by the electroscopic test of literary production.

'Resistances', on the basis of such examples, seem to be the expression of discordances which are often momentary but are sometimes lasting; discordances in the plurality of historical times and especially in the time-frame of the history of mentalities. From these studies and suggestions, there emerges the contrasting idea that the history of mentalities cannot simply be seen as part of the history of resistances (conceived in terms of inertia or periods of latency) but that the real possibility exists of sudden change, lightning creativity and periods or moments when a new sensibility brutally comes into being.

In conclusion, it seems to me that the problematic which I have tried to introduce can be very fruitful, if we approach it from a resolutely dynamic perspective. If our analysis only succeeds in unearthing treasuries or repositories of unchanging gestures and museums of misunderstood legacies located in geographically isolated communities or closed social groupings, it will doubtless be interesting, but it will remain poor and will not give rise to a future problematic. In my view, we need to see it as means of deepening our approach to the interlacing of historical times, in the sense in which Althusser defined the phrase, within the 'overdetermining' context of the mode of production. Using this framework, I think we can arrive at a more sophisticated approach to the notion of collective mentality, and perhaps succeed in breaking out of the magic circle of current and received ideas in all their verbal facility. 'The force of inertia of mental structures', the 'collective unconscious', are given concepts which are perhaps still workable today, but which cannot for much longer avoid being subjected to more searching explanatory analysis.

Note

This paper first appeared as an article in *Le Monde Alpin et Rhodanien* (June 1980).

9

The Prerevolutionary Sensibility

If I had to give another title to the paper which I read to the Göttingen conference on the origins of the French Revolution, I do not know that I would still choose the term 'sensibility', for fear of multiplying such terms, which are useful but vague. Yet, if the label can be objected to, the contents are unambiguous, dealing with the question of just what happened, sometime around 1750, to collective mentalities, at a time when France was undergoing profound change.

In the field of the history of mentalities, the notion of collective sensibility is one which must, of course, be used with the greatest of caution, if only because of the possibilities of purely verbal explanation which it carries with it. It can, however, turn out to be both accommodating and, I believe, fruitful. We will try to apply it in this way to a 'prerevolutionary' period drawn quite widely and covering, in all, the thirty years leading up to 1789.

From revolutionary to prerevolutionary sensibility

Although the field of collective mentalities is not one of the most widely exploited in the area of French revolutionary studies, we nonetheless possess a certain number of approaches, some of them very important, to what can be described as the revolutionary sensibility. Some of these are great classics, surprisingly modern in their bias, like Georges Lefebvre's *The Great Fear*. On the other hand, there are recent studies, like Albert Soboul's portrait of the Parisian sans-culottes, Georges Rudé's analysis of the sociology and behaviour of the revolutionary crowd and Mona Ozouf's approach to the revolutionary festival. I myself took part in this movement of exploration in *The Metamorphoses of the Festival in Provence, 1750–1820* and in *Religion and Revolution: the dechristianization of the Year II in the south-east*, which tried, while maintaining a sense of proportion and making necessary adjustments, to apply Georges Lefebvre's approach to the Great Fear to the equally panicky but also semi-spontaneous process of dechristianization.

This is an open field and one which, I feel, is undergoing a revival. Yet the scholar working in the short time-frame of the revolutionary period is constantly faced with the problem of origins, of the context of change in the *longue durée* of which these forms of revolutionary behaviour are perhaps only the result, the crystallization in the heat of the moment. This was precisely what led me to move from the definite and explosive dechristianization process of the Year II to the dechristianization process which took place during the Enlightenment, which I looked at in terms of the interaction between the traditional 'folkloric' festival and the revolutionary festival in Provence.

To what extent can we find the roots of revolutionary behaviour, or, conversely, measure the extent of revolutionary change, by using the longer time-frame – if not the long-term perspective in which things only change very slowly, at least the middle term of a number of decades, or a century? The data which we currently possess, can be said to be either profuse or scanty. We still need to reach a preliminary understanding of what we mean by a 'prerevolutionary sensibility'.

A primary interpretation and its limits; the prerevolutionary climate

We can give the term a primary, limiting interpretation by confining ourselves to what the old textbooks called the 'immediate' causes of the Revolution, meaning the years which immediately preceded and prepared it.

No doubt this kind of study of the revolutionary climate in both its spectacular and everyday manifestations from 1787 at the latest, or perhaps from 1774, is very important, even if it is open to the easy and somewhat dated charge that it reconstructs the past with the benefit of hindsight and that it permits cheap prophecy. From the Flour War to the actions of the *parlements*, the affair of the Queen's necklace or the Reveillon revolt, to stick deliberately to the confused catalogue of images which have come down to us, we can follow the maturing of a collective anxiety, which looked for and found its forms of expression as much in traditional kinds of social protest as in the framework of a progressively more mature and politicized public opinion. We see here the emergence of a climate of opinion rather than a collective sensibility and we will not linger over it. Not that it is devoid of interest, it must be said, but because it is already so well known to us, in its event-orientated aspect at any rate.

Such research into the premonitory signs of the Revolution also poses some important questions. The Flour War apart, the Revolution broke out at the end of a century which had seen nothing like the spectacular explosions of the preceding period, as Emmanuel Le Roy Ladurie noted in his study 'Rural protests and revolts in France, 1675–1788'. The 'angry outbursts', to quote Roland Mousnier, of popular uprisings which were repeated, and which spread beyond provincial boundaries, were more characteristic of the 'tragic' seventeenth century.

To this apparent paradox of a 'quiet' century leading up to the paroxysms of the revolutionary period, Le Roy Ladurie has proposed a number of interpretative hypotheses. These are suggested by a variegated geography of confrontations arising from his findings for the south, north and north-east of France. My own work on the south has stressed the less spectacular yet persistent and aggravated forms of confrontation in the villages, as they appear in judicial sources (the archives of the *senechaussées* and of the courts dealing with forests and water rights).

This initial type of inquiry in the domain of collective sensibilities is important. It avoids the all too frequent danger of conceiving of the history of mentalities as an end in itself, without reference to the promptings of the history of social structures and economic conjunctures. However, one can also say that it only touches on one level – essentially popular – of collective sensibilities, which is expressed in the gestures of social protest, whether everyday or explosive.

Another level of the prerevolutionary sensibility

There is a strong temptation to look for another, more secret level of sensibility which, quite apart from truly revolutionary gestures, would reveal a changed view of things and of the world in general. In a different context, this was doubtless part of H. Brunschwig's aim in his *Crisis of the Prussian State at the End of the Eighteenth Century and the Birth of Romanticism* (1947), a work which did not, perhaps, get the attention it deserved. In passing from the framework of the state to the role of human and class relations in the expressions of collective sensibility at a time of crisis, from the *Sturm und Drang* movement to Romanticism, Brunschwig used anonymous statistical sources and semi-anonymous sources like small magazines and treatises which reflected opinion, to move on to the level of aesthetic or literary expression. Here we have an example of a deliberately continuous study which we are far from possessing, even now, for eighteenth-century France.

We are not being over-critical of works which currently set out to give a panoramic view, with titles like 'France at the End of the Ancien Régime' or 'Remote Causes of the French Revolution' by noting the relative or complete absence of any study of changes in collective sensibility in the second half of the eighteenth century. Constrained by the limits of a very condensed synthesis, Jacques Godechot was unable to find a place for the subject in his textbook *The Revolutions* amid the space which he rightly devoted to economy, society and demography on the one hand and to the movement of ideas on the other. Albert Soboul found room, in the course of an analytic survey, for the forms of collective behaviour in his work *The French Revolution and Civilization*. He dealt with the peasant mentality, aristocratic ideology, the bourgeois mind and 'popular culture and mentality' – but such an approach does not favour a global view of the problem. Although Pierre Chaunu, in his *European Culture and the Enlightenment* does include mentalities, and other fields, in a study of secular change – something which is perhaps lacking in Soboul's book – he places the turning point sometime between 1680 and 1720 at the apogee of the Enlightenment, which is identified with the baroque period. This is an abrasive interpretation for Jacobins like us, who see everything as converging on 1789, and yet we are not certain that we have found what we were looking for here either.

If history seems to be hesitant here, another kind of history – literary history – introduced a basic periodization a long time ago. We are speaking here of literary history in the wider sense, which incorporates the history of art and of all forms of aesthetic expression.

We will not be so naive as to recount the now classic schema of Enlightenment periodization derived from D. Mornet's *Intellectual Origins of the French Revolution* and P. Hazard's *European Thought in the Eighteenth Century, from Montesquieu to Lessing*, which were based on literary sources. These surveys are far from dated. It was

Mornet who gave us a real history of the spread of the Enlightenment, based on an inventory of works in eighteenth-century libraries, and he insisted on the importance of 1760 as a turning point. For these authors, literary history included the history of sentiment and collective sensibility, a field happily explored since then by R. Mauzi in *The Idea of Happiness* and J. Ehrard's *Idea of Nature*, followed by J. Deprun's work on the theme of anxiety.

These studies dealt with the collective sensibility of the elite. In reading these authors, the historian's curiosity is aroused, and not totally satisfied. The triumph of reason in the *Aufklärung* was succeeded by the return of the irrational at the twilight of the Enlightenment. From Rousseauism to Sade's theatre of cruelty or the gothic novel, other currents emerged which suggest profound changes in ways of thinking and feeling. The question remains as to how we are to correlate these forms of literary and artistic expression with the collective attitudes of the majority. Is the way to be found in a history of culture, or cultures?

Transition: from literary history to cultural history

To describe the uses of cultural history in the study of the decades before the Revolution still does not bring us directly to grips with the history of sensibility. For this reason, we will content ourselves with giving a deliberately brief summary of the field. Yet in this way we are at least approaching the realms of the collective unconscious, by beginning with the study of clear thought and ideologies.

Over the last ten years we have been able to quantify trends in publishing under the monarchy in terms of the internal changes affecting the granting of public or of tacit permission to publish, provincial reprints and other, more sophisticated procedures for measuring opinion, such as the quantification of reviews in certain journals of the period (graph 2). The history of secular change in this field confirms the originality of the prerevolutionary decades. Public permits show a collapse of theological literature and corresponding increases in the area of arts and sciences, which took on their 'revolutionary image', to quote François Furet, in the grants of tacit permits, with the multiplication of political works.[1] The novel, too, took on great importance in the tacit permits, under the category of 'belles-lettres'. Such changes cannot always be seen in a linear way. A process of masking and exclusion meant that it was 'possible to read the *Journal des Savants* between 1785 and 1789 without for a

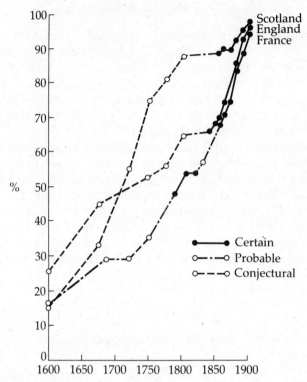

Adult male literacy in France, Scotland and England (including Wales), 1600–1900. (Source: L. Stone, 'Literacy and education in England, 1640–1900', *Past and Present* (February 1969))

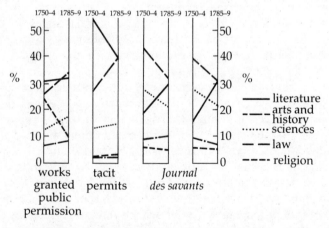

The culture of the elite: global breakdown of books printed in France between 1750 and 1789. (Source: Roger and Ehrard, *The Book and Society* (vol. 1, Paris, 1970))

moment thinking that France was heading for Revolution' (Ehrard and Roger).

A turning point has undoubtedly been reached, however, at least at the top of the scale. But the main problem is one of trying to find out to what extent such a change which involved both culture and affectivity – or, more generally, sensibility – was registered on the popular level. We will not venture much further in this area – which needs to be fully developed in its own right – than to outline a periodization to which we shall shortly return. That is, we will avoid asking about the content, as such, of popular culture, whose themes and constants have been inventoried by Robert Mandrou. In terms of the relationship between elite and popular culture we will content ourselves with a look at the progress of literacy, whose spread is reflected in statistics showing the ability of people to sign their names on the marriage register. This is an old field of study, initiated in the last century by the famous researches of Maggiolo between 1870 and 1880, recently rediscovered and now being used as part of more elaborate research procedures. The study of literacy has come into its own again in provincial studies like those of Champagne and Brittany, which echo the work of Parisian teams. I have summarized the results obtained for Provence under the no doubt presumptuous title, 'Was there a cultural revolution in the eighteenth century?'.

At the risk of making a sparse indicator appear even more sparse, we can summarize the work of Lawrence Stone, Furet and Ozouf and my own team under a number of headings. New analysis of Maggiolo's figures and new studies in the field largely confirm the generally accepted features of this landscape. There is the contrast between two Frances – a learned one in the north-east, in a line stretching from Mont-St-Michel to Geneva, and an ignorant south-west – a division which also corresponds to a marked sexual dimorphism. But we are more interested in change than in constants in this area. There is an unmistakable secular trend whereby the global percentages of literacy grew from less than 30 per cent at the end of the eighteenth century to nearly 50 per cent on the eve of the Revolution. François Furet's work has introduced some specific changes into this picture. The real 'take-off' in time occurs downstream of the Revolution, in the nineteenth century. Likewise in space, the far too simple split between learned northern France and the ignorant south is replaced by a split into three main divisions: a highly literate north which accelerated its progress and then reached a plateau in the second half of the century; the 'Atlantic' region, from Lower Normandy to the Limousin, which stagnated and became entrenched in its illiteracy; and finally the southern regions, which began to regain ground from the middle of the eighteenth century.

Were there rhythms in this, very relative, recovery? Provençal sources show a curve which can be generally divided into three sections. There was a period of growth between 1680 and 1710 or 1720, corresponding to the maximum level of post-Tridentine pastoral activism. This fell off between 1720 and 1750–60 and was followed by a new surge, which is very clearly marked, after 1760, which continued uninterrupted throughout the revolutionary period. This was perhaps the real cultural revolution of the Enlightenment. Can we extrapolate from the example of Provence, however? The answer is a definite no, even though our general schema bears a considerable resemblance to that proposed by Lawrence Stone for France as a whole in comparison with England and Scotland (graph 1).[2]

With all the questions raised by this graph, and primarily with the problem of the popular diffusion of the Enlightenment, we are faced with the need to go further, moving out of the realm of cultures and into that of collective attitudes.

From life to death, via the family: some significant series

As a result of the massive investment which has taken place in recent years into serial approaches to collective attitudes and forms of behaviour based on the anonymous sources of the history of mentalities, we now have the advantage of possessing a whole range of statistics or, so as not to frighten anyone, of changes observed in such diverse areas as attitudes to life and family structures, attitudes to death, religious practice, the relationships of sociability or, conversely, of violence, social pathology and protest against the established order.

Is it legitimate to look at this collection of indicators together and to assume that they have some mutual complicity? That can only be said once we have examined both the quantified data and the results of their qualitative interpretation.

If we look at the area of attitudes to life at the primary, most elementary and yet essential level of life as something given or received, it is clear that we possess a whole collection of statistics which are surprisingly convergent, though based on tests which are both specific and significant, including contraception, illegitimacy, premarital conceptions and abandonment of children. These are problems which we neither wish to nor are capable of examining in depth, but for which it may be legitimate, at this stage, to take an overview based on the very impressive quantity of specific or synthetic approaches which we nowadays possess. A number of recent studies call for this to be done, among which we would single out J.-L. Flandrin's work on *Peasant Love* and his recent synthesis on the history of sexuality.

On the origins of contraception, which has been widely discussed in the French school and elsewhere, we can briefly summarize two or three certainties and assumptions. These tend to reinforce the import- ance of the second half of the eighteenth century in the general picture which emerges from these concordant sources. We do not find any French equivalent to the precocity of Colyton or some other British sites, where such processes began in the seventeenth century. Similar- ly, it is only in the very limited milieu of the higher nobility that we find anything like the precocious familial Malthusianism of the Genevan patricians. Conversely, the exceptional adherence to the traditional model of which French Canada is the yardstick is, apart from a few provinces, not at all the rule in France. Something happened, therefore, to French reproductive behaviour. When did it happen, and how?

Some scholars, like Emmanuel Le Roy Ladurie in *Annales histori- ques de la Révolution française* (1965), tend to suggest that the real turning point in rural France came after the Revolution, in the 1790s. The debate which took place between A. Chamoux and C. Dauphin on one side and J. Dupâquier and M. Lachiver, on the other,[3] makes it possible for us to assess the current view of the problem. Signs of deliberate restraint on births appear in the towns, including the small towns, around the middle of the eighteenth century, in the 1740s. But Dupâquier and Lachiver, drawing attention to other areas, such as Meulan, which show a less linear development, distinguish between two different types of Malthusianism. The first was fairly general, but diffuse and limited in the number of families involved, and was marked by a systematic form of behaviour among a certain number of 'contraceptive families', comprising perhaps 10 per cent of the total. On the basis of this more refined typology, the authors suggest a change of pace rather than a turning point around 1740, succeeded by a 'slow but steady advance of contraception between 1765 and 1790', with 'the great divide' occurring around 1790 with the total dis- appearance of traditional demographic behaviour. We need to share the caution of these scholars, who are united in their insistence on the need for diversified research methods, and also on the perceptible contrasts between town and country, as well as between different parts of the countryside, from Quercy to the *bocage* country of the west. We are left with an outline periodization, however, which is obvious if we turn to the indices provided by the rates of illegitimate births and premarital conceptions, contenting ourselves, for the moment, with the brutality of statistics. In the two very useful series of graphs (3a and 3b) which J.-L. Frandrin has prepared, some marked trends are revealed. The rates of illegitimate births begin to rise, sometimes markedly, in the period 1750–60, in the half-dozen rural sites studies. This growth is modest, admittedly, by comparison with urban sites which we know about from other studies, such as Paris, Lille, Nantes, Bordeaux, Toulouse or Grenoble, where percentages ranging from 15 to 30 per cent or even more reflect both internal change and an influx of unmarried mothers from the countryside. Less decisive is the information provided by the data on premarital conceptions. For six graphs which show an increase, compared with just one showing decline, change is only apparent in half between 1740 and 1780; elsewhere change appears at the same time as, or subsequent to, the Revolution.

Before discussing the meaning of these graphs, we should note that the series of indicators chosen is not thereby limited. We could also add data on foundling children, for which we can refer to F. Lebrun's acute study (in *Annales E.S.C.*, 1972), which shows a similar eruption in Angers in the second half of the eighteenth century, leading us to think that it does not simply merge into the data on illegitimacy but might, in a wider sense, be a reflection of urban misery.

The convergence of these data, which is too striking not to be discussed, calls for explanatory schemas – and they are not lacking. Are we dealing, as Philippe Ariès has said, with a new view of the family expressed through the discovery of childhood, or with the 'sexual revolution' which Edward Shorter locates in this transitional period? We can keep our options open for the present, while retaining at least the awareness that all of these turning points in the second half of the eighteenth century reflect a changed view of family structures.

A certain number of the main themes involved in this process of change – which is more perceptibly registered in qualitative than in quantitive sources – were presented in Philippe Ariès's work. Thanks to him, the Rousseau of *Émile* has been placed in the context of a much wider change in sensibility by which the family, contracted in size and in its view of itself, began to attach a value to the presence of children, around which it organized itself. It might be said that

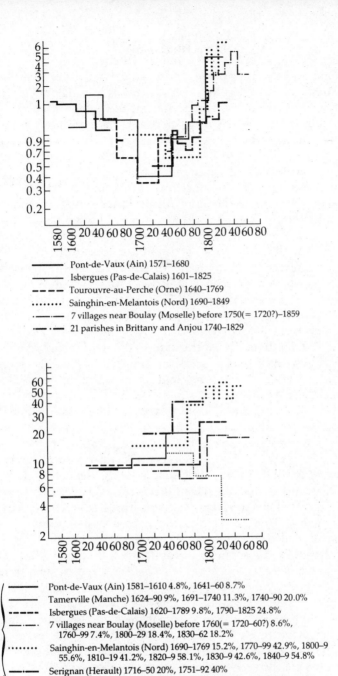

Pont-de-Vaux (Ain) 1571–1680
Isbergues (Pas-de-Calais) 1601–1825
Tourouvre-au-Perche (Orne) 1640–1769
Sainghin-en-Melantois (Nord) 1690–1849
7 villages near Boulay (Moselle) before 1750(= 1720?)–1859
21 parishes in Brittany and Anjou 1740–1829

Rising {
Pont-de-Vaux (Ain) 1581–1610 4.8%, 1641–60 8.7%
Tamerville (Manche) 1624–90 9%, 1691–1740 11.3%, 1740–90 20.0%
Isbergues (Pas-de-Calais) 1620–1789 9.8%, 1790–1825 24.8%
7 villages near Boulay (Moselle) before 1760(= 1720–60?) 8.6%, 1760–99 7.4%, 1800–29 18.4%, 1830–62 18.2%
Sainghin-en-Melantois (Nord) 1690–1769 15.2%, 1770–99 42.9%, 1800–9 55.6%, 1810–19 41.2%, 1820–9 58.1%, 1830–9 42.6%, 1840–9 54.8%

Falling {
Serignan (Herault) 1716–50 20%, 1751–92 40%
Bilhères-d'Ossau (Basses-Pyrénées) 1740–79 12.9%, 1780–1819 7.7%, 1820–59 2.8%

Premarital conceptions, 1580–1850 (percentages).
Source: J.-L. Flandrin, *Peasant Love* (Paris, 1975)

Philippe Ariès's chronology, more fluid by the very nature of the essentially qualitative sources on which it is based, does not attach the same importance to the second half of the eighteenth century as the preceding studies. In his view, the sanction of Rousseauism put the finishing touches to a process of change in the *longue durée* which covered the whole classical period, from the invention of schooling and the 'enclosure' of children at the beginning of the seventeenth century. Yet Ariès is very conscious of the changes in the structures of and sentiments about the family in the latter period, when he stresses that relationships were bathed in a wholly new climate of affectivity.

Whether we see these phenomena as constituting a change or a new, not at all unequivocal, series of nuances, new kinds of internal tensions emerged side by side with the turning-in on itself of the family group, in a dialectic of contradiction which must be explained. We can see these tensions in Y. Castan's very subtle analysis of Languedocian peasant society, *Honnêteté and Social Relations in Languedoc in the Eighteenth Century*. These include a change in the father–son relationship. At the core of the stem family, the eldest son is both privileged and dependent; younger sons are excluded from inheritance and, in the second half of the eighteenth century, we can see them freeing themselves, sometimes brutally, from family control, gaining an increasing mobility and a differently defined set of relationships with others of their own age.

The relationship between father and son and between parents and children changed and so, inevitably, did relationships between men and women. Both Shorter, in his study of the 'sexual revolution', and Depauw, in his study of illegitimacy in Nantes, see the free urban relationship of the modern type, which was then coming into being, as something very different from the unequal brutality of what Mandrou called the 'ephemeral couplings' of the preceding era. The idea shared by Rousseau and Marat, and by some of Albert Soboul's sans-culottes, of a couple which was idealized in new terms, was forged at this time. We should not be too quick to assume that positions were thus equalized. Although literacy statistics show that urban women were catching up on men in the male–female relationship in the lower bourgeoisie or the popular classes, a dimorphism of attitudes was nevertheless accentuated and took on a different aspect, as can be seen in the gestures of religious practice. Molière's *dévot* was a man, but it was female *dévotes* who were harassed by the irreligious sans-culottes of 1792.

Both attitudes to life and family relationships underwent profound change, therefore. We can see this clearly in literary sources like

Restif's or Sébastien Mercier's descriptions of life, tempered, however, with all the legitimate suspicions involved in the assessment of
such evidence. The same goes, more widely, for attitudes to death,
which are a vital means of studying the gestures of religious practice
and forms of behaviour.

Attitudes towards death and religious attitudes: anxiety or serenity

In order to summarize some of the themes and some of the stages
which marked the turning point in attitudes towards death, essentially in the second half of the eighteenth century, I will start with my
own work and with studies like F. Lebrun's work on death in Anjou
in the seventeenth and eighteenth centuries. In *Baroque Piety and
Dechristianization*, and more generally in *Death in History*, I started
from a description of the extraordinarily all-embracing system of
baroque funeral rites which took shape in Provence and which
culminated, in practically every part of Catholic post-Tridentine
Christendom, in what I called the 'grand ceremonial of death'. Fear of
and preparation for death took up a whole lifetime, giving rise to
public and ostentatious forms of ceremonial accompanied by a whole
series of rituals and offerings of good works, Masses and prayers
designed to ensure the salvation or reprieve of the deceased. The will,
a source especially valuable because of its social status, provided the
main resource for my research, which was then fleshed out by a study
of the semi-anonymous sources of minor literature, both sacred and
profane, comprising sermons and *artes moriendi* as well as major
literature. From this emerged a continuum of attitudes, which were,
of course, modified according to geographical and social factors, but
which were nevertheless extraordinarily homogenous as evidence of
the powerful hold on human life and death gained by the post-
Tridentine Church, based on people's desire for salvation.

The small number of graphs to which I have deliberately restricted
my argument show the destructuring of this system in the eighteenth
century in a trend shown in the rate of demand for Masses, the most
broadly based test (graph 4). After a phase of growth or consolidation
lasting up to the middle of the century, there is a remorseless process
of decline which saw the percentage of testators anxious to have
Masses said for their souls fall by nearly a half. One can apply a
number of modulations to this global trend. Thematically, we can
point to the decline in the number of funeral monuments erected, of

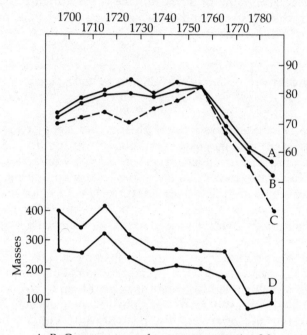

A, B, C: percentage of testators requesting Masses
D: average number of Masses requested

Requests for Masses in eighteenth-century Provence. (Source: M. Vovelle, *Baroque Piety and Dechristianization: attitudes to death in eighteenth-century Provence* (Paris, 1973))

acts of charity, membership of confraternities and funeral processions. Geographically, we can stress the mobility of some towns and districts and the stability of others. In sociological terms, especially, we can follow the increase in dimorphism by gender; in the mobility of the elites and also of the lesser bourgeoisie and of a section of the small urban manufacturers who were later to swell the ranks of the sans-culottes.

We are left with a reliable and homogenous graph which essentially validates the importance of the second half of the eighteenth century, starting from 1750 and proceeding at a more rapid pace between 1760 and 1770, although some sites – notably centres of Jansenism or of Protestant–Catholic contact – offer evidence of precocious change before 1730. Can we extrapolate from the example of Provence? Although François Lebrun did not use a comparable methodology, his very rich qualitative data on attitudes towards death in Anjou confirm the periodization suggested by the other site reasonably well. Subsequent studies have, of course, introduced more than just refinements of meaning. The application of our methods by Pierre Chaunu and his students to the Paris area showed that the capital was in advance of the general trend of desocialization of death, suggesting a link with the other upheaval in collective sensibility which took place at the end of the seventeenth and the beginning of the eighteenth century, the time of the 'crisis of European thought'. Yet is Paris, in all its precocity, not the exception which proves the rule? Monographs on provincial sites, which have since proliferated, tend to bear this out.

The transition from attitudes towards death to the totality of forms of religious belief is a natural one, and we will doubtless soon be accused of having put the cart before the horse by dealing with one before the other.

The eclipse of the sacred?

Can we speak of the dechristianization of the Enlightenment? I do not promise to settle the question out of hand. I shall briefly state the current state of the problem as I see it. There are hardly any historians who still believe that France was wholly Christian in 1789 and that the revolutionary crisis was the sole point of origin of contemporary dechristianization. In addition, there are many, whom I willingly acknowledge, to remind us of the universality of certain gestures of religious practice in a world of 'Christianity', where no formal separation of genres had been made and where daily life was impregnated with religious elements. The idea of a France which, in some rural districts, had never been fully Christianized, according to Gabriel Le Bras, or of a country already dechristianized, beginning with the Enlightenment elites, according to another interpretation, raise problems of their own. Starting from a very high level of religious practice, and possibly of Christianization, achieved between 1680 and 1750, to date it very crudely, current research into the most widespread gestures of religious practice show little if any change for the later period. The 'seasonal' sacraments of life, early baptism and even Easter practice were generally still going strong, which explains the relative setback suffered by those scholars who wanted to apply regressively the statistical methods of contemporary religious sociology devised by the Le Bras school. But there are other indices which show signs of movement. We have long been aware of the desertion of religious houses in the second half of the eighteenth century, and of the ageing of their inhabitants. Statistics for entry into religious orders and the ordination of priests compiled by different scholars (Berthelot du Chesnay, Julia, myself and, more recently, T. Tackett) for various dioceses (Reims, Autun, Rouen, Bordeaux, Aix and so on) show a growing crisis of vocations which was felt early on in some Jansenist sites, like Autun, and which became more general after 1750 or 1760. In this context, however, we should also note the slight revival which took place in the last decade of the *ancien régime*. Clearly, vocations were falling, especially in the cities, such as Marseille, and in whole regions like the Paris basin and Lower Provence, which made up numbers from areas which still had a surplus of vocations. The *bocage* of Normandy supplied Paris, while the Alpine region supplied the south. These areas appear as sanctuaries of Christianity, a trait which sometimes foreshadows the future contours of religious practice in the twentieth century.

This is the same turning point which was registered in most of the statistics derived from Provençal wills in my own work, dealing with Masses, the raising of funerary monuments, legacies and membership of confraternities. More profoundly, I was also struck by the secularization of the formulas used, which showed a steady retreat of the Virgin and patron saints from the preambles of wills.

Other indices and other kinds of exploration strengthen what might seem to be fragile in the information provided by these unique sources. A sustained analysis of representations of the hereafter in paintings on the altars to the souls in Purgatory confirmed the depopulation of the traditional pantheon of intercessory saints. In addition, we can call on the rich collection of studies carried out by Maurice Agulhon on the secularization of the southern confraternities, which were a traditional expression of religiosity as well as of sociability. The migration of the Provençal elite from penitent societies to masonic lodges from 1760, or especially 1770, is one of the major elements which can add to the file.

The debate on the meaning to be assigned to these changes is wide open. The Abbé Plongeron, commenting on Agulhon's work, states that we are dealing with a process of laicization rather than the beginnings of a real process of dechristianization. Philippe Ariès believes that the laicization of wills in the second half of the eighteenth century is not an index of the decline of religiosity, but rather of a change in feelings about the family. The testator, at a time of Rousseau-esque affectivity, is confident that his heirs will take care of the spiritual offerings which previously had to be specified, without implying any diminution of the strength of religious feeling. This does not, however, explain why priests and religious are increasingly rare within the family circle.

It therefore seems fairly certain that a process got under way in the second half of the eighteenth century of which the dechristianization of 1793 was the explosive form. Yet this still leaves the problem of the origins of the process largely unresolved.

It is necessary, before leaving this theme, to underline its known limits. It would be wrong to think that a 'pre-Tridentine' religiosity, based on folklorized, often magical practices had completely disappeared from the popular classes, especially in rural areas. The episcopal offensive of the classical period did not succeed in uprooting everything, and to believe that it did would make it impossible to understand a number of forms of marginal religiosity in the revolutionary period. Nor should we forget the very strong religious impregnation which took place in the towns and among the lower bourgeoisie, affecting women much more than men. Might it have been, as Le Roy Ladurie suggested, the terrorist power of indiscreet confessors which paved the way for the Sunday division between the women in the church and the men in the bar?

In the elite groups (a term which I use for the sake of convenience), there are also a number of distinctions to be made. We were struck by the continuity of religious practice among the aristocracy which was shown in the Provençal wills, despite the fact that this group had commonly been thought of as frivolous and disillusioned, according to the dictionary of received images. This was in contrast to the very marked abandonment of religious practice among the mercantile

bourgeoisie and the liberal professions. Does this mean that the newly
constructed landscape of collective sensibility in these circles reflected
the serene outlook of Buffon or the Encyclopedists? We can close this
section with an abstract look at a final reality which was, perhaps, the
prerogative of the elite, but which seems to have taken the place of the
confident religiosity which had formerly prevailed: this is the phenomenon of anxiety.

We would be justly criticized for attributing an importance to
anxiety in the prerevolutionary decades which it only attained at a
later period. The approach is difficult, possibly because the profusion
of literary sources uncovered by Hazard, Mornet, or the classics of
literary history such as Van Tighem, and recently brought to our
attention again by scholars such as J. Deprun, do not lend themselves
very well to a serial historical approach. Yet we do find signs of
anxiety in narratives and memoirs when studying attitudes towards
death. In a field which is still essentially unresearched, we are all the
more appreciative of recent studies which have been carried out on
the irrational in the age of Enlightenment, such as Robert Darnton's
work on mesmerism. Can the history of anxiety or instability be
written? They are, nevertheless, essential for our purpose.

From sociability to aggression; collective relationships

Solidarities and tensions are two complementary fields which have
recently been reopened by a series of studies which should allow us to
add some factors to our survey.

The idea of sociability, if not the term, was part of traditional
historiography. Maurice Agulhon had the merit of rediscovering it
and of reactivating research from a modern perspective, in his work
on the – admittedly privileged – site of the Mediterranean south. He
has described and analysed the different elements around which a
highly structured, masculine collective life was organized, ranging
from institutional or municipal confraternities to pious confraternities dedicated to the upkeep of a chapel. From the valuable material
provided in his book *Penitents and Freemasons* we can recognize a
major turning point in the second half of the eighteenth century of the
kind already rapidly dealt with in terms of religious life. This change
involved institutionalization, increased control by the municipality
and a trend towards secularization. Change of a quantitative kind can
also be seen. Confraternities declined and often collapsed, but
sociability flourished. While not abruptly moving away, the elites

gradually switched their meeting place to the masonic lodges. Penitential societies became more 'democratic' in their recruitment as they declined. Yet their meetings became more frequent. From being an annual event, the feast day became weekly. Sociability became multiple. Unanimism gave way to a class-based division, which is often an indicator of tensions and confrontations.

Can we not see the same process, expressed in different terms, in Y. Castan's recent thesis on social relations in Languedoc? A crisis and decline of the sense of community became apparent at the end of the eighteenth century. The younger groups went their own way, leaving the world of parents and of the well-to-do to one side. Thus there was a change in the sense of community, which had long been one of the major anchoring points of village solidarity. Some scholars, like F. X. Emmanuelli[4] have shed light on internal conflicts which pitted one community against another or, more frequently, pitted the community against the local landlord. Emmanuelli's work gives us a curve of such conflicts which shows little sign of growth and is, in fact, falling in the second half of the eighteenth century – most noticeably at mid-century.

In my own study *The Metamorphoses of the Festival in Provence, 1750–1820*, the same turning point is registered both in the forms of these important meetings and in attitudes towards them. That the festival had changed can clearly be seen by mid-century. The pilgrimage, or patron day, had never been so popular, and it multiplied during the summer months. But its secular character was accentuated, even though it continued to operate along traditional lines. The urban festival was especially modified. Traditional festivities at events like the games at the *Fête-Dieu* at Aix or the *Tarasque* at Tarascon began to seem exotic to travellers who had read Rousseau, who had little understanding of these events and thought of ancient Greek and Roman games. But such decline or fossilization was compensated for by the atomization of the festival, which became a permanent, or at least weekly spectacle, involving promenades in the streets and escape, on Sundays, to the country taverns.

Secularizing trends and crisis in the sense of community spelled the end of traditional unanimism, and were explicit characteristics of the new style of festival which emerged.

Amid its solidarities and tensions, traditional society created a 'great segregation' of the sick, beggars and the insane, whom it wanted to keep out of sight, in ways well known to us from Michel Foucault's work. In terms of the level of social practice with which we are concerned here, the Enlightenment period shows considerable ambiguity, but seems characterized more by the inheritance and adaptation of traditional practices than by any real innovation. The traditional system was not fundamentally questioned, but it showed signs of age and weakness. Using Provençal wills, I was able to study the crisis, in the period 1750–60, of a traditional system of charity in which the legacies of the faithful had gone to urban hospitals. The Christmas collection for the hospital of St Jacques in Aix also showed a markedly downward trend. It is at this point, however, that the secularized bourgeois concept of doing-good appears in the documents, to provide at least a verbal compensation for the decline of a form of charity, which henceforth began to dress in bourgeois clothes.

Conflict is delineated in multiple forms of protest and breaches of the social order ranging from delinquency to larceny or, most simply, tavern brawls and assaults on gossips. The most elaborate forms of social breakdown took a number of forms, visible in the *lettres de cachet*, in the case of the elite, and by judgements which sent poor wretches to the galleys, the gibbet or the wheel for crime, sedition, salt contraband or rioting.

Did such realities change in the prerevolutionary decades, and can one write the history of 'wickedness' which Lucien Febvre called for? Is there, at the very least, a form of aggression by which collective sensibility reflected the social 'climate' which we discussed earlier? In reading the chroniclers of the period one is inclined to say that there is. Sébastien Mercier's *Paris* or Restif's *Nights* are charged with aggression. The diary of Barbier the notary oscillates between Enlightenment humanitarianism and the pessimism of the urban bourgeois. We can modify the picture by comparing these impressionistic jottings with quantified data supplied by a great number of recent studies, at all levels, in the judicial archives of repression. To interpret the statistics we must look at the variables: the trends in criminality and reciprocal trends in the intensity of oppression. In this area, there was ferocity on both sides.

In an article on delinquency and criminality in eighteenth-century Provence, based on Aix prison warrants, we stressed the marked tendency of these statistics to peak between 1772 and 1774, with figures more than double those of 1750 (graph 5). By contrast, the decade before the Revolution saw an easing of tension. Studies carried out on a wider basis by research teams in Paris and Provence do not show trends as clear as this. Figures for the number of people judged in the criminal court at the Châtelet in Paris were fairly constant at between 450 and 520 between 1750 and the Revolution, although with varying levels of severity, and the annual statistics for

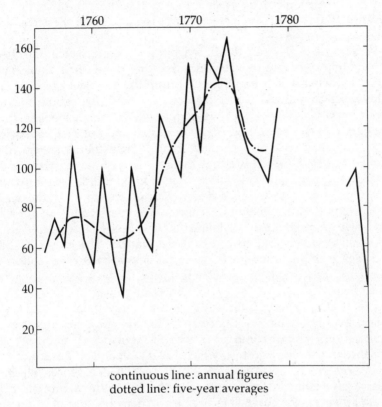

continuous line: annual figures
dotted line: five-year averages

Delinquency and criminality curve for eighteenth-century Provence:
number of cases transmitted annually to the Prisons Book of Aix.

criminal proceedings at Paris oscillate between 276 in 1755 and 216 in 1785 (with, however, a peak of 290 in 1775). Might the fall in the number of prosecutions, both in Paris and the south, in the last decades of the century indicate a change in attitudes to the accused by the judges themselves?

What conclusions can we draw from these data, which have been deliberately restricted to a few surveys? One cannot help thinking of the old schema which was inherited from the fantasies of Taine and others, which posited a link between renewed aggression and the revolutionary violence which was to follow. We can see its limits from the outset. If the revolution of the wretched and the dregs of society was going to break out, we have long known that it would have broken out in 1774. This is not to say that popular misery had no place in the explosion of 1788–9, which indeed it did. Yet, at the risk of seeming hurriedly to join a winning cause, we would readily share P. Petrovitch's caution with regard to Georges Rudé's work. The wretched population of delinquents of all kinds was not what essentially made up the force of the Revolution. This is not to deny that the brigand is still one of the most impressive figures in collective mentality, as a myth or mobilizing image, as was seen during the Great Fear.

This is all very well as far as delinquency or popular criminality is concerned. Drawing an arbitrary boundary for the purpose of explanation, we can compare it with the statistics of rejection and deviance in the 'elite' groups, which F. X. Emmanuelli has studied in the *lettres de cachet*. The curve is sustained in Provence, which is clearly tense and constantly litigious, even within the family circle. In Paris, however, the curve is in decline, perhaps because of a sapping of conviction among those in power. At any rate, as the author concludes, the approach offers another perspective, both in the geography of the zones of chronic trouble which he provides, and in its chronology, which is not at all negligible for the study of anxiety which we discussed earlier.

Assembling and interpreting: a provisional summary

This article was designed to show some significant series of results as part of a provisional summary of research carried out in recent years. We are aware of the limits of this procedure. Our assertion of the value of an anonymous mass of quantitive evidence may seem surprising in a field where it is easy to see the value of literary or

artistic documents – qualitative documents, in any event. We deliberately chose to adopt this kind of approach and have already explained
why. We are left now with the delicate task of going from these
quantified attitudes and forms of behaviour to elaborate individual
expressions, bearing in mind the fact that although our sources are
vitally important for the study of popular forms of behaviour by their
simple weight and number, a different approach is necessary when
dealing with literary sources.

A collective landscape emerges fairly clearly from the data at which
we have looked. It is characterized by the image of a world of changed
collective attitudes in the three decades leading up to the French
Revolution. The collective values of this world were shaken, as were
religion, family structures and relationships between people –
whether we look at sociability and the festival or at aggression, their
reverse and complement. Individual or affective values were also
changed, including love, relationships within the couple or with
children and, finally, the sensibility of death, which declined and then
reappeared in a different form. This transitional sensibility was not at
all simple, as can be seen by juxtaposing the new certainties of the
Enlightenment and the invasion of affectivity which accompanied it
on the one hand, and, on the other, the growth of anxiety and
tensions.

It might seem difficult, or artificial, to integrate all the changes
registered in the statistics into a common rhythm, and yet we are
almost surprised by the convergences which emerge. Doubtless we are
seeing changes of different frequency superimposed on one another
and we are tempted, though not in any spirit of naive plagiarism, to
treat them in terms of an economistic model of periodization by
secular change, intercycle and cyclical crisis. The change in familial
attitudes to the child is a pluri-secular movement in the *longue durée*,
if we believe Philippe Ariès, who has traced its evolution from the
seventeenth century. The change in attitudes to death, in terms of
increasing individualization, is another process of change in the
longue durée according to the same author, whereby a growing
consciousness of the 'death of the self' (egoistic death, associated with
an obsession with salvation) was replaced by a Romantic interest in
the 'death of the other'. In this interpretation, the prerevolutionary
decades seem to be the culmination of a long process and also a
turning point which saw the beginnings of a new sensibility.

The general turning point which took place between 1750 and
1770 seems to be much more clear. It is not much of a discovery,
some might say, which confirms Mornet and the most classic

interpretations of literary history. Yet we are working on a different level, the level of mass behaviour, where certain changes which had been in progress among the elite from the end of the seventeenth century were being massively diffused. The statistics of illegitimacy and religious practice eloquently testify to the destructuring of the world-view of the classical period which was extended into the *Aufklärung*. By following these trends we can help to overcome the paradoxical impression left by Pierre Chaunu in his *Age of Enlightenment*, when he associated both these cultural manifestations with the age of absolutism. There are crises and accidents in the destructuring process which can be seen in most of the indicators from 1700 onwards. The pressure evident in the period 1770–5 is one example of these crises.

Some differentiations are apparent in the process of change, within a wider synchronism, such as the town–country distinction, where isolated communities which preserved traditional attitudes contrast with regions of mobility. Social distinctions are especially important, between groups which show signs of change, like the bourgeoisie and small urban tradesmen and groups which seem to stand still – except that they secretly invent new ways of avoiding having children.

Neither a primary cause nor an epiphenomenon: the place of prerevolutionary sensibility

From these interpretations and from some certainties, the question of what real place mentalities occupied in the lead-up to the French Revolution has been reformulated. In a word, we are asking to what extent this sensibility really was prerevolutionary. It might be best to begin with the traditional interpretations, if only as a foil to our own conclusions. These older views certainly integrated the various indices which we have looked at into a unified vision. If we read De Ribbe or some of the other conservative writers of the late nineteenth century, we can see that they saw changes in traditional attitudes towards religion, the family and authority as part of the sequel to the spread of philosophism which caused the fall of the *ancien régime*. This view, which lays a heavy stress on mental – we would say superstructural – forces, also has its image, or negative, in the liberal interpretation which saw the progress of individualism and the retreat of superstition as products of the spread of the Enlightenment and as a prelude to revolutionary emancipation.

It is easy to respond to these historically dated interpretations by pointing out the technical problems which they raise. What was the role of Voltaire or Rousseau in a society which was over 50 per cent illiterate and where, out of the 10 per cent of the population who were relatively well-off in Châlons-sur-Marne, whose wills give a listing of their libraries, only a tenth possessed more than 100 books? The whole question of the spread of the Enlightenment needs to be reformulated on the basis of this falsely innocent question.

Nowadays, emphasis is certainly placed on the weight of material factors in conditioning changes in collective sensibility. Demographic change made its effects felt in many ways during this period, disturbing the equilibrium of the family in the rural world, already swelling the ranks of rural migrants to the cities and banishing, to some extent, the traditional obsession with death. Not for nothing did the theme of the evils of the city already figure prominently in the obsessions of Sébastien Mercier and others. Changes in social relationships in the village, as well as in the cities, called into question the traditional unanimist fictions of social equilibrium. In terms of global developments in the dominant groups, involving the rise of an enlightened bourgeoisie on the one hand and the crisis of the nobility on the other, different forms of sensibility hid behind a common language, where moralism was expressed both in Rousseau-esque effusions and neoclassical heroism, while the declining status of the nobility was registered in the expressive revolts of a Sade or a Mirabeau.

We know all this, at least in general terms, and there is no need to go over it in too much detail. This is also prudent, because we know that the dialectical relationships which united the different social levels were not expressed as mechanically felt influences. F. Lebrun has demonstrated this in his work on death in Anjou, showing how the collective interpretation of death could change in a province where practice did not change in the eighteenth century, and where the traditional way of death remained in style. Thus we find anticipations, inertias and latencies as often as not. Such examples show that we cannot reduce collective sensibilities to an epiphenomenal role, but that they occupy an important place at the heart of ideological superstructures.

Forms of behaviour, sensibilities, ideologies

If we wish to adopt these assumptions, then the 'how' seems to be even more important here than the 'why', meaning, that if we admit the principle of a global relationship between changes in structures, as socioeconomic relationships, and changes in mentalities, it remains true that the screen of culture and ideologies stands between us and the level of sensibilities. Are mentalities and sensibilities only a reflection of culture and ideology?

In concrete terms, we are faced once again with the question of the role of the diffusion of the cultural model of the bourgeois elites, built into the corpus of Enlightenment philosophy, as a factor in changes in collective sensibilities in the course of the eighteenth century.

It seems undeniable that a number of the changes which we have been following were propagated (in ways which are still not clear) by the acquisition of different ways of seeing. This is the case with changes in behaviour towards death among the merchants and judges in Marseille from 1730, which can then be followed through to the artisans and shopkeepers and their wives between 1750 and 1770. This is why it has been possible, in all cordiality, to disagree with Philippe Ariès's interpretation, which is a prime example of the kind of analysis which banishes ideology, whether it be philosophical or religious, in order to stick to the development of a 'collective psychology' which is gifted with its own, quasi-autonomous ebb and flow.

This is not to assert that all changes in collective sensibility between 1760 and 1789 can be explained by the adoption, or vertical transmission, of an elite model. One can ask whether a new model of collective behaviour does not also emerge, specifically or locally, even within the popular groups. Edward Shorter's *Sexual Revolution*, which offers a typical portrait of the sans-culotte as described by Albert Soboul, among others, suggests, at the very least, a free adaptation of the bourgeois values of the Enlightenment. Many of these behavioural characteristics were borrowings which emerged from an older tradition with which the bourgeoisie could not identify. The revolutionary representatives, as Enlightenment materialists, sometimes recoiled with horror from the carnivalesque dechristianizing festivals of 1793. Does this mean that, after all, forms of popular revolutionary behaviour, in their continuity, can be assimilated to the panicky and backward-looking mass forms of behaviour which had not changed, either in their outlook or their reactions, from the time of the Fronde or the League? This would be to ignore the fact that, for the masses too, the vision of the world had changed.

Notes

A paper read at Göttingen in 1976 and published in *Vom Ancien Regime zur Französischen Revolution*, ed. Ernst Hindrichs, Eberhart Schmitt and Rudolf Vierhaus (Göttingen, 1978).

1 Public and tacit permits were two different categories of state permission to publish books in eighteenth-century France. Public permits (*permissions publiques*) were issued for books which had passed through the formal censoring machinery of the state. Tacit permits (*permissions tacites*) were issued for books 'that censors would not openly certify as inoffensive to morals, religion, or the state' (R. Darnton). [translator]
2 *Past and Present* (1969).
3 *Annales E.S.C.*, vol. 24 (1964).
4 In *Revue Historique* (1974).

10

The French Revolution: Change or Crisis of Values?

Is this paper a continuation of the same discussion? There is an undeniable continuity between the paper delivered at Göttingen in 1976 and the one presented at Bamberg in 1979 at the Conference on 'The French Revolution, an inevitable or contingent event?'. Here I look at the 'moderately-long' period of fifty years leading up to the Revolution and the short time-frame of the revolutionary explosion itself. Cultural revolutions bring about lightning changes in a world-view. What is the importance of such hereditary and creative processes?

To approach the French Revolution as a crisis or change of values requires some preliminary justification. One might be justified in seeing a considerable naivety in this enterprise – hammering on a door which has been open for a long time – in recalling that the world-view which emerged from the revolutionary crisis was quite different from that of the *ancien régime*. It might even be seen as a backward-looking approach, since traditional historiography, which began shortly after the Revolution itself and developed during the course of the nineteenth century, centred its interpretation of the revolutionary event on the collapse of the traditional values of the *ancien régime*. Since then, the pathways of more intensive scholarship on the problematic of the Revolution have led us in a different direction, for which we should be grateful. Recent historiography has concentrated on changes in the structures of society and on social dynamics in this period.

Rather than going back over old ground, I believe that we are adopting new approaches to what we nowadays call collective representations during the revolutionary period. We are responding to the interests of contemporary historiography in applying to this essential historical crisis methods which are often formulated over wide stretches of the *longue durée*.

That a crisis of values, as reflected in collective sensibility, took place prior to the event itself, and shaped some of its characteristics, goes without saying. I have tried, in the preceding essay on prerevolutionary sensibility, to answer the impertinent and naive question, 'what happened around 1750?', by using the trends of current research.

I was asked a number of questions as a result of that paper, some of them central. Were the 'indicators' chosen (religion, attitudes to life and death, sociability) the most appropriate or significant ones? Since then, too, research has moved on and no longer concentrates on origins so much as on the revolutionary moment itself, approached through such themes as the festival, culture, language or dechristianization in Year II of the First Republic. Sometimes, more at the level of conceptualization than research, the revolutionary event has been seen as an essential trauma, not so much hereditary as constitutive, the locus of a 'transfer' of sacrality or legitimacy. Whatever reservations I might have had about François Furet's theory, I nevertheless think it touches on an essential problematic. I think it is necessary today to move on to the heart of the revolutionary episode in order to gauge the shattering impact it had on collective representations.

Yet I want to do this in my own way, as a historian in the field, that is, on the basis of current research as it is taking place, or in terms of areas which have yet to be explored and which are just being opened up.

Developing new sources

In order to place our study of change in the context of a crisis of hegemonic or received collective values, both on the level of theory and of social practice, we need to have recourse to a range of apparently disparate sources. These include proclamatory or discursive sources, whereby the Revolution presented its new view of the world; sources of 'noble' or popular iconography by which key ideas became current and by which they were symbolically translated into imagery; also musical sources, especially songs, which, like popular imagery, tell more about the way in which new values were received than about their formulation at a higher level. From these sources we are led on to a final series of material which reflects the way in which these new ideas were put into practice. This includes narratives and images of life as found in reports and speeches or, in a less stilted way, in the reports of police informers and judicial records. In addition to the written sources, songs and imagery, gesture occupies an essential place in this demonstrative age. The revolutionary festival, a proclamation organized as a total spectacle, repeats and explicates the discourse of the official proclamations, but it also sometimes introduces an expression of popular aspirations, more as a counterpoint than a complement to the official discourse.

The festival has come in for a good deal of attention in contemporary research, as a microcosm which reflects the universe of collective representations in a condensed but singularly suggestive form. In a more secretive way, the very intimacy of gestures and forms of behaviour, as reflected in demographic data, for example, allows us to appreciate the extent to which the world changed for those who lived through the revolutionary period.

All this confronts us with a host of sources and characteristics which, it must be noted, give us access to various levels and different perceptions of reality. An entire dialectic emerges between such diverse sources as the direct proclamations or voluntarist discourses by which the world-view of the revolutionary bourgeoisie was expressed and the way in which these new values were received and put into practice. This is a dialectic which needs to be investigated, but it can be grasped, at a primary level of description, through a certain number of characteristics.

The second stage of this process is the need to establish a hierarchy of the data which we have obtained. The new system of values, as they were proclaimed and put into practice, was far from homogenous. We can see these differences in the different approaches to various sources. We can adopt an approach based on proclamatory sources, involving discourses, imagery and songs, which were often as much, if not more, the expression of a dream rather than of a reality, whereby bourgeois values made progress by compromises with popular aspirations. On the other hand, we can adopt an approach based on the gestures and expressions of social practice, involving demographic sources, narratives, reports or police records. Between these two spheres, the revolutionary festival is the supreme expression of an intermediary level which registers the interaction between a voluntarist impulse and the way it was received – the way it was translated. The festival is not the only example of this kind of intermediary level, and in this context we can also point to the various forms of spontaneous religiosity. In this closed field of comparisons and confrontations we come up against one of the least understood aspects of the Revolution, the Revolution in 'hearts and minds'.

An inventory of new values: the questioning of the family

The inventory of new values, born out of the heat of action, which I am going to offer under this heading, should not, at the risk of sounding mystificatory, be seen as the expression of a new consensus, but rather as the reflection of conflict and of a gradual process of elaboration.

It may be useful, in the Manichean, black-and-white outlook of the period itself, to begin with the great refusal, that is the system which the Revolution, in its discourses and proclamations, wished to exorcise and proscribe, what it reactively defined as the hated values of the *ancien régime*. We have been able to reconstruct this system in a rather crude, but nonetheless suggestive fashion on the basis of a corpus of speeches and addresses produced during the dechristianization of the Year II, as studied in the south-eastern quarter of France, an area which offers massive, though qualitatively poor sources. The Manichean outlook encompassed the two major systems associated with the political and social structures of the *ancien régime*: feudalism and 'superstition'. On the one hand there was slavery, arrogance and oppression, all the labels which evoke hierarchy, subservience and arbitrary rule. On the other hand was the nebulous complex which included fanaticism, error, lies, hypocrisy, idolatry, dogmatism and absurdity, with their complements of ignorance and credulity. But this toppled world was also defined in terms of moral condemnation, being associated with imposture, corruption, egotism and cruelty. A heavy weight of radical reprobation was applied to this abandoned world of shadows.

By contrast, the new system of positive values with which the French Revolution was identified needs, at this exploratory stage, to be pedagogically simplified so as to describe its key ideas, whether explicit or otherwise.

It might seem artificial to start with the idea of the family, given that the expected ideological reference point might be the individual, as affirmed and recognized both in the Declaration of the Rights of Man and in the new legal system. But the complementary notion of 'family', which had been prepared by the considerable emphasis placed on the theme by public opinion in the wake of Rousseau, also emerged both in literal and metaphorical terms. 'The Bastille has gone, we are all one family' was the chant in 1789 when unanimity was still the dominant word. The emphasis on the family as an elementary structure arose as a counterpart to the condemnation of celibacy, illustrated by the attack on monastic celibacy from 1790 and, later, on priestly celibacy, up to the crisis of the Year II. One thinks of the popular print showing a double line of monks and nuns emerging from the cloister, united in civil marriage by the mocking citizen who jokes that it is a useful way of avoiding the risk of being cuckolded. We also have the self-image of the sans-culotte printed in the Year II under the title *An answer to the important question, 'What is a sans-culotte?'*, in which the hero presented himself as a family man, concerned with providing for his wife and children. This image corresponds quite well to the results of research into the sociology of the sans-culottes in Paris and Marseille, where they were generally fathers of families, with an average age around forty, as in the stereotype.

Does the image of the couple show any evidence of change? We should begin with the naive but essential test of assessing the link between the proclamations and the realities of the situation on the ground. Institutionally, the laicization of marriage; the abolition of the forbidden periods (Lent, Advent, etc.), the easing of restrictions on consanguinity and the introduction of divorce cannot have failed to have modified perceptions of these realities. But, in order to judge properly, we need to have more studies of the impact of divorce, both in the countryside and in the cities. Divorce seems to have been quite marked in the great cities (although one wonders to what extent this reflected the regularization of existing situations) but was often negligible elsewhere. The picture of free unions among the sans-culottes, as they appear in the Parisian environment studied by Soboul, were a popular reflection of the relationship of Jean-Jacques Rousseau and Thérèse Levasseur, but they were also rooted in popular urban practices established in the second half of the eighteenth century. They also need to be studied in their real extent. Were they a phenomenon peculiar to Paris, or to the great cities, which were already experiencing their 'sexual revolution'?

The ambiguity of revolutionary discourse and practice is affirmed here. Under the Directory, one of the moral elements of the revolutionary festival was the celebration of wedlock. Yet, to judge by the indices of diffusion and participation which I found for Provence, this does not seem to have been one of the more widely followed rituals.

This was an ephemeral urban liturgy, even if we do find the occasional southern village ready to congratulate an old couple who, in fifty years of marriage, 'had never said a cross word to one another'.

The celebration of marriage and of the couple was not an innovation of the Directory period, the characteristic of a bourgeois anxiety for a return to order. It is directly inscribed in the moralism of the Jacobin period and its mentality, in which moral degradation and libertinism were aristocratic vices. Marie-Antoinette and the Princesse de Lamballe were, in this period, images of the 'she-wolf', the great prostitute of a corrupt world. Doubtless Hébert's reference to the trial of Marie-Antoinette as an assault on the decency of motherhood, or, at the very least, an offence against good taste, can be understood in this context. This is also a context in which, ultimately, an element of misogyny played an important part. Popular or *petit bourgeois* misogyny left its mark in terms of the Jacobin opposition to women's involvement in the Revolution. This is to say nothing of the strong dislike, indeed the murderous hatred, of the counter-revolutionary aristocracy and bourgeoisie for the 'amazons' and 'furies' who, as goddesses of Reason or simply as participants in the revolutionary crowds, had departed from their traditionally allotted roles.

Deepening the study of the new image of the family as reflected in the couple will lead us in many directions which can only be suggested here. They include the faces and expressions of love during the Revolution, from platonic and deferred love, as in the case of Robespierre, or of Buzot and Mme Roland, to Danton's voracious sexuality. This is an area which is too encumbered by received images to delay us for very long, however, although perhaps it should. A more austere direction, based on demographic statistics, would include an attempt, based on a wider range of sites, to verify or modify the working hypothesis advanced by Le Roy Ladurie in his essay 'Demography and dark secrets in Languedoc'. Was the Revolution the real turning point in the generalized use of contraception amongst the peasantry, registered in a fall of between 38 and 32 per cent in the birth rate? We are aware of the early roots of this change, from 1770 and even before, in the cities and certain parts of the countryside. Yet this does not undermine the importance of the Revolution as an immediate or deferred turning point, nor of the essential change which took place with respect to a way of life and to religious ordinances.

The murder of the father

The representation of the family in the collective revolutionary imagination has been dealt with under a certain number of headings. Among these is the emphasis placed on the symbolism of age in the revolutionary festivals, to which Mona Ozouf has rightly drawn our attention. Was this a mystificatory theme which (to simplify greatly) was consciously or unconsciously designed to disguise real social divisions? At the very least it reflects, in an allusive and filtered way, the profound readjustment of family relationships which took place in this period. In what has to be a programme of suggestions for further investigation, there is an important place for the study of the image of the father during the Revolution, at the different levels at which the image is encountered. The Revolution carried out by forty-year-old fathers of families is symbolically conceivable in terms of the murder of the father in two previously all-powerful forms: those of the king and, at times at least, of God himself.

We can trace the stages of a gradual process of emancipation, seen by the actors themselves as a tragedy, in the development of the image of the king. This image changed from that of the king as a father-protector, to whom the *cahiers de doléances* were respectfully addressed, to the image of the king as an enemy, whose symbolic death, anticipating the real event, was expressed by the glacial silence which greeted his return from Varennes, before becoming the subject of a fundamental debate in the Convention.

God – God the Father meting out eternal punishment, whose terrorist image haunted Manon Roland from childhood – also suffered an eclipse. It is, perhaps, not reading too much into the imagery to ask why God the Father was momentarily replaced by the feminine image of the Goddess of Reason. There is, of course, no simple answer to the play of creativity of the collective imagination, especially when God the Father, deprived of his terrorist aspect and seen as dispenser of rewards to the good and punishment to the wicked, is to be found rehabilitated in the figure of the Supreme Being, 'father of the universe, supreme intelligence . . .'.

To return, which is not always easy, from the level of symbolic representations to that of lived social practice, we can also find, in the exemplary scenography of the revolutionary festival, two coexisting images of the grown male: the adult and the old man. But even this event did not quite give pride of place to the aged patriarch.

The Spartan imagery of the festival represented the old man as the guardian of the wisdom and experience which he will transmit to the younger men and soldiers who bear him aloft in town squares, entitled to the respect which, under the Directory, took a symbolic form in the Festival of Age. As a living symbol of continuity and tradition, the old man was present to pass on the torch and to preside over the calling to arms of younger men. Dominating the scene was the figure of the warrior, of the young man in the prime of life, as in David's painting *Brutus*, showing the lictors carrying the dead bodies of his sons to him. This is hardly surprising in a period where Roland seemed an old fogey in the assemblies, a time in which the Revolution meant the massive promotion of a whole galaxy of young men between the ages of eighteen and forty, on all fronts, both internal and external. As the promotion or victory, however temporary, of youth, the Revolution had its child-heroes like Bara or Viala and its young generals like Hoche, Marceau and Kléber, whose names persistently figured among the most popular names given to children during the nineteenth century and right up to the beginning of the twentieth. Yet if the young hero was most strikingly revealed at the moment when he became a warrior, this does not devalue the formidable investment in youth which was made during the French Revolution. Youth became the bearer of a great many hopes. The place of children in the revolutionary festivals grew from 1792 onwards. It is true that this happened in different ways, ranging from the young battalions of 1793–4 to the schoolchildren who figured in the Directory's festivals; the latter, if not returned to the ranks, had at least been reduced to a more subordinate role.

Throughout the exemplary test represented by familial values, revolutionary change is already apparent in all its complexity, and also in its limits, contradictions and fluctuations. It is appropriate, in moving on, to extend the study to the invisible family, the span of generations, tradition and inheritance. We need not be surprised by the pompous bad taste of Maximin Isnard, who urged the people of Marseille, in the Year III, to dig up the bones of their fathers to fight against the Terrorists. At its climax the Revolution did exhume bones (at Saint-Denis and other places) but only to scatter them. Here we see the major limit of the revolutionary use of the family as an element of continuity. As a constitutive event, it began by rejecting tradition. As one famous quotation put it, the old men no longer brag about their young days, 'they are embarrassed by them.' This sense of radical cleavage was forcefully expressed, and with some grandeur, during the most traumatic events, such as the trial of the king. It was Cambon, less prosaically than usual, who used the metaphor of the island on which the revolutionaries had landed, burning the boats which had brought them there.

The rediscovery of tradition, in the widest sense of the term, took place at a later stage, and we will deal with it in due course. But clearly, the Revolution wished, at least temporarily, to strain the links established by tradition. Individuals found themselves integrated into a wider space and time-frame – that of the collectivity, the nation, the nation which could enlarge its frontiers to the limits of the universe.

If the Revolution kept the family as the indivisible knot of its value-system, it broke ancient solidarities, whether horizontal ones, involving social groups, companionship and confraternities, or vertical ones, involving the links of dependence and subordination of a society of 'orders'. Yet it also proposed a new framework and renewed norms to this collection of individuals.

The remodelling of time and space

For some of its citizens, the Revolution provided new social contexts by breaking through the limited horizons of the village or the urban district. It was a period of great demographic mobility. In the increased mobility of men and women shown by marriage statistics, it showed itself to be innovative in much more than a momentary way. Three-quarters of married couples in Chartres, a medium-sized city of about 10,000 people, were 'natives' in 1788; under the Revolution no more than half were native, and this change survived the ephemeral aspects of the crisis, such as the marriage-fever brought on by conscription.

Such change was particularly noticeable among young males between twenty and thirty years of age and was certainly most especially felt as a result of the impact of the conscription of men. Yet it went far beyond these limits. Intermarriage and contacts of the most varied kind, ranging from fraternization during the revolutionary festivals to the military raids on the provinces conducted by revolutionaries during the winter of 1793, represented forms of contact which went far beyond the traditional kind, even if these too were reactivated by the crisis, as in the emergence of vagrancy and begging in the great agricultural plains.

In this period there was a link between the explosion of the limits of space for a growing section of the population, brought into contact with national realities by their own displacement or by the fact that they encountered the Revolution in the form of the Great Fear or the process of dechristianization and, on the other hand, the deliberate reconstruction of space and time after 1793 by the new calendar, the introduction of the metric system and, more revolutionary still, the remodelling of place names. These were gigantic undertakings, if we think about them, and they go well beyond a mere change of framework, in terms of our current theme. The new calendar, like the desacralization and defeudalization of place names, removed a whole deep-rooted heritage from the rhythms of collective life and the places where it was expressed, introducing the banal or neutralized regularity of the new calendar and, even better, reclaiming possession of space and time by populating them with the new symbols of the Revolution and the values which they promoted.

The metric system was successful, in the middle term at least; neither the new calendar nor, generally speaking, the new toponymy survived the Revolution. It is nevertheless true that by this remodelling of space, geographical as well as social space, the Revolution tried to promote new values and new solidarities.

Solitude or community: the new solidarities. The nation and the people

The solitude of the individual, isolated in his own adventure, remained the tragic appanage of the revolutionary hero: Marat immured in his role of prophet; Saint-Just and Robespierre conscious of the fatal character of the adventure on which they had embarked. 'Virtue has always been in the minority in the world.' Such a sentiment, in many different forms, only became common during the period of the Directory, with its dominant motif of 'every man for himself'. 'We have all lost our titles,' wrote one Parisian journalist of the time, meaning that everyone had, in one way or another, broken with their social past, whether mental or familial, and with the framework of their former lives. These expressions reflect one aspect of the 'revolution in manners', but clearly, the revolutionary discourse was differently expressed during its triumphant phase.

Almost from the start, the Revolution proposed the image of a community of citizens, through the medium of fraternity. The fraternization of the Feast of the Federation in the summer of 1790 remained for many, in the collective memory, the prototype of the revolutionary festival which was unanimous in intent, even if the iconography and songs around the theme were immediately contradicted by a spirit of comic rejection:

Aristocrat, you're really done for now.
The Champ de Mars will cook your goose for good!

The myth of unanimity and of the practice of fraternity was one of the most obstinately reasserted of all the repertory of revolutionary values, through a whole series of reverses which it suffered at the hands of events. It inspired all the 'fraternizations', which were repeated up to the middle of the period of the Terror, as in the fraternal banquets of the spring of the Year II. It gave rise to its own symbolic expressions, of which the festivals of the Directory provided the most sophisticated expression, but which can be seen in earlier models involving rituals of exchange and the ritual of the revolutionary oath. The Revolution, which began by trying to abolish oaths because of the limitations they placed on individual liberty, as was also the case with the abolition of perpetual vows, ended up by rehabilitating them in the form of civic oaths, like the oath of the Federation, as links by which to provide a structure for its new solidarities.

Two new themes, or new values, emerged among the range of key revolutionary ideas: the Nation and the People. A new collective consciousness took root between the Federation movement, a kind of antidote to the Great Fear of the previous year, which swept through France and sanctioned a sense of guilt which abolished the old divisions of particularism, the beginnings of the revolutionary war and the proclamation of the fatherland in danger. This collective consciousness was able to survive the storms of federalism, conscription and centrifugal tensions. To this extent, national ideology, which was revived by the war, resisted the pressure of events better than the idea of 'the People' as a collective *persona* which alone was capable, in its gigantic reality, of defeating the kings, as in the popular print which shows the popular Hercules crushing the crowned pygmies.

It we try to follow the evolution of the idea of the people through the course of the history of the Revolution, it is not difficult to see the birth, assertion and disintegration of this key idea, even without calling on the resources of historical lexicography, which we shall consider presently. From 'the peoples' referred to at the time of the Estates General, when France was still, in Mirabeau's phrase, 'an aggregate of disunited peoples', we can trace the emergence of the monolithic and total reality of the people in the unanimist period of the bourgeois Revolution. From this, by a process of successively identifying the enemies of the Revolution and excluding them from the picture of national unity (as aristocrats, suspects, reactionaries,

federalists) there emerged the restrictive image of the people as the
petit peuple, the lower orders. This group, which was 'so interesting
and so neglected', in Marat's phrase, took shape and became dominant during the Terror. The realignments of the Directory revived the
pseudo-unanimist image of 'the awakening of the people ... The
French people, a people of brothers', mitigated by the protective tone
which some other chants of the time adopted towards the 'good
people'.

In this new framework, the French Revolution was experimenting,
not without difficulties and contradictions, with the forms of a new
humanism, the intense experience of which made it into much more
than just an extension of the message of the Enlightenment.

A new humanism: the shortness of life and the search for happiness, dignity and virtue

A sense, or feeling of life was born in this period which was marked
by brevity and, at the same time, by an ardent search for happiness,
the kind of happiness which was truly, as in Saint-Just's phrase, 'a
new idea in Europe'. One thinks, as an echo of this, of the remarkable
oath which Fauchet, a future constitutional bishop, made the congregation take under the vaults of the Sacred Temple: 'We vow today
... we vow that we shall be happy.' Happiness here is more a claim
and a battle to be won than a state of being. True life consists of
conquering and creating, but only on earth, since we know, with
François de Neufchateau, that:

> Paradise is found on earth
> And hell is in remorse.

This search for happiness, happiness to be experienced immediately
or, at the latest, tomorrow, modelled a number of the characteristics
of the revolutionary *homo novus*. These, not surprisingly, contained
certain contradictions involving the period and the environment.

The first, or at least the most constant, of the individual values
promoted by the new humanism is perhaps dignity: the respect for the
person expressed in the laconic formula by which the Jacobins signed
themselves, 'your equal before the law'. My dignity goes beyond the
respect accorded it by others. It presupposes the right to life and to the
most ambiguous forms of existence. It certainly includes security and
the respect for physical integrity which led to the abolition of the
tortures and degrading punishments of the *ancien régime*. The

substitution of the guillotine for older forms of execution was itself a step forward and a reflection of a new view of humanity. It implied a respect for the right to life. For the bourgeoisie in power, it was called the respect for property; for the popular movement, in its most extreme forms of expression, it extended, by contrast, to the limitation of that right by the affirmation of the right of all people to a decent existence.

The respect for my dignity which I require from others presupposes that I respect myself by the exercise of virtue, another key word, second only to liberty, in the new ethic. Moral, and moralizing, the Jacobin revolution defined itself by contrast to the corruption of the old regime, even if Robespierre's pessimism ('Virtue has always been in the minority') set limits to the hopes for a new world. Daily practice, or the circulation of the proclamations issued by the assemblies of the Sections, testified that this key idea was not just a declaration of pious intentions. In its wars against prostitution and luxury, the Spartan tone of the Jacobin episode remains one of those marked characteristics which define the atmosphere of the period.

In its wake, virtue brought a whole series of connected assertions, such as the dignity of work in contrast to the idleness of the great or of the parasitic groupings of the *ancien régime*, and the necessity for personal and collective discipline. On his masonic tombstone, the Jacobin Joseph Sec, the self-made man from Aix whose mental universe I studied from the evidence on his monument proclaimed:

> Freed from a cruel slavery,
> I have no master but myself
> But with this liberty, my only wish
> Is to obey the law.

This is merely the expression of the new ethic at an everyday level. The pressure of events and revolutionary necessities led to an ultimate formulation which was subliminal, in the form of the heroism and heroic mentality of the period. The revolutionary period appears as the age of the hero, whether individual or collective and anonymous. The revolutionary festivals and the construction of a revolutionary pantheon are the unequivocal expression of this heroism.

The practice of equality, or 'the republican level'

Equality and a later arrival, fraternity, are the two values which we expect in the ethical repertory of this new world. We are not directly concerned here with their abstract proclamation, but with the ways in which they were practised, or at least dreamed about. As profoundly 'shattering', on reflection, as the great reconstructions which were attempted in space and time were the ephemeral changes, such as the use of '*tu*', the revolution in dress among the sans-culottes, the wearing of the red bonnet or the fraternal banquets of the spring of 1794. In the more extreme forms, which can still surprise us, such as the demolition of church towers in the Alps, so as to place them 'on the republican level', in the phrase of the emissary Albitte, we see the concrete translation of this egalitarian impulse at a time of liberation, which testifies to the extent to which such ideas were accepted. Even though acceptance was not universal, we can see that it was taken up by a popular sensibility which found in it a response to its own aspirations.

The symbolism of the revolutionary festival, in the often spontaneous forms invented in 1793–4, as well as in the liturgies established under the Directory, metaphorically translated the new code of values which had been dreamed of into gestures. In this process, the gestural system of exchange, the gift, occupied an important place.

This repertory which I have all too briefly enumerated might well be said to have been familiar to us for a very long time, from the time when the triad of 'Liberty, Equality, Fraternity' was inscribed on the walls of public buildings at the end of the nineteenth century. What is less well known, to say the least, is the way in which this new system of representations was spread, to what profound harmonics it responded, with whom, for how long, and how deeply.

Some vital centres of expression, such as festivals, form a good introduction to this area, and lead on to a level where key ideas are illustrated, if not embodied, in symbols. At the same time they reflect both the official discourse and the way in which it was adapted, and also spontaneous creativity on the ground. Yet there remains the problem of discovering to what extent these values were really 'lived', and in what measure they represent a momentary turning point or decisive change at the level of the 'collective imagination'.

The answer – in a field which has hardly been explored – is not unambiguous. Did life change for the men and women of this period? Again at the proclamatory level, in song, the *Leavetaking Song*, praising Bara and Viala, proclaims:

They are dead but they have lived . . .
The coward weighed down with years has never lived . . . ..

Real life is going to be different from now on. The most directly involved actors of the Revolution have experienced it as something short, intense and heroic. Did they have the privilege of a sensibility which values the moment, but values even more the urgency of the task to be accomplished? At the humblest levels of everyday militancy, or in the lower ranks of the movement, we find the same perception expressed in identical terms. I think, out of the host of possible examples in this context, of the justificatory autobiography of Barjavel, public prosecutor in Vaucluse in the Year II, on the eve of his trial and execution in the Year III. His self-sacrifice, devotion and commitment are beyond measure – and these are qualities which Richard Cobb does not in the least deny to the middle ranks of the Jacobin movement, which are his area of expertise.

Yet, as a complement to this Jacobin self-portrait for posterity, Cobb is not alone in wishing to trace a 'realistic' image of the Jacobin or sans-culotte as the demystified hero, restored to human dimensions.

The punitive will; violence

Against this system of values, whose themes have just been recalled, in some of which the bourgeoisie could recognize its own referential norms, the revolutionary movement opposed the consciousness of a very vital tension. On the one side, we have the values of 'peaceful and victorious liberty', in Robespierre's phrase; on the other the emergence, momentarily at least, of very old and very new ideas of vigilance, violence, punishment, all things of which Saint-Just might have been thinking when he wrote: 'It is possible that the force of circumstances will lead us to results which he had not foreseen.'

One section of contemporary history, like the historiography of the nineteenth century, has not been particularly open to this 'awkward' aspect of the revolution of hearts and minds. We have been reminded of its backward-looking characteristics, rooted in a whole tradition of violence and popular upheavals. The punitive impulse, as expressed in the killings and massacres leading up to and including the September Massacres, has been seen as a continuation of attitudes and gestures whose monotonous repetition can be traced back to the Fronde, the League and even beyond. This was the opinion, fifteen years ago, of Denis Richet and François Furet. The latter's interpretation is now very different. He insists, not on tradition or on the past, but on the future of the Revolution as a transfer to legitimacy, an essential part of which is the myth of the plot, one of the major forms of revolutionary 'delirium', in his phrase, being both ancestor and nurse of 'all the gulags to come'. At this level, Furet paradoxically finds common ground with Richard Cobb's psychological portrait of the sans-culottes, which stresses their spontaneous and brutal intolerance.

Without becoming involved in polemic, it is certainly necessary to make room for a whole series of new ideas in the revolutionary mentality which are unexpected in terms of an Enlightenment heritage. Even before the myth of the plot, vigilance is symbolized by the open and attentive eye which is to be found in the headlines of the committees of surveillance, and elsewhere. Vigilance, an anxious form of consciousness, and of virtue, appropriated to the revolutionary moment, is only one of the domesticated forms of the punitive impulse. This impulse arising out of popular practice, and supported by the bourgeoisie, re-imposed on Enlightenment philanthropy the idea that violence was necessary to ensure the triumph of the objectives of the Revolution.

Vigilance, plots and legitimized violence form a notional system which, at the level of the discourse of dechristianization, was expressed in a determined vocabulary dominated by terms of action: terms like energy, hatred, vengeance, thunder, destroy, crush, vigour, exterminate, execrate, ardour, vomit, annihilate. This kind of emphasis and its frequent repetition allows us to see the important place it occupied in the revolutionary mentality. Yet was it not simply the product of circumstances, a momentary distortion of the bourgeois value-system which would very shortly repudiate, as alien, these excesses of the moment? Yet there is one essential fact which cannot be passed over in silence. Very naively, it is the fact of the Revolution itself – the collective consciousness of a sudden, violent break with continuity, tradition and heritage.

Contemporaries felt the significance of this constitutive event and expressed it in awe-struck tones. Listen to Desmoulins: '*Fiat, fiat*, yes, all this is going to be accomplished ... we have become invincible.' The revolutionary event, in all its magnitude, which, as the birth of a new era, justified the violence which it unleashed, is the pivot of the change in collective mentality.

The Year I of Liberty; reason and the heart

The Revolution was presented as the Year I of Liberty, as a new birth.

The feeling of a beneficial and total break with the past lies at the heart of the revolutionary sensibility. It pervades the new symbolism, as in the theme of regeneration, or of a new birth, which can be seen in the majestic fountain of 10 August 1793 built to mark the promulgation of the new constitution, when the members of the Convention filled their cups with water flowing from the breasts of a colossal statue in Egyptian style.

On the declaratory level, we only have to look at the speeches and writings of some of those involved. 'Our freedom came like a tempest, and its triumph was like a clap of thunder,' wrote Saint-Just in his famous subsistence speech of October 1792, echoing Marat, who wrote in the 'Offering to the fatherland': 'Know just once the price of liberty; know just once the value of an instant.' The feeling of an abrupt break with the past was combined with the feeling of the invincibility or irreversibility of the Revolution. 'A people in a state of revolution is invincible,' wrote Isnard in 1751, for once in agreement with Marat: 'The Revolution will unfailingly succeed, and no power on earth will be able to stop it.'

The new system of revolutionary values, the keystone of the new humanism whose characteristics we have all too briefly outlined, was also rooted in the legitimation of the radical change, or total subversion, which the Revolution represented. This is not to say that it was presented as a *tabula rasa* or a creation *ex nihilo*. We also need to take account of the securities it sought in a new sacrality and the indebtedness it felt to its heritage of moral and cultural models.

In the dechristianizing discourse of Year II, which was the ultimate expression of this process, the Promethean force of change, here pushed to its climax, was primarily described in terms of a rapid process of emancipation or liberation. Here the key words were: regenerate, open one's eyes, unmask, unveil, liberate, extricate, uproot and extirpate, but also restore – in the context of what was claimed as a moral revolution.

The first process, as a *tabula rasa*, led to a new system of references, based on a double appeal to reason and the heart. The essential themes are all found here, in varying proportions depending on place, time and the people responsible for the dechristianizing discourse. On the one hand they include reason, truth, enlightenment or philosophy and even good sense, and on the other an appeal to the heart based on nature, truth, sentiment, morality, sensibility, even instinct and on the the inspiration or even the 'transports' which these deeply rooted values can provoke in us.

Was this double system of reference to reason and the heart

sufficient to fill the vacuum left by the exorcism of fanaticism and superstition? This was certainly the belief of promoters and activists of the Cult of Reason, in the course of its brief but eventful existence between the months of *brumaire* and *ventose* in Year II. In what can only be a brief inventory of directions and areas of research, we can hardly avoid asking just what the personification of Reason by living goddesses of Reason in the cities, towns and villages meant to ordinary sans-culotte spectators. Current research has rendered obsolete the caricatural image of Bacchic Saturnalias inherited from nineteenth-century historiography, which nevertheless survives in the present century.

The Cult of Reason was certainly better received by popular groupings than had previously been thought. This is proved by maps showing how far it spread. It remains to be seen how it was perceived and put into practice. When we read in the family diary of Coulet, a weaver from Avignon, the simple statement: 'Today, the living mother of God was paraded in public,' we can see in what unexpected ways the event was experienced by popular groups.

The Supreme Being and the new hereafter

The question just raised about the real impact of collective representations of this kind recurs in the case of the other sacred image by which Robespierre and Saint-Just tried to replace the Cult of Reason, which was a disguised version of the atheism banned by the Jacobins. We have long been aware of what the Cult of Reason meant to its promoters, through writings and speeches, of which Robespierre's are the purest and most complete examples. It answered the needs of the heart as much as those of the mind and was the indispensable complement to belief in the immortality of the soul, which was itself an essential extension of the need to know that one day the good would be rewarded and the wicked punished according to their crimes.

Whereas the heirs of one part of the Enlightenment – the materialism of the second half of the eighteenth century – banished all the ghosts of the hereafter and the old system of eternal punishment at the hands of a vengeful God (listen to the representative Lequinio: 'No citizens, there is no future life, no ...'), another view of the hereafter was affirmed in the Cult of the Supreme Being, which was at once very abstract and a response to the claims of sentiment more than those of reason.

What is currently being investigated, beyond the theoretical level of proclamations, is the way in which these forms and expressions of a new hereafter were experienced, perceived and imagined. This is an important area in the study of collective imagination, which is often discussed nowadays. We can very generally discern its themes and characteristics through the key ideas of the discourses, terms like universe, humanity, progress, prosperity, immortality, and also from the redeployment of a great many ideas derived from traditional religion in the service of revolutionary ideology: sublime, martyrs, adore, apostles and missionaries, grace, wonders, miracles, preach, marvels, oracles, gospel, dogma, revelation, etc., etc. Having been chased away, the supernatural comes galloping back!

The supernatural returned not merely in the important redeployment of words, but also even in the forms of expression of the new religiosity which made use of original forms, including the cult of martyrs of liberty – Marat, Le Peletier, Chalier – a new trinity which was eventually enlarged by the addition of the child heroes Bara and Viala; spontaneous local devotions were associated with revolutionary saints, such as St Pataude of the tricoloured wings. Here we have a new popular level of sacred experience in which is reflected what Mona Ozouf has defined as a 'transfer of sacrality', expressed in the symbolism of the revolutionary festivals.

Social practice is thus validated and sacralized by new key values which provide it with legitimacy. These new values range from the civic cult, limitless endeavour for the public good, the investment in happiness to be constructed by future generations and the new hereafter which justifies all sacrifices, even that of life itself, where survival is guaranteed in the collective memory: 'I leave you my memory, it will be dear to you and you will defend it . . ..'

At this level one feels that the revolutionary *homo novus*, having proclaimed the *tabula rasa* of the heritage of the past, presents himself, consciously or unconsciously, as an 'heir', heir to moral and cultural models, either consciously asserted or, if unconscious, deeply rooted nonetheless.

At the stage which we have now reached, with an inventory or programme of research, we can move on to a description of the ultimate sources of this revolutionary heritage.

The Bible, fable and history; the revolutionary as heir

Religious heritage is represented by the Bible, even before the reading of the New Testament Jesus as a sans-culotte. Jean Marsin, in his timeless writings, has very subtly analysed the prophetic side of a personality like Jean-Paul Marat, and of others like Jacques Roux, who were voices crying in the wilderness. This kind of prophetism was expressed in actions and situations, the isolation of the forerunner, for example, but it also emerged in *topoi* directly inherited from the discourse of preaching, as in the denunciation of the idleness and flabbiness of the rich, or in apocalyptic visions.

The millenarian dimension of one part of the revolutionary discourse, both on a popular level and among some sections of the *petit-bourgeois* activists and some of the leading spokesmen, is an area of research which is currently being explored but which still requires a good deal of work. This is also the case with the direct legacy of Christianity, which was violently rejected and yet also cultivated in the theme of Jesus the sans-culotte. The nature of the compromise, which was dramatically and painfully embodied in the figures of the constitutional clergy, caught between Christian values and revolutionary involvement in the Year II, also needs to be examined and deepened. We can see something of this compromise in the naive yet serene and controlled syncretism of the fine masonic funeral monument of Joseph Sec, the citizen of Aix about whom I have written. In a single iconographic discourse, Sec portrayed his own personal adventure: his ascension as a succesful bourgeois, the collective adventure of the French Revolution, which he had experienced, and finally the ascent of humanity, as it flies to the apex of his monument into a blazing sun like the prophet Elijah. Sec's case presents a model, or example, doubtless less isolated than it seems, of the way in which such an experience was lived and felt. Yet it is only one model among many. Many people had to live out the crisis of values of which the Revolution was the culmination in an infinitely more painful way than Joseph Sec.

There is one other heritage which must be taken into account in this history of the 'costumes' with which the new world clothed itself, namely the classical heritage. To paraphrase Marx's famous statement, we can say that the major and minor actors of the Revolution lived out their adventure in Roman costume, finding the heroic references they needed in classical models learned from Plutarch in their schooldays. How and why did this neoclassical framework, of which David's art is the exemplary expression, become the central and most useful pillar of the new symbolism and, even more profoundly still, of the new ethic and world-view? This is not at all a futile question. Why do we have this paradox between a sensibility which was already Romantic – that of the hero, isolated in the pesssimism of an adventure which he knows will be fatal – and yet which censored itself, one might say, by adopting the framework of Neoclassicism? This is an open field and one which a study of the ample corpus of neoclassical painting, engraving and design, as we have seen in recent exhibitions, should allow us to deepen and modify.

From this inevitably summary inventory of problems, which I felt should be offered, we can now pass on to the fundamental problems to which it gives rise, and with which I would like to conclude.

The ways and means of change

At the primary level, the clear extent of the change, the profound split, which took place during the Revolution in the area of collective mentalities leads us to investigate the ways and means by which it took place.

The programme which takes shape from such research will shed light on the destructive forms of what has been qualified (by P. Goujard and C. Mazauric) as a veritable 'cultural revolution' in the French style, though this will be an inevitably artificial dichotomy. In this respect, the campaign of dechristianization unleashed between the months of *brumaire* and *germinal* of the Year II, and beyond, constitutes the most important and original period. The dechrist-ianization of the Year II, which was neither a wholly spontaneous movement nor one imposed by a regime which very quickly dis-avowed it, took place in the intermediary realm where an active minority came up against a public opinion which was sometimes restrained and sometimes ready to welcome, or even to practise intensively, the various forms of rapid liberation from received values. Autos-da-fé, vandalism and the expulsion of priests went hand in hand with a frequently simultaneous process of 'defeudalization' which attacked the direct or symbolic expressions of the old order, including the destruction of armorial insignias – the 'toys' of the old regime – and the changing of place names. We can see why interpretations of revolutionary vandalism form part of the pioneer-ing frontiers of current research. Such vandalism, in all its complexity, went far beyond the bestial, savage expression of a blindly destructive impulse.

There is a far from simple dialectic between this first order of collective behaviour, from the first killings of the Great Fear to the autos-da-fé of the Year II, and the second order, which, by contrast, proposed the spread of a new system of values and the building of a new world of representations in which a new 'collective imagination' found expression. Are we dealing with a simple complementarity here, as was thought at the time, with the closing of the church being succeeded by the opening of the temple of Reason? Or are we dealing with a more complex phenomenon of 'recuperation' whereby the Jacobin bourgeoisie, having given free rein, willingly or otherwise, to the expression of popular subversion, as in the 'carnivalesque' phase of the Year II, regained control of the situation in order to establish a basis for their system of stabilized values? Some recent studies help us to discern more precisely the mechanics of this turning point, based on a study of the system of gestures and discourse in certain specific areas. Thus, B. Conein's work on the September Massacres shows how the popular expression of primitive impulses, expressed in gestures and attitudes, was translated by the spontaneous spokesmen of the uprising, who ensured a process of transition by means of improvised tribunals which prepared the way for the ultimate control of the movement within the legal framework of the Terror of the Year II, which thus represented a return to a form of bourgeois legality – even in a revolutionary form of expression.

We have begun to understand, or at least to explore, these vital mediators of the French revolutionary period. In the demonstrative and experimental form of the revolutionary festival the new system of ideal values was expressed in the form of a scenography. In the absence of a fully developed pedagogic system in the schools, where the brevity of the revolutionary episode did not allow enough time for any really thorough development, the main development was in the politics of language, the gallicizing process, of which Grégoire's famous report on the national language in the Year II was the most important – and far from just symbolic – expression. Just as the auto-da-fé was the most spectacular and symbolic expression of the politics of the *tabula rasa*, the birth of the museum in the more cautious period of the Directory marked the end of one turning point. Works of art, manuscripts and other parts of the heritage were readmitted, but with a radically modified status. Bourgeois society and civilization reappropriated the now inoffensive vestiges of a heritage which had been completely divorced from its initial function. Beginning with the problem of the ways and means of innovation, we are thus led to a total assessment ranging over sociology, geography and chronology.

Sociology and geography can be grouped together as different expressions of the same reality. Quite simply, when speaking of turning points, crises and changes in values and, more widely, in collective mentalities, we cannot avoid one final question: who was affected? Are we dealing, as was traditionally thought, with a diffusion of bourgeois values accelerated by the Revolution, values which were the product of the Enlightenment and whose hegemony was affirmed at the very moment of crisis? Yet the examples and the changes which we have discussed, the vocabularies of the revolutionary festivals and of dechristianization, clearly show up the irreducible reality of popular attitudes. The incongruous return of popular culture via the auto-da-fé and the carnivalesque festivals of the Year II, to take only two examples, highlight the complexity of the problem. Then again, we cannot ignore the importance of the world of rejection; the survival, not just of an aristocracy which discovered the elements of an important ideological renewal during the Emigration, but also the survival, in a whole section of the popular classes, of traditional values which were not just unchanged, but hardened or renewed.

We must not underestimate the part, or place, of what Richard Cobb has called 'life on the margins', the lives of those French people who lived through the Revolution without living the Revolution. Not all of these people were marginal, of course. Such compartmentalization is geographically registered in the existence of 'areas of conservation' which were only superficially affected by the Revolution. These are areas which clearly show up in maps which test for collective attitudes, such as those showing the distribution of the constitutional oath, dechristianization and the success or failure of the revolutionary politics of place names.

To replace this problem in time – the short time-frame of a revolution and the longer time of the evolution which it crowned or of the century which followed – is to summarize its complexity.

A legacy of the *longue durée* or a constitutive event?

Are the phenomena which we have been discussing in terms of 'crisis' or rapid change, not in fact the culmination of a process of evolution in the *longue durée*, or the 'moderately long' time-frame of a century or half a century, when seen in relation to what went before? For my part, I am convinced that this is the case, having devoted an important part of my own research to studying the dechristianization of the Enlightenment, which operated in depth from about 1750 across a wide spectrum of French society. There is evidence of a decisive change in collective sensibility which went far beyond the simple domain of detachment from religious practice.

Yet, conversely, recent studies have replaced this view of an inherited revolution, which merely fed on a change in hearts and minds which had already taken place, with the image of a revolution which was not merely creative, but was the vital locus of a 'transfer of sacrality', to quote Mona Ozouf on the revolutionary festival, and of 'legitimacy', to quote François Furet. The importance of the Revolution as a turning point, in these views, is enhanced far more by the succeeding period than by its own achievements, as it became the starting point for a new view of the world.

I am not preaching a bourgeois compromise when I repeat that the creativity of the revolutionary episode seems to be both undeniable and yet bound up with the process of change which it completed, accelerated and often expressed in unexpected vocabularies and forms. The revolutionary event retains its catalytic role as an activator of historical change. Yet among the novelties which it introduced and the creativities of the collective imagination to which it gave birth, some were only creatures of the moment which did not survive the revolutionary episode. The last carnivalesque outburst of popular culture in the revolutionary festival is a case in point. In other areas, the ephemeral impression with which we are left by some of the manifestations of a new sensibility might be the product of a short-term perspective. The entire phenomenon of the revolutionary festival can only appear as an incongruous curiosity without a sequel, in the light of an apparent restoration of tradition after 1800, if we fail to acknowledge its historical importance as part of the establishment of the new civic values which were part and parcel of bourgeois society in the nineteenth century.

In distinguishing between the profound changes brought about or brought to light by the Revolution and those which were merely 'the transient froth of days', we must not underestimate its role in shaping what we can call a 'new imaginary universe', to quote a phrase which is currently being used. This is a phrase which, of course, needs to be thought about and defined more precisely, yet it is one whose usefulness is, in this context, very clear.

Note

Paper delivered to the conference on 'The French Revolution, an inevitable or contingent event?', Bamberg, June 1979.

11

The Event in the History of Mentalities

We finish our journey with a question – not in order to be coquettish, but to illustrate, with a precise example, the many questions raised by the history of mentalities, an area of study which is still developing. These few pages are my contribution to a collective discussion which will soon take place on the theme of the 'constitutive' event, or 'trauma', depending on the approach adopted, the event, in any case, which weighs so enduringly on destinies and on consciousness.

Does the event have a place in history? It goes without saying that we all understand it in our own different ways. Previously, one would have answered 'no' to this question without any hesitation. This continues to be true if we are dealing with the category of events which the *Annales* tradition has taught us to banish: the mossy, time-worn achorage of historizing, battle-oriented history which is no longer written, if we exclude that other race of historians who are more concerned with the still profitable means of exploiting this exhausted Potosi.

So be it. We do not intend to rehearse the uncontested victory of the *longue durée* and the new kinds of perspectives which it has made possible. We accorded it its well-earned place at a recent conference held at Aix-en-Provence in a paper called 'History of mentalities, history of resistances, or the prisons of the *longue durée*'. Elsewhere we expressed the reservations shared by many of us with respect to the *longue durée* as it tends to melt into 'immobile history'. Let us not go back over a quarrel which is in danger of very shortly becoming purely academic.

Let us instead address ourselves to another area, that of the event. Not that we need to rediscover the event, by a somewhat retrogressive indulgence. Rather, we need to constitute it, to appreciate it in its historical significance. We will not call it change, for fear of being rapped on the knuckles, but will cautiously hazard the term 'rupture', or, even more modestly, suggest that we are concerned to reflect on or re-evaluate the impact of the shorter time-frame. Pierre Nora, in *Writing History*, was the first to raise this problem, but did not see it as more than the concern of very contemporary or immediate history. Yet the shorter time-frame is not just the unique prerogative of the sociologist or of the historian of the present.

In the first instance, we shall gather together a range of indicators from current historiography, where we can see the elements of a much wider and fresher reinterpretation of the idea of the event. Preaching for our own cause, we shall venture to assert that these reinterpretations bring us into the field of mentalities.

We can take some examples, without multiplying them. We now know very well that the 'Black Death' never existed, that 1348 is only significant as a function of what had already emerged in Flanders or in Tuscany from 1315 or even earlier, just as recurrent outbreaks of the plague followed each other in subsequent periods. It has been shown that the frescoes of Campo Santo in Pisa date from before 1348 and we can no longer believe, as Millard Meiss did, that Florentine or Sienese painting can be divided into a period before and after the 'Black Death'. We therefore need more subtle, less linear mediations in this area, and yet it is just here that we are struck by the imprint of the shorter historical time-frame. Similarly, we should no longer be surprised that Georges Duby was able to study a whole stretch of history on the basis of the battle of Bouvines. This was much more than an accommodating method of historical writing.

The new-style event excites our current curiosity in three ways. I shall provisionally call this new-style event a 'historical traumatism', to get it through customs, as it were, without pretending to elegance or even to any greater precision than is necessary for an exploratory study. This triple form comprises the event itself, as a crucial moment, the event as a legacy and the constitutive event.

The event as a legacy? One expects objections. Many scholars say they are tired of it and we have been told that we should dispense with it, as in the study of the origins of the French Revolution, where only our German colleagues, at a recent conference on the problem of the French Revolution as a 'necessary or contingent event', seem to be interested any more. For fear of the reek of vulgar Marxism, we have perhaps been a little bit too quick to declare, with the sneer of rigour, that the dossier is closed and the affair wound up. Roots are all very well, but in the context of a history without events in the *longue durée*, revolution . . .

Nowadays, fashion favours the constitutive event! The event, like the Supreme Being, has no past but has a glorious future. More than one historian, previously pledged to banish the event has rediscovered it in this guise. I too read, with great interest, Mona Ozouf's pages on the revolutionary festival, defined as a transfer of sacrality, and also those of François Furet, in which the revolutionary event was seen as a point of departure rather than a terminus.

In addition, we have to give some predecessors the credit which is due to them. Paul Bois was the first to confront us, in very difficult but convincing terms, with the reality of historical traumatism in the turning point which took place at a moment in the history of the western French countryside, the impact of which is still being felt, two centuries later, in popular attitudes and beliefs. In what ways and by what means did this come about? A host of problems confronts us, and to solve them we have to await the findings of current scholars who have undertaken research on the forms and processes of collective memory.

There is another vast area which, one suspects, has great potential. Why not study the cleavage of the Reformation, for those who are tired of the French Revolution? Our German colleagues, suspicious of our Gallocentric Jacobinism, who amicably reproach us for having neglected the weight of events, will doubtless see no obstacle here.

This leads us to a third possible interpretation of the event which, I state quite baldly, lies in what it says about the moment itself – the things to which it gives rise, the vocabularies and systems of gestures which it invents, mixing old legacies and hopes for the future – and also its ephemeral expression, which is not to be derided for all that. This is why I passionately read what is currently being written about the September Massacres, or about the vocabularies and systems of gesture involved, as scholars decipher them.

I was even slightly tempted to reopen the not too distant file on the dechristianization of the Year II, curious about what the Abbé Godel suggestively, if inelegantly, called 'the explosion of the pastoral network'. The reaction of the guardians of classical religious history convinced me that the theme retains all its bitter novelty. Yet see how Alain Lottin and Solange Deyon have strayed back onto this shocking path by speaking of the 'watershed of the summer of 1566'. Do they have any greater right to indulgence?

In any case, we have here the return of the event. Is it coming into its own? What is the significance of this current interest? Is it just a swing of the pendulum after the strong emphasis placed on immobile history? This is an idle question, really. What matters are the answers, so that we can understand, through the traumatic event, the dialectical encounter of the short and long time-frame.

Note

A contribution to the 1983 conference of the Centre Méridional d'Histoire Sociale, des Mentalités et des Cultures in Aix-en-Provence.

Serial History or Case Studies: a Real or False Dilemma in the History of Mentalities?

Is this a real or a false debate? We have become accustomed over the past ten years to equate serial history and the history of mentalities. This equation arose from the kinds of analysis in which we have been involved, and there is no shortage of examples in current areas of exploration and production. Seen from afar, and especially from the other side of the Atlantic, these two connected traits have constituted the two inseparable facets of an intriguing and sophisticated 'French-style' history. Recently, a reverse process has taken place. The return of a qualitative approach, based on the rediscovery of the individual or case studies, has taken place in Italy and the English-speaking world, and doubts have emerged in France. Does this mark a simple swing of the pendulum from one fashion to another, or a real deepening of what is one of the most open areas of contemporary research? The question is not just an academic stylistic exercise, if we see it in the context of a process which, in the 'medium term' of the last thirty years, has seen the history of mentalities refine its concepts, define its objectives and propose working hypotheses, thanks to which it is now a success story.

In the 1960s it was possible to speculate, with justifiable pessimism, about the future of biography. Traditional biographies of great and not-so-great men are still one of the main categories of popular and academic history. But by remaining part of the traditional, historizing history, biography seemed to exclude new areas of research. When it did incorporate them, it was as a result of a distortion of the genre, of which Lucien Febvre's *Martin Luther, a destiny* or *Rabelais* are still the most elaborate and demonstrative examples. The odyssey of the individual hero is transfigured, in these cases, by the evocation of a collective mentality which both justifies and negates the irreducible character of the individual experience.

In the precise context of the 1960s, when social historians of the cities and the rural world were discovering the methods and advantages of quantification, based on fiscal or notarial sources which had been newly developed, and were attaching themselves to the school of economic history, it was almost inevitable that the history of mentalities, which was itself looking for an identity in the shadow of social history, should be tempted by this method of investigating worlds of silence. By this we mean the universe of people who could not afford the luxury of an individual biography of whatever kind. This includes the vast majority of our ancestors, whose anonymous traces we need to research and organize.

It is not surprising, therefore, that serial studies started out, cautiously at first and in a series of stages, with research into the history of the popular masses and began to assert its role in the domain of the history of cultures and mentalities. Robert Mandrou's work *Popular Culture in the Eighteenth Century*, which was based on a study of the hundreds of little books in the *Bibliothèque Bleu* of Troyes, and which provided a cultural inventory of the groups who bought this pedlar's literature, remains an essential reference point for me in this respect. Without any quantitive affectation or needless sophistication, the value of a thematic inventory was shown in this instance; subtly listing the categories of what we would nowadays call the collective imagination and opening, in this field, a pathway which is now well trodden.

What Mandrou studied in the area of popular literature, others began simultaneously to analyse in the archives of the book trade in France during the *ancien régime*. Under the direction of Alphonse Dupront and then of François Furet, what can be called, with a good deal of simplification, the literature of the elite, was analysed according to its categories, and its ebb and flow were charted in the different studies collected under the title *Books and Society*. This ebb and flow were studied at source, through the statistics of publishing privileges and tacit permits, while others studied it at its point of reception, through inventories of particular booksellers and through collective inventories. This is a new area of study which has now assumed the dimensions it deserves since the initial exploratory surveys carried out by Daniel Roche and others.

The quantifying process thus began with an approach to cultures, based on books, in the realm of ideas and then moved on to the realms of attitudes and collective representations. But during the great enterprise of decoding which took place in the 1960s many other new areas were opened up, without much concern for any mutual continuity. Connected with social history and the history of collective attitudes or consciousness, we saw the development of a sociological approach to traditional delinquency and criminality, as in the analysis of the revolutionary crowd. This was another means of breaking through into a world of silence. Whereas urban social history in the 1960s had aimed at the head of the western bourgeoisie by studying the notables, or the top 500 of the consular and imperial period, the new history tried to smoke out the most beggarly and wretched wherever they were to be found, from prison records to the archives of the Great Confinement and the brief-bags of the provincial *parlements*. But in doing this, it very quickly bypassed traditional sociography, which was rather impoverished from the start, and discovered other, newer problematics in the crossfire between repression and marginality, which directly involved the history of mentalities.

Would it be a false interpretation of the sources to link these approaches to 'social pathology' and new interpretations in demographic history, a discipline which seems to have become more flexible, going in search of both social and mental realities in looking for the secrets of conjugal or family behaviour in the parish registers and the archives of the ecclesiastical courts? In this area, too, the history of mentalities annexed new territories through the use of quantitive methods.

Yet it also devised new sources for itself. I shall assume my share of the responsibility for this, arising out of my 'rediscovery' of wills as a vital resource in the study of attitudes towards death. I am conscious, by having done this, of having participated in a collective movement involving a generation of social historians, which led them to work on mentalities without renouncing any of their methods, their interests or their statistical approach.

Nowadays the most suggestive fields of conquest appear to be in the area of iconography. Bernard Cousin's 5000 Provençal ex votos, M. Ménard's 1000 Le Mans reredoses and Vovelle and Bertrand's 5000 southern French tombs form a new corpus of material which we have begun to decipher through its structures and through the successive shifts which it registers as a reflection of the collective imagination. The generalization of this practice, from modest and sometimes controversial beginnings, now presents an image of real hegemony. Is 'serial study at the third level', to use Pierre Chaunu's phrase, now a successful cause?

One is inclined to think that it is, judging by the common use (in the best sense of the term) of these models. Wills have long ceased to be a Provençal speciality, since the method has been applied to Paris and to sites as diverse as Lyon, Alsace, Champagne and Brittany, not to mention the Veneto, the Basilicata and various parts of the Iberian peninsula. Likewise, private libraries are being analysed in all regions, just as the canons of normality and deviance in the sphere of the family and sexuality are being studied in parish registers and judicial archives.

I realize that this argument can be criticized. There are fashions in history as elsewhere. Yet the trend has been sufficiently sustained to be worthy of reflection and, one might even say, the beginnings of theorization. Thus, in a 1963 paper entitled 'A definition of the lower classes in the modern world' (*Annales E.S.C.*, pp. 459–74), François Furet saw only 'number and anonymity' as being of use in the study of these inevitably 'silent' social categories. Quantification was thus a means of cheating the silence of the poor. Yet others have gone further. Pierre Chaunu in his paper, 'Serial religious history; the quantitive at the third level', felt that a definitive conquest was involved, demanding precision and penetration in analysis and, at the same time, a reflex expression of the questions which a period asked of itself. Hitherto, this analysis was conducted in terms of economic growth; more recently in terms of social history and the history of structures; and nowadays it operates on the level of mentalities and identity. For many people, the acceptance of serial studies, these flexible forms of the quantitive method, finally sanctions the idea that true history is the history of the anonymous masses, research into the normality or average truth of a period, which comes into being not through the actions of the great (whether actors or authors), but is to be found in what is current and ordinary in the repetition of gestures, images and fragments of discourses among the majority of the people.

The strength of this kind of history is that it demonstrated the validity of the impulse that produced it as it progressed. The clarity of its results, which showed meaningful modulations in time, space and the density of the social fabric, provided an initial response to the preliminary objection which was raised to this history 'from the traces' – that it could only provide a poor reflection of social convention, the outermost crust of collective behaviour. Deliberately choosing my examples from different fields, without trying to be exhaustive, I would cite, almost at random, the map presented by Bouissy and Brancolini in the second volume of *Books and Society*. This map, based on the statistics of provincial book production in the eighteenth century, already shows the striking contrast between that part of France, in the west and north-east which remained traditionally faithful to religious books, and, on the other hand, the southern part of the country, which was already opting for secular literature. In the field of time rather than space, I hope I may be allowed to recall the naive and impertinent, yet inevitable question which arose from my own study of eighteenth-century wills. What happened around 1750 (between 1730 and 1760 to cast the net wider), when a whole system of gestures and attitudes towards death was brutally restructured?

This question arises again when we turn to other sources, including demographic sources, which, among other things, provide information about the origins of contraception and, more widely, of familial attitudes, sources of repression, which give evidence about collective forms of behaviour, not to mention the book which, as a source, reveals much more than the simple shifts of fashion.

Yet at the same time as the serial history of mentalities has won acceptance by the multiplicity of what it has produced, the reliability of its results and, better still, the importance of the problems which it raises, the subject has encountered objections from the start, as well as a whole series of questions which have been progressively refined.

From the beginning, to go back to my discussion of preliminary questions, the problem has been raised in different but globally convergent ways, as to what these traces can permit us to discover, scanty as they often are, and set in the mould of a formalized, codified expression, whatever the source may be. I was warned about the distorting effects of social pressure or, even worse, of notarial convention, when I first started to delve into vast numbers of wills. Did I not realize that the notary held the pen? The argument can be transposed into all fields of research. Thus, we can also mention the figure of the ex-voto painter, waiting at the door of the pilgrim shrine with his template already prepared to receive the 'individualized' complement to the stereotyped image of the miracle. There are other objections of a similar, yet different, kind. Furio Diaz and others have asked questions about the statistics of the book trade. Who knows what happened to these books, how they were passed on and, most important of all, how they were received? By the same token, what is the real life of an idea? This is a question which the complementary study of the contents of individual libraries can only partly answer, given its fragile assumptions about the reception of the book's message.

Given the assumptions on which Dupront and Furet's surveys of eighteenth-century book production were based, their decision to accept the categories of classification and coding used in the period in order to avoid the risk of anachronism, there is a danger that such a restrictive framework can lock us into a closed system of questions and answers as hermetic, or possibly even more so, than the formulas of the notary. In order to describe a change in sensibility as important as the development of the novel, scholars were forced, very happily, into the necessary iconoclasm of breaking up the category of 'belles-lettres'.

The argument can be transposed once more to the domain of judicial sources, including court cases and interrogation records. Translation is a form of treason. In thinking that we are grasping the reality of behaviour, what we are actually seeing is the moral code of a society which creates its own criminals and delinquents, and even prompts their answers to interrogation.

Here we come to a potentially radical objection to the serial history of mentalities, which, among its recent spokesmen, is based on a feeling which goes far beyond the initial reflex action of mere opposition to change.

The first and most anodyne reproach is that it produces a superficial view of the questions involved. Thus, J. C. Schmidt objected that inventories of funeral monuments confined themselves to external elements of identification, hovering around the object without really penetrating it and focusing the analysis on the problematics of economic and social history, with their inbuilt limitations. This argument can be applied to more than one of the failed attempts at a serial analysis of images at an early stage in the development of the method (as in the case of V.-L. Tapié's *Baroque Reredoses in Brittany*), but it shows a lack of awareness of recent work in this field, such as Bernard Cousin's analysis of Provençal ex votos.

More profoundly, the most radical objection of all, as formulated by Carlo Ginzburg and since taken up by Roger Chartier, questions the very validity of the procedure. Even worse than an impoverished or generalized reading of the subject, serial methods produce a profoundly distorted image. In referring to François Furet's arguments, which have already been discussed, Ginzburg saw them as reflecting an interpretation which sought to banish the Revolution itself. We have to admit that to some extent the serial approach represents the triumph of processes of average mobility and thereby tends to erase not just accidental but also abrupt change, and in this way minimizes the importance of all expressions of tension or conflict, however revealing they may be.

In Ginzburg's view, by erasing sudden change, the serial approach is also a means of masking conflict and eliminating difference, which leads back to a mystifying unity of collective mentality seen as an all-embracing reality, a consensus purged of all the tensions of which it is actually the vehicle. This is an unjust criticism, in general. Without wishing to plead *pro domo*, I should recall that this was not my research perspective when I worked on collective attitudes as expressed in eighteenth-century wills, in the context of the Provençal baroque, eager as I was to understand difference and to show contrasts between various forms of social behaviour.

For Ginzburg, as for Chartier, the cultural approach involved in the analysis of the book trade and of literary production provides a good example of the problems of serial sources. Such sources emphasize normalization and the diffusion of cultural models, of which they are the vehicle, whereas it is necessary to replace this approach with an analysis of the mechanisms of production and creation so as to grasp these realities as they come into being. This is a kind of research which can only be carried out on the basis of case studies and individual confessions, which are more direct even though they are more exceptional. A move from global, macroscopic study, which is not just over general but also potentially mystifying, to microscopic study is demanded as an epistemological necessity.

I believe that these criticisms can be placed in the wider context of a whole collection of new tendencies in historiography in recent years. Given that my approach may involve an element of simplification, perhaps too much, I shall try to place this change of perspective in the context of a return of the qualitative approach, which is currently reflected in the multiplication of biographical studies, primarily, but not exclusively, in history.

At the heart of the matter is the new questioning by historians of rebellious or obstinate silences, one stage of which was represented by the serial approach to history. The need for a greater degree of authenticity and, ultimately, the desire to come to terms with culture 'in the flesh' has been expressed in various ways. I do not think it fortuitous that the current fashion for 'life-stories' has developed at the same time as the emergence of oral history in recent years, just as it was not fortuitous that the serial history of mentalities emerged in the context of a social history which 'counts, weighs and measures' in Simiand's famous formula. In oral history, as in biography, there is an implicit assumption that 'truth comes out of the mouth'. This is a certain kind of truth, in relation to which the practitioners of this new history are certainly not dupes, maintaining a certain distance from the discourse and the fabrications and reproductions which it can contain.

In addition to this factor, a number of other convergent tendencies explain why the rediscovery of individual experiences, drawn from life, are seen as a vital reference point. Some go back to deeply rooted traditions, as in one branch of English historiography which has long been interested in prosopography; other studies have been adaptations, resulting from the development of a new approach to the treatment of the archives of repression – trials, evidence and confessions which, although they may have been extorted, nevertheless contain expressions of individual experience which are inexplicable if read reductively. The experience of the Friulian miller Menocchio, recounted by Carlo Ginzburg in *The Cheese and the Worms*, based on the archives of the Venetian inquisition, is the prime example of this kind of approach, and we can also point to the heroes of the tale of Martin Guerre, recently retold by Natalie Zemon Davis. The confession *par excellence* is, of course, the one which is shouted out rather than extracted, in Michel Foucault's *I, Pierre Riviere* . . .. The history of this most irreducible of lives is formulated as a cry and ending as a massacre.

Without turning to this extreme case (which nonetheless continues to pose questions), we can see from these references how, and by what paths, the case study has come to seem important as a more direct and especially as a more authentic means of understanding a text, one which sustains an analysis that is not just limited to the 'how', but also deals with the 'why'.

Grenadou, the peasant from Beauce, who quite plainly revealed, almost without prompting, the elements of a mental inventory in narrating the story of his life, gave many of us the initial encouragement to research this valuable form of evidence. In the wake of that pioneering work, examples have multiplied, forming a portrait gallery which is now practically teeming with characters. From the industrial worker of the north to the shepherd from the *Landes*, via the railway mechanic, this gallery of witnesses from life is constantly being enriched. These studies are often illuminating in the revelations which they offer along the way. Sometimes they are repetitive and as such they seem likely to liven the debate we are discussing. This general tendency, not just limited to France is, I believe, (if I can be permitted another simplification) one of the provinces of the search for identity, for 'roots', which is so much part of our collective curiosities at present. In trying to make the village speak, as in Lawrence Wylie's portrait of Roussillon in *A Village in Vaucluse*, which may have been the first of its kind, or in Bouchard's immobile village or even Le Roy Ladurie's *Montaillou*, individual history becomes one of the means of finding the typical in the particular.

Without the benefits of the tape recorder, historians have to manipulate the archives to obtain at least a substitute for, if not the equivalent of, direct evidence. The individual or family diary offers what seems to be the closest source for what we are looking for, and we can see a revival of interest in these documents. Not to multiply examples, Daniel Roche's recent work on the life of the Parisian journeyman, and later master glazier, Menetras is, I believe, an exemplary illustration, both by the wealth of the document and the analysis which accompanies it, of the possibilities which this kind of study offers.

When the subject is silent and beyond the scope of the written word, we can try to cheat the difficulty by using other means of investigation. Twenty years ago I tried to give a hearing to the Aix carpenter Joseph Sec, the self-made man of the neighbourhood, who left, not a diary, but a monumental Jacobin-masonic cenotaph which contained the elements of his individual mental inventory in iconographic form. When confronted with the ideological handiwork with which this obscure hero proclaimed his truth, in imagery which syncretically combined Christian and Enlightenment elements, and also those of the Revolution, which he preached, I felt I was beginning to understand the interior experience of the Provençal individuals whom I had looked at through the statistics of the various stages of dechristianization. When I retraced *The Irresistible Rise of Joseph Sec, Citizen of Aix* case studies or biographical writings were not fashionable, and only one provincial publisher was prepared to risk publishing what might have passed for a mere curiosity.

French publishing, which reflects the fashions of the time in a somewhat distorted way, was for a long time oblivious of the existence of Carlo Ginzburg's *Night Battles* and even of the miller Menocchio from *The Cheese and the Worms*. It is only a few years since these strange tales seemed to be on the fringes of serious history. We are even more surprised by the liveliness of the debate which is currently taking place. Menocchio, the Friulian miller who made a compromising confession of his world-view to the Venetian inquisitors around 1580, with a daring cosmogony in which God and the angels were generated from matter after it had formed out of original chaos, has nowadays become a familiar hero. Judicial sources, through a profusion of procedures and interrogations allow far more truth to filter through the prison walls than we might have thought. They were also used by Natalie Zemon Davis in *The Return of Martin Guerre* as the basis for a study which looked beyond the story of a soldier coming home from the war and saw more clearly the universe of the village or, even more simply, the way in which the minds of people abusively called simpletons functioned in the sixteenth century.

At this point, without multiplying examples, we see that we are now faced with a new series of questions – just as we were previously by the triumph of the serial approach. Apart from the evident enthusiasm which they inspire, case studies also raise, if not hesitations, at least a whole series of new questions. The very success of the method, and the enthusiasm which it arouses, prompt questions and even criticism. What are we researching in a case study? Is it real life which, as everyone knows, is to be found elsewhere? We very quickly realize, however, as was pointed out at the conference devoted to these biographical studies held at Nanterre in January 1982, under the aegis of the Centre de la Semiotique Textuelle, that 'the spontaneity of the cry, the transparence of a confidence vouchsafed'[1] is a lure. One life-story is all very well, bristling, jumping with novelty. Ten life-stories or twelve life-stories later and recurrent factors begin to emerge, the cliches, the fact, evident *a posteriori*, that these individual testimonies are themselves very structured, that they are vehicles of a discourse which is itself the reflection of received models and forms of conditioning. From this point, when measuring the recurrences and the stereotypes, it is useful ... to organize them into series, one might ironically say, so as to avoid redundancies, repetition, the *déjà vu*.

This, of course, takes nothing away from the extreme wealth of this multi-faceted type of evidence, insistent in the abundance of what it contains. The story of Menetras the glazier is at one level the history of the journeyman, but it is not just a simple variation on a theme already known through the model of Agricole Perdiguier. It is an immersion in the rhythms of popular life; the brawls, the fleeting encounters, be they pleasant or bitter. It is also, in its final sequence, during the French Revolution, when the clarity of the narrative begins to become cloudy and the machine starts to break down, a marvellous way of realizing how a militant from a Parisian district could actively and intensely live the Revolution without understanding anything about it. The flowing narrative of the years of apprenticeship and training – fluid because he retraces a career which was signposted right down to its accidents, and also because he reconstructed it as a function of existing moulds and of a model which was received and imagined as much as it was lived – disintegrates when it comes into contact with a great event.

Here too, we get a sense of the limits of the procedure, beyond its exceptional success. We look for spontaneity and find the norm, even if the norm is refined, and capable of in-depth analysis, which is quite considerable. If we do not do this, and I say this with a certain fear of being rapped on the knuckles, we run the risk of descending to the level of anecdote, a popular version of the old-style biographies of the great. As if, it will be said, there was ever a purely anecdotal level in history which is truly devoid of meaning. Yet, when stripped of all the contextual facets in which Natalie Zemon Davis placed it, does the story of bigamy and imposture in *Martin Guerre* not remain a *curiosum*, as contemporaries also experienced it? *Curiosa* do exist, of course, and all history is not rigidly exemplary.

We are faced with a curious dilemma. Either the case study leads us back to a more general model, and we find ourselves in the comical situation of the marvellous will which E.-J. Leonard cited as an example of Protestant faith in its pure state and of which, being difficult and mischievous, I found hundreds of examples in both Protestant and Catholic documents – or else it offers an irreducible rebelliousness and ends in a cry, like Foucault's Pierre Riviere.

But what then becomes of history? In responding to this dilemma, I am particularly aware of Carlo Ginzburg's argument in his introduction to *The Cheese and the Worms*, where he stressed the importance of the *eccezione normale*. It is in this realm of the exceptional, which is not at all anecdotal, that we can discover a ray of truth in this vital type of evidence. If I wanted amicably to bait the author, I would suspect him a little of wanting to win on all fronts; stressing the unique value of his discovery on the one hand, while saying that there are lots of other millers, and Menocchios by the dozen. Not that I wish to cast doubt on the well-hidden and therefore unrecognized reality of this kind of protest, whether popular or not. But it is really as an extreme testimony that we are interested in the story of this obscure hero, both in itself and beyond itself.

As an appendix to *The Irresistible Rise of Joseph Sec*, I inserted a more general piece entitled 'Some keys for the interpretation of *naifs*'. The useful term *naifs* was only an initial, and in reality somewhat inadequate prop for an investigation of what André Breton once called *'les inspirés'*,[2] meaning those people who suddenly emerge from what seems like a vow of silence to communicate a message – their message – whether through writing or some unconventional form of expression. Because it transgresses the norms, such a cry from the heart lights up hidden places and may even reveal whole stretches of reality which would otherwise be unknown. This kind of evidence is irreplaceable, not just because it lets us see invisible environments (which we do not really need to know about in great detail!) but because it reveals hidden moments. We find abrupt change at the very heart of the monolithism of autobiography, the apparently placid chronicles of immobile individual lives. The clarity of Ginzburg's interpretation helps us to revise a somewhat lazy view of biographies as individual reflections of the great consensus of immobile history by discovering the fissures and conflicts which they contain. We need to rid ourselves of the facile and dated stereotype of Fabrice del Dongo's *Waterloo*. The case study is not, in my view, a way of looking at history through the other end of the telescope, neither is it a confirmation of that other history of individuals where, it seems, nothing ever happens. Menocchio, in his tragic obstinacy, is a far better guide than Lucien Febvre's Rabelais to the problem of unbelief in the sixteenth century, because he gives us the keys by which we can understand it. Daniel Roche's hero, Menetras, who wrote for his own personal pleasure and enjoyment, helped me to understand the sans-culottes of Marseille from within, whose collective experience in the revolutionary period I had analysed in massed ranks using the most austere methods of the serial approach. By the same token, Joseph Sec helped me to understand how the dechristianization of the urban bourgeoisie was lived 'from within' at the end of the eighteenth century.

I do not want to conclude, at this stage of analysis, with a compromise, either dismissing the two opponents, or proposing a nonaggression pact for peaceful coexistence. We need, modestly, in the light of these experiments, to specify what we can expect to see achieved in the field of the social history of mentalities from both serial and case studies.

Serial study, which I believe to be indispensable, and which has not yet had its final say, must not fall into the statistical illusion (which was also present in the neoclassical period, between 1770 and 1820) of believing that it can grasp the whole of reality by the magic of quantification. In bourgeois thought during the Enlightenment this illusion represented, consciously or not, a means of control, of standardization of the masses, as well as the beginning of scientific knowledge. If carried out undiscerningly, serial history, taking place in the context of another social crisis, runs the risk of itself becoming mystifying and misleading. It is up to us to make it into an instrument of analysis which, of course, rejects sterile sociography, especially in the light of the changes the latter has gone through in its recent phases. The serial is not the only means of analysing cultural objects (as was seen in the analysis of the book trade), but when it deals with the basics of wills, ex votos, reredoses and the like, it is operating in the vital arena where we can observe the compromises, choices of and also the rejection of, cultural models and downward processes of acculturation, as well as responses to them and even the counter-models which it can reveal. To this extent, a serial history of mentalities is not fatalistically linked to the mystifying notion of a collective mentality which transcends class barriers, the norms of which it actually fixes.

Conversely, to believe that the case study can be a corrective, a panacea, a 'truth coming straight from the mouth' of which we spoke earlier, would be to give in to an illusory quest for identities – the oracular myth which is so much in force nowadays. Yet none of the well-informed current researchers into case studies, life-stories or oral history are in danger of succumbing to this illusion.

When we look at their respective needs, the two approaches do not seem to be antagonistic except when seen from the perspective of a reductionism which ignores the dialectical exchange between a global understanding of the kind which can only be gained by serial study, and the exploration in depth which is possible from a case study. I am convinced of the fruitfulness of a process which, from stage to stage, has allowed us to realize the objectives of the history of mentalities. I also believe that we are only at the beginning of the road, and I especially believe that one of the next steps will be to break out of the 'popular' ghetto in which the study has so far been confined. What if, in this way, we rediscover the expressions of an 'elite' culture (if I may, for the sake of convenience, be allowed the simplistic dichotomy)? This is a very large ambition, if we understand all that it entails, including the understanding of literary and aesthetic evidence at the highest levels. Here we are again faced with the voracious appetite characteristic of historians of mentalities. I hope, at the very least, that they will show, even in their voracity (of the best possible kind, I hope), all those qualities for which we are indebted to the intrepid discoverers who launched the discipline, of whom Robert Mandrou will always be, for me, the model.

Notes

Essay published in *Histoire sociale – sensibilitès collectives et mentalitès mèlanges Robert Mandrou* (P.U.F., 1985)

1   F. Gaussen, *Le Monde*, 14 February 1982.
2   A. Breton and G. Ehrmann, *The Inspirés and their Houses.*

Index

Index by Ann Barrett